Classic Clint

The Laughs and Times of Clint Murchison, Jr.

Dick Hitt

Wordware Publishing, Inc.
REGIONAL DIVISION

Library of Congress Cataloging-in-Publication Data

Hitt, Dick.
    Classic Clint : the laughs and times of Clint Murchison, Jr. / by Dick Hitt.
       p.   cm.
    Includes index.
    ISBN 1-55622-146-0
    1. Murchison, Clinton Williams, Jr., 1923-1987.   2. Businessmen—
Texas—Biography.   3. Entrepreneurship—Texas—Biography.   I. Title.
HC102.5.M87H58   1991
338'.04'092—dc20
[B]   91-23127
                                                                                      CIP

Copyright © 1992, Wordware Publishing, Inc.
All Rights Reserved
1506 Capital Avenue
Plano, Texas 75074

No part of this book may be reproduced in any form or by any means without permission in writing from Wordware Publishing, Inc.
Printed in the United States of America

ISBN 1-55622-146-0
10 9 8 7 6 5 4 3 2
9107

All inquiries for volume purchases of this book should be addressed to Wordware Publishing, Inc., at the above address. Telephone inquiries may be made by calling:
(214) 423-0090

Contents

Greetings and Salutations, Etc. v
1 Clint and the Social Graces 1
2 Adventures with Dook and Jane 19
3 Thanks for the Memories 33
4 A Funny Thing Happened On the Way to the N.F.L. 67
5 The Creation of the Dallas Whatsits 73
6 The Hole in the Roof Gang 111
7 Almost Strictly Business 137
8 Not-So-Strange Bedfellows 151
9 Inspirations and Other Outrages 171
10 Letters from the Stomach 193
11 Miscellaneous Mischief 209
12 Public Wobblies, Private Strength 219
13 'The Other Side Of Silence' 233
14 P. S. 249
Afterword 257
Index 261

Greetings and Salutations, Etc.

Dear Reader:

This is a book mostly of letters. Most of them made somebody, somewhere, smile. Most of the letters were written by Clint Murchison, Jr., who at various times of his life was described as a precocious Marine, a multimillionaire sportsman, a Texas wheeler-dealer, a cold, shy recluse, an habitual imp, an arrogant gadfly, a gallivantin' rascal, a burrheaded hedonist, a downhome gourmet, a lovable grandfather, a greedy NFL owner, an acerbic wit (he liked that one a lot), a feverish entrepreneur, a hounded paradigm of the Texas bust, and a born-again invalid.

He found the time and had the money and opportunity to afford these careers and pastimes. Much of his fame, pleasure, and pride came from his creation and ownership of the Dallas Cowboys Football Club of the National Football League, which came to be known, to its greatly mixed emotions, as "America's Team." Clint was a slight man of immense wealth, public inwardness, and private flamboyance. Not many knew of his authentic intellectual talents, such as the master's degree from Massachusetts Institute of Technology, which gave him the ability not only to introduce computerization to the grimy arts of football, but to understand it as well.

At various high-water marks, the real estate holdings of Clint, Sr., Clint, Jr., and his brother John, and various partners ranged across the world, from German industrial property to Australian Gold Coast high-rises, Mexican cattle ranches and silver mines, downtown Dallas office buildings, a private island in the Bahamas, and residential and commercial developments in Florida, California, and Hawaii. There were other properties in New Orleans, New York, and Washington, D.C.

There were also such assets as Alleghany Corporation, the Dallas Cowboys Football Club, Dallas taxicab franchises, Centex

Greetings and Salutations, Etc.

Corporation, Daisy Air Rifles, *Field & Stream* magazine, Holt, Rinehart & Winston Publishers, James Heddon's Sons fishing equipment, Delhi-Taylor Oil Company, Delhi International, Delhi-Australia Oil, Canadian Delhi Oil, Southern Union Gas Company, Tecon Corporation, Lamar Life Insurance Company, Roma Corporation (the Tony Roma's restaurant chain), and Clint, Jr.'s acronymic pride, Calorific Recovery Anaerobic Process, Inc., of Guymon, Oklahoma. It processed cow manure to produce first, methane gas, and later to produce a protein-enriched cattle feed supplement. He was pleased to refer to it by its initials, C.R.A.P.

The letters, telegrams, memoirs, and napkin notes that make up the bones of this collection were diligently saved by his secretary of many years, Ruth Woodard, and conserved in a roomful of long boxes by his children, Burk, Robert, Clint III, and Coke Anne. The man they reflect stretches from the moony bravado of a wartime officer-candidate to the bulletproof audacity of a 35-year-old magnate who kidnaped the Washington Redskins' Fight Song to create the Dallas Cowboys franchise.

He wrote as easily to presidents as to his plumber. In our era of video eyestrain and galloping rudeness, when we're told we don't write enough letters and have forgotten the protocols of basic manners, the files of Clint Murchison, Jr., may help to show the power of postal etiquette. Purists will note his fondness for the semicolon; shade-tree analysts will think they see a difference in his attitudes toward people whose letters he closed with "Sincerely," as opposed to those he signed "Very truly yours."

Most of the rest of the collection is oral history, savored by his friends from boyhood, recounting tales of the heady times and the goofy jokes; memories treasured by his companions from trips to barbecue joints and Persian Gulf vaults; testimonials from the witnesses to his wit and later to his courage; and remembrances by the affectionate victims of his elaborate practical jokes.

Clint's most famous moment in mail came from a letter that wasn't even addressed to him. It was a shrill note from a large former creditor of a property in downtown Dallas that Clint's company had sold to Canadian developers. The mortgage on the property in question had been paid off in the 1960s—a fact apparently unknown

Greetings and Salutations, Etc.

to the mortgage clerk who had watched, goggle-eyed, a TV news report on the spectacular, controlled implosion of the building, and who then hastily notified his bosses that their collateral had been destroyed. This was the letter that resulted:

CERTIFIED MAIL
RETURN RECEIPT REQUESTED

Southwestern Life
Investment Department

May 28, 1982

Mr. Ken Vallens
Bramalea Limited
1867 Yonge Street
Toronto, Ontario M451Y5

Re: Loan Number 30021
Bramalea Limited
(Formerly Dallas Texas Corporation, Old Texas Bank Building and Parking Garage)
Downtown Dallas, Texas

Dear Mr. Vallens:

It has come to our attention that you have totally destroyed the 12 story office building and parking garage that were an integral part of the security for the above captioned loan. This action is clearly in violation of the Deed of Trust covenants.

This letter is formal notice to you that the above captioned loan is hereby declared entirely due and demand is here made that the loan be paid in full by no later than July 1, 1982. The amount required for full payment on June 1, 1982 is the principal balance of $1,471,551.61 and interest after June 1, 1982 is $408.76 per day calculated at 10% as provided in paragraph one of the Note. Payment in full should be by bankable funds and include the daily interest through and including the day of receipt of payment at the offices of Southwestern Life here in Dallas.

Sincerely,

James F. Robinson

JFR: lw

cc: Bramalea Limited
    858 One Main Place
    Dallas, Texas 75250

SOUTHWESTERN LIFE INSURANCE COMPANY • POST OFFICE BOX 2699 • DALLAS, TEXAS • 75221

Ignorance is not always bliss. According to Pete Kleifgen, a Murchison executive, that mortgage no longer even existed. On the site of the old bank and garage, Bramalea was about to erect a 70-story spire in the Dallas skyline called InterFirst Tower. In the

Greetings and Salutations, Etc.

subsequent Russian rouletting of the Texas banking industry during the '80s, its name would change to NCNB Plaza.

The Canadians sent a copy of the letter to Clint, who was beginning to have serious, and real, financial problems exacerbated by his failing health. He was happy to have a chance to reply to a bum rap. Clint sent a copy of the letter back to its querulous writer with his own customarily brief comment, which was even briefer than was his custom.

CLINT MURCHISON, JR.
DALLAS, TEXAS

June 7, 1982

Mr. James F. Robinson
Southwestern Life
  Insurance Company
P. O. Box 2699
Dallas, TX   75221

Re: Attached Letter

Dear Mr. Robinson:

Picky, picky, picky!

Yours very truly,

Clint Murchison Jr.

Greetings and Salutations, Etc.

It was a David & Goliath shot, devilish drollness bringing down portentous indignation. It was widely and feverishly quoted, first by phone and interoffice mail and then on its way from office bulletin boards into business-news journals and on into squelchdom's hall of fame. But in fact Clint Murchison, Jr., could relate to pickiness. He was picky in the ways that accompany perfectionism, a passion for meticulous detail, mathematical genius, relentless intelligence, and class leavened by the perspective of humor. I hope you enjoy the record of his laughs and times.

Yours very truly,

DICK HITT

Chapter One
Clint and the Social Graces

". . . the key elements to success in business are hard work, dedication, and having a rich father."

In the book she wrote about Clint's father, Clint Murchison, Sr., Ernestine Orrick Van Buren observed, "He liked the personal touch of a letter in which he could express ideas he might have been too shy to put into spoken words."

The Clints, Senior and Junior, shared a sepulchral shyness that was often mistaken for aloofness or coldness. Sociologists and police still argue over whether heredity or environment plays the bigger role in producing a person's character; Clint, Jr.'s chronic shrinking from even pleasantries like "Good morning" could well have been a genetic legacy from "Pop," as the children and grandchildren called him. But a point in environment's favor is that the son could hardly have grown up around Pop without noting the power of the thank-you note.

Clint, Jr.'s thank-you notes were terse, functional, and, at the slightest excuse, funny. The bounty of the Christmastime deliveries to 6200 Forest Lane in 1974 reached such a volume that he took most of January 3, 1975, to send notes of thanks to Evelyn and Roy for the pecans, John for the turkey, Nancy and Mark for the popcorn, Joan for the condiment dish ("Please send some caviar to go with it"), Janet and Gus for the caviar (but no mention of needing a condiment dish),

Bob for the grapefruit, Martha Anne and Steve for more grapefruit, Effie for more pecans, Morin for still more grapefruit, Gloria and George for cheese, Warren for fruitcake, Kathleen for pumpkin bread, Uta and Paul for an alarm clock, and Sandra for an executive fly swatter.

Other friends had sent cans of "Good Luck" black-eyed peas from a canning company in the family hometown of Athens. It is a Texas tradition that eating the peas on New Year's Day assures good luck through the year. "Dear Gertrude and Doc: Thank you for the black-eyed peas. I hope they work."

To Jack Peeples of Miami: "Thank you for the belt buckle. I walk with a slight list now—but don't worry, I am getting in shape." *To Tom and Alicia Landry*, for a photographic "coffee-table" book of Dallas scenes: "Dear Tom and Alicia: Thank you for the folio on Dallas. It is an interesting history and will complement very well a similar volume I have, entitled *Miami*, which Don Shula was kind enough to send to me." *To Dallas banker William D. Breedlove*: "Dear Bill: I want to thank you and Tack and Dick for the very handsome lithograph of the first issue of the Texas Duck Stamp; it folds nicely into my wallet." The largesse in 1982, the year of the NFL players' strike, included a needlepoint box from Mrs. Bobby Frase: "Dear Bobby: Many thanks for the needlepoint tissue dispenser; it is really good looking. Now I will know where to go when I am crying over the strike."

In 1975 Phyllis George was working with Brent Musberger, Irv Cross, and Jimmy the Greek Snyder on CBS-TV's "NFL Today," and she had recently become the bride of Kentucky Governor John Y. Brown. Clint acknowledged the couple's holiday gift, which may have come for both corporate and personal reasons:

> **Dear Phyllis and John:**
>
> I appreciate the white wine; I only hope that I can keep it away from Bedford.

The punchlines let his friends know that he was acknowledging their specific gesture; that he had actually looked at the book, hefted the belt buckle, or had plans for the needlepoint tissue dispenser.

Clint and the Social Graces

> Joe Perrin
> 9300 Flicker Way
> Los Angeles, California 90069
>
> Dear Joe:
>
> I certainly appreciate your sending me an illustrated edition of *B-26 Marauder at War*. I have already read the first eight pages and so far I haven't come across a reference to you. Should I keep reading?
>
> Sincerely,
> Clint

At Christmastime of 1982, writer John D. McDowell sent him a copy of his newly published book, *More Than a Carpenter*. The title was a reference to Jesus' original occupation.

> Dear Josh:
>
> Your book, which I enjoyed, reminded me of an Associated Press release of several years ago. Golda Meir, then prime minister of Israel, had an audience with the Pope in Rome. While awaiting his entry she fidgeted nervously, saying "What am I, Golda Meir, daughter of Moshe Mabovitch the carpenter, doing here with the Pope of all the Catholics?" "But Golda," one of her aides interposed, "carpentry is a pretty respected profession around here."

To Robert Ramey, engineering professor at the University of Virginia:

> Dear Bob:
>
> I appreciate your bringing back memories by sending me your latest textbook. Naturally, however, time doing what it does, its pages are somewhat obscure to me; I'll do a lot better talking to you about football. Incidentally, Charles Vail is now vice president of Southern Methodist University; I know because I ran into him at a football game. As I said, I'm a lot better talking about football.

He was particularly pleased when an author sent him a book. He was a prolific and quick reader, especially of sportswriting. Three of his favorites were the *Dallas Times Herald* triumvirate of Blackie Sherrod, Bud Shrake, and Dan Jenkins, who covered the Cowboy beat during the team's teething years. By 1962 Jenkins had moved on to write football for *Sports Illustrated*, on the way to writing his classic Texas-inspired novel *Semi-Tough*. Clint enjoyed discovering the tiny ironies of running across people in news stories who had fitting names: a bank teller named Dollar, plumbers named Piper and Nutt, or a cobbler named Shoemaker. One of Jenkins' *S.I.* articles had mentioned a sports press agent with a perfect name:

> March 29, 1963
>
> Dear Dan:
>
> My ordinary practice in reading a magazine article is to skip the credit, observing it only when some particularly adroit combination of words recommends the writer. Last week, as I was perusing SI from the vantage point of a Spanish Cay terrace, I encountered just such an expression, "the happily named Flack." As I raised my eyes to ascertain the name of the author, just before I became dazzled by the sun, I discerned the name of a friend.
>
> Then, I retreated into the shade of a pandanus, thinking of you all the while.

Shrake, another sportswriter destined to be a novelist and screenplay writer, had been a partner in a determinedly dilapidated Maple Avenue saloon, called Bud Shrake West, in the early sixties. The bar featured a photographic hall of fame of local sports and media celebrities. One of the portraits, of *Fort Worth Star-Telegram* columnist Elston Brooks, hung in the men's room and was inscribed: "Dear Bud—Good luck. Here's the picture you asked for. Hope it escapes the men's room." There were pictures of Clint in bizarre poses and props on more than one wall.

By 1968 Shrake, too, had served a stint at *Sports Illustrated* and had recently moved from New York to Austin to write novels and screenplays. One of the novels was *Blessed McGill,* an epic of an 1880s Texas frontier trapper whose adventures ended in his beatification.

> May 23, 1968
>
> Blessed Bud:
>
> Jane and I appreciate your sending us a copy of your latest novel; we will keep it with our edition of *Poor No More*. (I'll tell you about that when I see you next.)

> I was particularly impressed by the Shel Hershorn photograph of you on the back cover; it reminded me of the photographs of me which have been exhibited variously at a Maple Avenue saloon, now boarded, and a famous local taco house. I recall that it was difficult for me to achieve the comic effect in my photographs, which was apparently no problem in your case. This is certainly indicative of an innate talent.
>
> I haven't read the book yet.

In gratitude for our corporate goodwill, most of us expect to receive little pop-up calendars from our insurance agents or a handsomely Xeroxed "Merry Christmas" circular inside the bank statement at Christmastime. Clint played in bigger leagues. In 1981 a Pacific Northwest bank sent its favored clients a collection of color lithographs of Mount St. Helens' epochal explosion.

> Mr. Mark Potter
> Seattle-First National Bank
> National Department
> 1001 Fourth Avenue
> Seattle, Washington 98124
>
> Dear Mark:
>
> I really appreciate the folio of photographs on Mt. St. Helens. I was impressed by the pictures in the current *National Geographic* until I saw these.
>
> I would like to send you some photographs in return, but all we have down here is that sinkhole out in Wink County and people have stopped talking about it since they pulled the cow out.

To Sabine Corporation's Ashley Priddy, who had sent a commemorative company anniversary collection of specially inked historic lithographs:

> Dear Ashley:
>
> Many thanks for the set of lithographs. They are quite handsome. Incidentally, I have had some experience with the fade-resistant inks; it happens that my bankers have suggested for several years that I use such a product on my bank notes.
>
> I was also considerably impressed with the GOLD Anniversary seal on your stationery. I have given the one on my letter to my grandchildren with the suggestion that they hold it until the price of gold goes back up to $400 per ounce.

> Sam Katz
> United Exposition Service Co.
> 1555 W. 44th Street
> Chicago, Illinois
>
> Dear Sam:
>
> Thank you for the clock radio. I like the "sleep" feature better than the "wake-up" feature.

One of the logistical culture shocks faced by globetrotting businessmen in the late sixties and seventies was the growing incidence, and inconvenience, of airline strikes in those days when the routes were more exclusive, connections were more limited, and options for the stranded were fewer. One of Clint's California banking friends had been marooned in the Middle East by a strike but made it back in time to send out the corporate Christmas gifts.

> Dec. 20, 1974
>
> Mr. Al Rice
> Executive Vice President
> Bank of America—World Headquarters
> 555 California Street
> San Francisco, California 94104
>
> Dear Al:
>
> Many thanks for the Persian rug. Since it is from the land of flying carpets, I am unsure, in light of your historical transportation problems, whether you came over with it or on it. Temporarily, I am placing it on the floor, but the next time we have an airline strike I may take it outside and give it a try.

The sprawling home that Clint designed and built at 6200 Forest Lane in Dallas was the talk not only of the city and region, but of the architectural nation. Its exterior was a blend of the design philosophies of Frank Lloyd Wright and Mies van der Rohe. Its acreage approached the size of a city park, spread across some of the most expensive land in North Dallas. The main house was all one story. ("My father had a fetish against stairs, for some reason," says his daughter Coke Anne Murchison Saunders.) There were eight bedrooms, Italian Travertine marble walls, an industrial kitchen that was itself the size of some ordinary houses and which had one of the first microwave ovens. It was under construction for 10 years. The basement had a wine cellar and a room devoted to the switches and controls for the electronic conveniences Clint himself designed.

After its years of construction, delays, and redesigns, the scene was set for Clint's plaintive thank-you note to his plumbing contractor for another in a lengthening series of Christmas fruitcakes:

> Mr. Ward Downs
> Dallas Plumbing Co.
> 2425 McKinney
> Dallas, Texas
>
> Dear Ward:
>
> I would like to thank you again for remembering me with the gift of a fruitcake. If we do not hurry up and finish the house, you're going to be out of fruit.
>
> Sincerely,
> Clint

Among the amenities the house never had was a collection of exquisite Venetian glassware, which had been offered to Clint by Neiman-Marcus president Stanley Marcus:

> Dear Stanley:
>
> That Venetian glassware is extremely handsome, but I must admit the Italians have finally reached my choke price. I have too many unruly friends who insist upon throwing their goblets into the fireplace.

Usually, sometime around each important juncture in his affairs, a little letter fell from Steve Schneider, Clint's Pen Pal from Hell. This was Schneider's housewarming letter:

> FRIENDLY FINANCE COMPANY
> 1201 ½ Main Street
> Dallas, Texas
>
> Mr. Clint W. Murchison Jr.
> 1201 Main Street
> Dallas, Texas
>
> Dear Mr. Murchison (pronounced Mur<u>k</u>ison)
>
> Well, ha! ha! ha!, the old first payment on the new house is now due, and we know you want to start off on the right foot (for your convenience, a draft for $16,543.13—$13,434.15 interest—is attached) ha! ha! ha! This, of course, is the first semi-monthly payment. Unfortunately, due to government regulations, we are

unable to group the car payments on your new Pontiac with the house payment. This would preclude your idea of grouping your washing machine, your icebox, your lawn-mower, your golf clubs, your golf balls, etc., into a hell-of-a-big-one-payment-loan account.

But we know you are good for each and every one of them, Mr. Murchison (pronounced Mur<u>k</u>ison), we think. You **are** good for it, aren't you, Mr. Murchison, ha! ha! ha! Please say you are good for it, please! John Dabney will stand behind you, won't he, Mr. Murchison (pronounced Mur<u>k</u>ison)? Oh, God! No, sir, we are not worried. No, sir—oh, God!

Your Friendly friend,
O.G. COLLIGAN
Hong Kong Real Estate and Touch-and-Go Loans
p.s. Golf balls?—Oh, God!

The house at 6200 and its legends were worthy of such grotesque parody. Watching it being built helped nudge Clint and Jane's daughter Coke Anne toward the college study of architecture at Princeton and Columbia. "I can remember the early days out there, even after we'd moved in, they were still building the pool house. I'd come home from the sixth grade and in the distance I'd hear the constant chipping and chiseling of the stone; it came in great huge pieces to the site, and the workers would chisel it by hand into these four by four by twelve-inch blocks. I think that experience had a definite effect on my decision to study architecture; that's what I wrote in my applications to the schools.

"Generically, the house was modern and in the *oeuvre* of Frank Lloyd Wright and Mies van der Rohe. He appreciated their work and designed it in their styles. Wright's was organic, with a look and materials indigenous to the local terrain, using materials that are native to the setting. Van der Rohe was very technical and mathematical in his approach. The I-beam was his favorite form; he used it a lot. It focused a lot of attention on the details of the structure and how the parts went together, as simplistically as possible. That's difficult to achieve, because you can't hide anything or cover it up with other materials.

"The house had long, low, overhanging eaves, the Wright influence, so that the roof came down and sheltered the windows from the sun's rays in a kind of natural air-conditioning, and yet it didn't have the kind of arts-and-crafts detailing that Wright would have put into one of his houses. There was a lot of glass and exposed steel, and the Travertine marble walls were very much like, say, Mies van der Rohe's Barcelona Pavilion. It was very sprawling, maybe 10,000 square feet. There were eight bedrooms and one large industrial kitchen with lots of commercial restaurant equipment, like the orange-juicer and special dishwashing machines, and the bun warmers that you get in restaurants but don't really find in homes. It was set up for big parties, lots of storage space and stainless steel counters and sinks. The basement was huge and could be used as a bomb-shelter"—the house was still under construction at the time of the 1962 Cuban missile crisis and the national bomb shelter craze.

Clint's only daughter Coke Anne was his little princess.

"There was a wine cellar and a room just for Christmas presents and wrappings. There was a room with all the electrical equipment for the house. Because of his background in electrical engineering, the house was way ahead of its time in terms of the electronics that were installed; but they were also rudimentary. He was ahead of the electronics industry as well, and most of his designs had to be specially built. Whereas now you would have a small light panel to control all the lighting, there was a door that looked like a coat closet off the living room. The whole interior of the closet was switches for controlling the lights. The basement was inhabited by our electrician, Benny—he rode a motorcycle. That was his life, keeping the gadgets running; he was still hooking things up at the very end. He was there nearly 20 years, on staff. There were still elements that had been dreamed up and designed but hadn't been installed. And Benny was always repairing something; some wire would blow or something. There was a sound system; all over the house, in practically every room, there was a little box with 12 buttons on it, and you could punch into one of 12 radio stations. But it wasn't sophisticated. There was a little room in the basement with *12 different radios*, each one tuned to a different station."

Clint's Pen Pal from Hell, Steve Schneider, a Dallas-based consulting geologist, delighted in his 25-year role as a self-appointed sort of postal Greek Chorus during big events in Clint's life. Their friendship was based in part on a mutually sardonic rapport. Schneider was an Army Air Corps pilot in World War II and, after contracting polio, had to walk with metal cane braces. Schneider's favorite story defining their bantering relationship: "Everybody thinks Clint was a cool fish. He didn't talk much, we know that, but I know he was sentimental. I know, because one time I was traveling across the room and Clint turned to me and said, 'Steve?' You know it shook you up anytime he called your name.

"He said, 'When did you get polio?'
I said, 'In 1949.'
He just looked at me and smiled."

Clint and the Social Graces

Clint and Steve Schneider, dressed to the nines in the sixties.

Another time, when he was hospitalized for hip surgery, Schneider recalled: "I'm layin' up there with my damn legs hanging on a chain, and I get this gift-wrapped box from Clint. I open it up and it's a pair of ice skates."

(Schneider got even by never acknowledging the gift. His wife Martha Anne says, "Much later, Clint finally couldn't stand it and he asked me if Steve had gotten the skates. I told him, 'He not only got 'em, he *kept* 'em.'")

Another acquaintance was Elroy (Crazy Legs) Hirsch, the collegiate All-American running back and L.A. Ram star, who had entered the nickname hall of fame with a churning, splay-legged running style. In 1976 he wrote Clint to tell him that a mutual friend was living in the Bahamas, a convenient stop on the next Murchison outing to Spanish Cay.

Classic Clint

> Mr. Elroy Hirsch
> Director of Athletics
> The University of Wisconsin
> 1440 Monroe Street
> Madison, Wisconsin 53706
>
> Dear Elroy:
>
> I appreciate the note about Jack Olson and will certainly look him up on my next journey to the Bahamas; while we are having our third coca-conga, I am sure your name will be casually mentioned. Incidentally, I notice that you signed your latest letter "Legs," although I generally refer to you when speaking with our mutual friends as "Crazy"; I guess when you get into higher education this is one of the changes that occur.

The era of the weather satellite has made the view of earth from space as commonplace as the 10 o'clock news, but in 1968 such photos were stunning and miraculous novelties. It was even better when you personally owned that segment of the earth that was captured in the space camera's lens.

In late 1968 during the series of Apollo fights leading up to the moon landing in July of the next year, NASA shot from orbit panoramic views of many places, including that idyllic spot fifteen miles northeast of Green Turtle Cay in the Abaco Group of the Bahamas: it was Clint's island, Spanish Cay.

> **NATIONAL AERONAUTICS AND SPACE ADMINISTRATION**
> **MANNED SPACECRAFT CENTER**
> Houston, Texas 77058
>
> Mr. Clint Murchison Jr.
> 2300 First National Bank Building
> Dallas, Texas 75202
>
> Dear Clint:
>
> Enclosed are the photos and transparencies I promised you when we met at Tom Webb's a few weeks ago. Instructions for finding Spanish Cay are on the reverse side of the print. Both of these pictures were taken in October on the Apollo 7 flight.
>
> Sincerely yours,
> GEORGE S. TRIMBLE
> Deputy Director

Clint's first letter in reply, sent the same week, was,

> **Dear George:**
> **I certainly appreciate the two photographs which you sent. Someday, I hope that you will be able to come to Spanish Cay and see what it looks like at a slightly closer range.**
> **Sincerely, Clint.**

A few weeks later, with time to frame and savor the shots and to look out the office window at the slush and blear of a Dallas February, he sent an afterthought note:

> **Mr. George S. Trimble**
> **Manned Spacecraft Center**
> **Houston, Texas**
>
> **Dear George:**
> **Spanish Cay does look small in that photograph, but it certainly looks inviting. If you really want to do something nice for the first man to land the lunar module, you ought to arrange a splashdown off our beach.**
> **Sincerely, Clint.**

Neil Armstrong and the Apollo 11 crew would splash down, as scheduled, on the other side of the world in the Pacific. But it hadn't hurt to ask.

The Coca-Conga mentioned in Clint's letter to Crazy Legs Hirsch was the official drink of Spanish Cay, a concoction that had the taste of the Islands and the effect of a coconut landing on the head. "It was a real tradition, almost from the moment of your arrival at the island," says Coke Anne. "When we'd fly there we would land and then take a Jeep to the house. Ready and waiting for us on silver trays were the drinks called the Coca-Conga, which was coconut milk, rum—lots of rum—and maybe a little lime juice. The key ingredient was a powdered coconut milk mix called Coco-Whip. You could only buy it in Nassau, which was why it was so hard to duplicate a Coca-Conga anywhere else. Once you'd had just one, it did you in. You felt no pain.

"We would sit on the porch of the house, drink Coca-Congas and look at the view of the ocean in the distance. Farther away from the house were the coconut groves. We'd walk on down to the beach, and in the process of doing that, we had to walk under some stands of Australian

Pines that had these little one-inch cones. They were totally painful to walk on. (You immediately took off your shoes upon arriving at the island; everyone stayed barefoot.) But no one felt the discomfort of walking on the pine cones because of the Coca-Congas, very efficient pain-killers. It was only in the morning, before the drinking, that it hurt.

"And then my father quit drinking in 1976. And lo and behold, the next time I went down to the island, those pine trees had been cut down." With no more painkiller around, had he gotten rid of the source of the pain? "I think there was a definite connection between his temperance and the cutting down of the trees," his daughter says.

There was another arrival ritual on flights to the island. As his son Clint III recalls, "Just before the plane would start to land, Dad would get up and go into the bathroom aboard the plane. Usually he'd have boarded the plane wearing a business suit, having come to the airport straight from the office. In a couple of minutes, he'd bound out of the toilet, into the aisle of the plane, wearing his bathing suit. He was ready for Spanish Cay then. It was a little like watching Clark Kent leap out of the phone booth."

Clint enjoyed going to Spanish Cay as often as possible; he also enjoyed showing it off:

> Mr. August A. Busch, Jr.
>
> Dear Mr. Busch:
>
> Bill Georges told me that you were going to be in Florida shortly and would probably be sailing through the Bahamas. As I mentioned to you, I have an island down there and it happens that Jane and I will be there for several days starting February 24, and again for several days starting March 21. If you can join us on either of these occasions, I hope you will do so.
>
> If you think you might be in the general vicinity of the island on any other occasion, please let me know and I will advise Paul Reinholm, the manager, to expect you. I am sure that after a difficult cruise you would enjoy a couple of days at a landfall, even if we do serve Heineken's.

Clint and the Social Graces

> The name of the island is Spanish Cay. It is located fifteen miles northeast of Green Turtle Cay in the Abaco Group of the Bahamas. There is a landing strip on the island and the dock will easily accommodate a boat with a draft of six or seven feet.

Busch, the Budweiser beer baron and owner of the St. Louis baseball Cardinals, did indeed visit the island. Clint had the island's food-and-beverage staffer Willard Hutchinson see that when Busch was served beer, it came in the distinctive stubby green bottles of Heineken—whose labels had been removed and replaced by Budweiser labels.

Getaway to paradise: Clint's island, Spanish Cay.

Classic Clint

Some people would rather speak in public before a large group than learn quantum physics; Clint had the opposite problem. His consistent shyness was the stuff of legend and was often misperceived as aloofness. When a man's constitutionally ingrained shyness prohibits him even from saying "Good morning" to colleagues on an office elevator, it is not hard to predict the response he would make to an invitation to speak in public. Even so, he usually managed to decline the invitation with a disarmingly puckish approach.

Because of his financial success, his worldwide travels, his many connections and, indeed, the mystique of his phantom celebrity, his opinions were all the more sought after by groups in the business community. In 1981 he was asked by Richland College in Dallas to be a speaker at a business leadership seminar. The college's official, Mary Menig, asked if he would address the group on his ideas of the keys to success in the business world.

> January 13, 1981
>
> Dear Ms. Menig:
>
> I regret that I will be unable to speak at Richland College in April. I would suggest, however, that the key elements to success in business are hard work, dedication, and having a rich father.

He even shied away from public writing:

> October 14, 1963
>
> Mr. E. Gordon Smith
> Lawyers Title Insurance Corporation
> Dallas, Texas
>
> Dear Gordon:
>
> I appreciate your offering me a forum in the *Lawyers Title News* to give my opinion of what will happen to our economy in 1964. However, in order not to disturb any reputation which I may have for prescience, I would prefer to write this article in January, 1965.
>
> Will this help?

Clint and the Social Graces

An East Texas college student wrote to ask him for a summary of his philosophy of life, perhaps for a thesis.

> March 26, 1969
>
> Miss Marsha Spivey
> Tyler, Texas
>
> Dear Miss Spivey:
>
> Frankly, I am of the opinion that a person should not begin stating his philosophy of life until he is 60 or 70 years old. In fact, I believe that most of the successful people I know spend very little time philosophizing and a great deal of time doing.
>
> Maybe that's a philosophy, but if it is I don't want to think about it because if I did I would be breaking my own rule.

For the last quarter century of his life, Clint's pet charitable project had been the Boys Clubs. In his debut column of July 1970, in the Cowboy Newsletter, he had written that his remuneration for the columns was being donated to the Boys Club of Dallas. In a later column on Oct. 2, entitled "Better Boys, Better Men," he wrote "In the first of these weekly pearls of wisdom, I mentioned that the publisher of the Dallas Cowboys Newsletter was making a modest (my terminology) contribution to the Dallas Boys Club in lieu of direct payment for my efforts. This has turned out to be an excellent arrangement: the publisher cannot be accused by his stockholders of overpayment, and the Boys Club can use the money.

"So what is the Dallas Boys Club? I'm sure that many of you are no better informed than I was about 15 years ago when my interest in these organizations began. I had heard the name, intuitively thought well of them, but that was about it..."

He went on to tell the history of the national and Dallas Boys Clubs and to give examples of the impact the Dallas club particularly had made in stopping the drift of many kids into law trouble. He neglected to mention that ever since his interest had begun, he had become the single biggest benefactor of the clubs.

Considering his long-standing image as Mr. Boys Club, he may have been bemused 12 years later, when a letter addressed to him in care of the Boys Club of Dallas arrived from E. E. (Buddy) Fogelson, a Dallas oilman and husband of actress Greer Garson.

Classic Clint

> **Dear Clint:**
>
> Enclosed is a Cashiers Check in the amount of $2,212.90 made payable to the Boys Club of Dallas, Inc. This check represents funds which have been sitting in a bank account I started many years ago from contributions solicited to start a Boys Club in Dallas. Inasmuch as we now have a fine Dallas club, I thought it was time to turn over these funds to you.

Clint's reply seemed to pull the difficult trick of combining a thank-you with a scolding:

> **Dear Buddy:**
>
> Thank you so much for cleaning out the old account for the Boys Clubs of Dallas. It is too bad it wasn't a savings account! At present rates we could own half of Dallas County by now.

Along with time, money, and affection, Clint lent his terseness to Boys Club business. John L. Schoellkopf served on the club's board of directors for more than 20 years, beginning in 1965. "The original director of the club," Schoellkopf recalls, "was a lanky and loquacious Alabamian named Emory Gulledge. Emory did a good job and he was forever trying to extract more money from Clint for various projects—usually after telling some heart-wrenching story of a youngster saved.

"One time I remember he told Clint, 'Why, just the other day, I sat down on a big rock with two youngsters and talked them out of what could've been a life of crime.' Then he said he could save even more kids if Clint would come up with the money for a new gym.

"Clint's reply was characteristically short: 'I'll pay for all the big rocks you need, Emory.'"

Chapter Two
Adventures With Dook and Jane

"Wednesday is too far away to worry about."

The urgencies of World War II swindled thousands of American teenage boys out of the rights to their last years of callowness. Boyhood was over. It often ended overnight. The study of war was added to everyone's curriculum.

After prep school at Lawrenceville and an undergraduate year at Massachusetts Institute of Technology, Clint entered the V-12 program of the Navy, an accelerated college program ending in a military commission. As a wartime innovation that churned out officers at the same near-miraculous rate as America's industrial machine was turning out bombers and tanks, the V-12 program funneled thousands of top-rank candidates into a handful of universities geared up for the studies. They were the elite of the country's college students, including athletes and scholars. Among the exotic results of V-12, schools like Southwestern Louisiana Institute suddenly started beating schools like Michigan State on the football field.

V-12 sent Clint to Duke University in Durham, N.C., as, officially, a Marine private who could expect a commission upon completing his accelerated degree work in electrical engineering. In wartime Durham, there were still echoes of an exceptional event: the one and

Classic Clint

only asterisk that appears in the list of Rose Bowl results happened in Durham on Jan. 1, 1942, when the Rose Bowl game was moved to North Carolina from Pasadena out of concern for a possible Japanese attack on the West Coast. Pearl Harbor had been barely three weeks before. Duke had been invited to the Rose Bowl to play Oregon State but ended up as the home team. Oregon State won the game 20-16.

World War II: as a Marine at Duke University in the accelerated officers' training program. —photo courtesy of Virginia Linthicum

Adventures With Dook and Jane

The precise, businesslike look of a Clint letter, crisply and immaculately typed on an IBM, was to come later. His letters home to Clint, Sr., and to his stepmother, Virginia, were written invariably, and meticulously, in ink on Duke University stationery in a blockish and upright script. They showed early signs of his terseness and economy in language. At times they suggested signs of a young man who was capable of a droll self-examination. They could also be dutifully, if carefully, chatty and occasionally smacked of homesickness.

> Sunday.
>
> Dear Daddy:
>
> When I was in Lawrenceville I stayed in pretty much. The proctor, name of Bill, wouldn't let us out. I figured that I was the smartest boy at Lawrenceville; under those conditions I may conceivably have decided that I was the smartest boy in the world, as you said. Anyway, when I landed in M.I.T. I met several of the boys who were enough smarter than I that I decided to leave the scholastics to them.
>
> Since then I have not considered myself a scholar. I get fairly good grades here at Dook, but that is Dook's fault.
>
> My door is never locked, and it isn't even allowed, as an officer may want to inspect. Last week I went to six dances and one movie; this week I only made two dances and a movie, since there weren't any more dances, and the other movies were no good.
>
> Tonight we of the Engineers are putting on a sing, followed by an open house; tomorrow we have to go to a training film, and Tuesday I'm going to another dance. Wednesday is too far away to worry about.
>
> I say all this merely to indicate that I'm not anti-social; but even so your fears are not unfounded. If they keep me around these ignorant swabbies long enough I'm liable to decide that I'm the smartest man in the world all over again. Then I'll have to go back to M.I.T.
>
> It is axiomatic that no Marine shuns a beer or a babe. With love,
>
> Clint W.

Classic Clint

Saturday

Dear Virginia:

We find ourselves now in the midst of Dook's famous midwinter social season, which inevitably comes at the end of the winter instead of the mid. Harry James, Glenn Miller, Kay Kyser, etc. What an assortment we have for our dances! All, of course, on record, at the protest of Petrillo.*

Speaking of music, I've been feeling pretty glum in the early morns of late. My little radio, after coughing and stuttering and generally wrecking itself, has finally ended up in ye olde repair shoppe, and I do mean ended. It's been there for five weeks, and I'm told it has a rather chronic case of no-tubitis. At first they thought the trouble was that one of the condensers wouldn't condense, but after I gave them $4.12 ($0.12 for parts, $4.00 for labor) for replacing it they became quite satisfied that that wasn't the trouble at all.

(After a weekend pass) I arrived at dear old D.U. three hours late. However, I had a note from an MP saying the train broke down, so nothing happened to me. The surprising thing about it all is that the train really did break down.

You'd never know it, but it's still before breakfast—the most beautiful part of the day, called that, no doubt, because it looks so much like bedtime. I am looking forward excitedly to seeing the sun come up.

I got a letter from J.D.,** and he says he's swinging out nightly in the Orange Grove, or whatever the name of his night club is, to the hep jive of five or 10 boys from a local colored division. Till 10 p.m. He reports they have Pabst *in cans* direct from Cairo, and that the happy natives are still willing to bum a cigarette off a soldier.

And that's the news from here; I will return you to our correspondent in Tamipolo.

*James C. Petrillo was the militant head of the American Federation of Musicians and preferred that Americans hire live bands rather than playing their records.

**His brother, John Dabney, was an Army Air Corps pilot serving overseas.

Adventures With Dook and Jane

Wednesday

Dear Daddy:

I'm pretty sure I'll be home on Feb. 23 or 24 for a few days. It seems to be cheating for them to let us know ahead of time.

Last week I wandered back from wrestling practice and who should be here but Bob Thompson & Co. * Previously he had walked in my room looking for "Little Murchison" and scared heck out of my roommate, who looked upon him as a prelude to a presidential inspection. We went downtown and had supper and discussed the weighty problems of the Corps as only a major and a private can discuss them.

I just got a letter from my old buddy Ricardo and he's not going to Parris Island next month after all. They had such an influx of officer candidates last term that they have to restrict them this time; doing it according to age and college standing—now instead of six terms, liberal arts boys have to have completed seven, and be a certain age, depending upon the quota of the particular college. All this doesn't affect me, as I'm an engineer (in training). The Navy has also decided to take out all the Naval ROTC students in the junior year or higher, even the engineers. So my class of 12 loses four. They get their commission immediately, why, I don't know. That's the Navy.

My chances of getting to M.I.T. are even less than my chance of flying; some boys are leaving for technology at the end of this term, but they aren't Marines—there isn't a Marine unit there. I couldn't get my diploma from M.I.T. now anyway, even if I changed back, or at least not the kind of diploma I want, so I'd just as soon wait and do some graduate work, what amount depending on how they accept Dook credits. With love,

*His father's young protege from Dallas, Bob Thompson, was already a blustery Marine major. After the war he and Clint formed Centex Construction.

Dear Daddy:

Enclosed is that excess train ticket I had several months back.

We went into khakis today, which pleases me no end. And also went to another (of many) training films. This one had Bob Hope and Betty Hutton in it, though . . . I'm almost sunburned; Friday and Saturday I played about seven hours of tennis, which wore me down no end. At this point I would like to place a request for my tennis racquet; it's

Classic Clint

in my closet. I think there are two there; if so, send me the one with the leather grip on the handle.

There are only going to be four EE* seniors left next semester—all but eight of the engineer-civilians are now 1-A, and the eight are 4-F. So we will fight it out alone, no doubt. I have to give a speech before a bunch of North Carolina electrical engineers in a couple of weeks; the professor in charge of the meeting (of the Amer, Inst. of E.E.'s) told me to make it simple so they could understand it. You better write me another of those letters.

I got a letter from Dick, who says he's doing the same thing I'm doing, to wit, *nada*.

I've recently come onto a good little "Short Course in Japanese" which I plan to mince over in boot camp and thereafter so that I'll be able to tell it to the natives in style:

All of which reminds me of today's history lesson: In 1799, John Paul Jones, in the *Bonhomme Richard*, was attacking the British HMS *Serapis*. The Marines were in the rigging keeping up steady rifle fire and throwing grenades, but nonetheless the situation was pretty bad. One particular Gyrene had just had his rifle shot away, and the flames were licking up his pants legs, when Jones waved his sword over his head and said, "I have not yet begun to fight!" The Marine looked down and said, "In every outfit you always find some knucklehead who never gets the word."

*Electrical Engineering majors

Dear Daddy:

Your letter didn't say anything about the big SAE party, but I guess it occurred anyway. They were probably held in by the Coca-Cola ration, though. Reynolds is at Parris Island now. It must be pretty tepid there, as they recently had the red flag which means 'too hot to drill' waved in their happy faces. They've also opened a new OCS*, twice the size of Quantico, with the announced purpose of getting the V-12 overseas by November—due to Saipan, no doubt.**

Now I just have four months of the old college life left, and it certainly is a nice feeling. That will finish off two years of almost solid schooling which is too solid for this kid. My eyes have fallen considerably below standard as well, so this semester I'm going to do as little reading as possible. I have little or no desire to spend the rest of this war as a private, I'll tell you. I assume I'll get a degree from here, although they haven't said so. They may decide that Duke is too good to accept M.I.T. credits. One way or the other doesn't make me a lot of difference, as I expect to return to M.I.T. anyway.

They have a dorm full of girls here in which you can speak only Spanish. Obviously this is the place to go to practice up on the *Espanol*. However, they're all a little too fast for me, since I'm slightly out of practice, to say the least. And it's embarrassing to have to say that a wild and woolly Texan learned most of his Spanish in New Jersey.

The word 'Texas' is really a magic word, and performs all manner of miracles, as I'm sure you've noticed in the past. However, you did miss the pleasure of wearing a Marine uniform, to which people react similarly. In fact, I have been encouraged to believe that a Marine from Texas is something of an unbeatable combination, and at the same time I have encouraged that belief.

I got a letter from J.D., and he was feeling pretty bad, as he'd just finished the last bit of beer he'd flown in in his wing trays. You ought to seal some bottles of Scotch in cans and send them—probably raise morale all over China.

Love,
Clint W.

*Officers' Candidate School.
**Saipan was a costly Marine Pacific island battle.

In the summer of 1941, Clint had met Jane Katherine Coleman on a blind date in Dallas. She was petite and sixteen. Their courtship continued by phone, mail, and occasionally in person when Clint visited her at school in San Antonio and Austin. It was war time, and Clint, Sr., noted one inconvenience: "Clint W. would get a long-distance girl during gas rationing."

Jane would later say she found Clint's sense of humor to be the thing that most attracted her. After Duke, he entered Marine training at Parris Island, South Carolina; Camp Lejeune, North Carolina; and

Classic Clint

Officers Candidate School at Quantico, Virginia. His letters to Jane while in the service showed his deep affection for his wife-to-be and clearly demonstrated that his Marine experience had not affected his classic sense of humor.

> Saturday
> 5 Feb 45
>
> My Darling,
>
> I guess you think I've just forgotten all about you but I haven't, really Jane. It all happened this way. Thursday morning they woke us up 20 minutes early and we laid around in bed awhile so they got mad. That night we had a field day. No, I take it back. That all happened Wednesday. Thursday they were still mad so they gave us a fire drill at 4:00 a.m. In a fire drill you jump out of bed, grab a bucket, run outside, run around in the cold for a while, then get back in bed and drop off to sleep just as reveille blows. We've been thinking it over and have about decided that we were gypped as this building is fireproof. Another night, another field day. Friday comes with a conditioning hike and of course a field day (as we always have Friday night for the inspection Saturday). Don't feel bad though as the picture is now brightening. The NCO's are now not so mad, and it's Saturday, big weekend, etc. So we get up this morning, chipper as usual, have the old inspection, then watch the O.C. Battalion drill team competition. Nobody from dear old Plat 4 was on the team as our lieutenant didn't hear about it, but with only 4 days practice, only a little each day, those boys from "C" put on the best drill exhibition you'd ever hope to see. No kidding, they drilled 15 minutes and didn't do a single thing by the book, spinning rifles like batons, etc. We hadn't seen it before, and they snowed us as much as the judges, who were amazed. We started the big snow job on the judges with a V pointed toward the judges, the leader saluting from the point of the V, and two boys coming out from each side doing a rifle twirling salute, the rest being at present arms. Well, the judges could take that, but when they saw the two from the sides were identical twins they gave up. Our captain told us to keep up the good work and we'd be in Quantico in two weeks. That sounds pretty good if it's true, doesn't it?
>
> I went to a movie tonight which you really must see. In the first 20 minutes Dracula had appeared, killed someone, and been killed (stake through heart, rays of sun, etc.). Next came the mad scientist, the Wolf Man, a hunchback, and, of course, Frankenstein's monster. I'm not kidding either; it got so that every time a new fiend appeared the

audience laughed. Incidentally the Wolf Man was killed by a silver bullet, necessarily from the pistol of the girl who loved him (more laughs from spectators) and the Monster went down in quicksand, scientist in his arms, but only after hurling the hunchback from a castle tower.

I've been eating my mint tablets all week, Jane, and they are so good. How did you know I wanted some? But really, I'm awful with candy & things you send me. I hardly let anyone else get any at all. I guess I shouldn't, but goodness me . . .

I love you with all my heart.

Your Clinton

Friday
10 Feb 45

My Darling,

Just to illustrate what "fouled up" means, I'd just started writing this letter when those of us going to Quantico fell out. They called the roll, then in we went again. I don't know, maybe they thought someone had gone over the hill . . .

I imagine that there's a lot more field work at Q-co than here, so it'll probably be mucho more fun, except for the cold of course. For instance, yesterday we ran a compass azimuth out thru a swamp, coming eventually to the conclusion that the compass is on its way out; and then we made a small scale banzai charge on some unsuspecting soul who maintains he riddled us with machine gun bullets. At Quantico there probably won't be any "I got you — no you didn't" arguments as there they use live ammo. That is one of my grievances, but that's life. I plan to do all my maneuvering in subterranean caverns.

We just ate and so it's off for the field day. I'll write you more tomorrow.

I love you, Jane.

Clinton

P.S. PFC Clint W. is happy to announce that his address is now

    c/o Officer Candidates Class
    Marine Barracks, Quantico, VA

I hope to get most of my mail there. But really sometimes we get some here; the boy next to me got a postcard last Monday. The mail clerk is really popular here. Everybody always has a good word for him. I can't repeat the word.

Classic Clint

Monday
14 Feb 45

My Darling,

Today I got the sweetest letter and the cutest Valentines card, both from you, and it makes me so happy. If the surprise you mentioned in the letter doesn't get here tomorrow I may not get it, since they're pretty slow on forwarding things. Isn't that the worst? But even so, thank you so much, darling; you're so sweet to me, and I love you so very much. It's so much fun getting something from you. I wish I had a desk so I could sit my little card up on it; you know the bottom folds out and the little girl can stand up . . .

Leaving here surely will be nice. They'll probably let us *walk* in and out of the barracks there. I'll tell you all about it as soon as I can.

There have been dice games going on almost continuously since Saturday. Pretty big games too — one boy won $300. About half of that came from one of the sergeants. Of course everyone grieves . . .

I miss you so tonight Jane. You're just starting dead week now, and I won't be able to keep you from studying at all. Isn't that awful? Just think, if I could just walk in the night before the government exam and save you all that studying. By the way, when we're in Boston what are you going to do while I'm studying? I guess I just won't study much. You know you're going to have to go up there about a week before me because you said you wanted to pick out the apartment by yourself. I hope we can get the place I'm thinking about, though. It's just perfect — the right size, the right place, and they paint it & carpet the floor to suit you. Really the best for Janeson.

I love you with all my heart,

Your Clinton.

Monday
20 Feb 45

My Darling,

Another day, another dollar sixty-seven. We've just finished the quiz and have 45 minutes to go before the sandman arrives. This morning we switched to taking apart and putting back together against time the machine gun. We get a minute to do it. I only cut myself in three places & broke two fingernails, so I got off pretty easy. If we should ever have a car and go driving someday, don't be surprised if I stop in the middle of the road and try to field strip it in 38 seconds sometimes. I'll probably be in the habit by then . . .

We haven't been having to do calisthenics in the mornings since we got here, but the word just came that tomorrow we start. I'm not so hot for the idea, but I haven't bothered to contact the colonel yet. It certainly is frigid out there, though. I think the idea must be to make us hungry so we will eat their breakfasts — yesterday for instance, we had a helping of pork & beans, a piece of bread and a cup of coffee, period, no seconds, final. After Duke it wouldn't have been bad but after Lejeune it's a little discouraging. Let us hope our move Wednesday is for the better.

It's almost time for lights out now. Boonas nochas.

I love you,

Clinton W.

Monday
1 Mar 45

My darling,

Goodness, I haven't heard from you in so long. You just hurry up and get caught up now; I just have to hear from you. I got a letter from Virginia* today. She was giving all the dope on you, you know. However, at one point she said that we were a perfect match, which is a heck of a thing to say about you I guess. Oh well, you'll live it down. She said Frank & Norinne** talked about coming up in June; if all the Murchisons come we may have a pretty big wedding after all. (The crowds lining the streets parted to allow the bride to enter the church. There appears to be some confusion due to the absence of the groom; he's only six hours late though, and everyone expresses great confidence in his ultimate arrival. There was a stir several hours ago when an usher from the Majestic Theater attempted to break thru the police cordon. He was removed to the county jail.

"Wait! Here's a flash! Sheriff Smoot Smith just reported that it wasn't an usher, but a Marine in a white uniform. He claims he's the groom. It will have to be cleared thru Marine Corps Headquarters, Washington, however, so for the next 23 hours we will hear Jerald Gay play the famous WFAA mouth organ. For further developments stay tuned to this station.")

It's supposed to be spring now, but it certainly has been staying cold for a long time. It's pretty nice for field work though, and we do a lot of that this week. You don't get too hot, that is. I always like some

Classic Clint

real hot weather during lunch though. I lay out in the sun and doze off in nothing flat. It's certainly dee-lightful when you consider that someone has to go thru here when there's snow on the ground.

We had a parade tonight. They're great sport, as they come during your quote free unquote time. You get in at 5:00, get ready for the parade, finally finish at 6:30, get to chow an hour late, fall out for thisa and thata, et cetera. I may as well warn you now Jane, it's going to take you 6 1/2 years to get me to eat my meals slow, "slow" being anything over 3 1/2 minutes. I guess that's about the worst habit they get us in, and the hardest to break. Even when we're at the hotel in D.C. we knock down the beef before the waiter can get the steak knives on the table. We'll probably have to work out a system for a while whereby I eat my meals in the kitchen first then come out in the open and play like I'm eating.

I'll write again tomorrow. So until then I remain

Your secret admirer,

Clinton Q. Murch. Jr.

*Clint's stepmother Virginia
**His uncle and aunt, Frank & Norinne Murchison

Second Lieutenant Clint Murchison, Jr., in dress whites married Jane Coleman in Dallas on June 12, 1945.

Saturday
21 April 45

My darling,

... It's now Sunday. I tried to call you this morning but the service is rather poor here. I guess we're too close to Washington. Yesterday afternoon we were scheduled to go out on the field (to the range to fire BAR's) for the first time, and so true to form at 9:00 yesterday morning it started snowing. They issue us long woollies, sheepskin coats, mittens, fur caps, etc., so we weren't supposed to get cold. That held true except for the old feet. The mud was about 6" deep, had the consistency of soup, and will probably replace Freon as a refrigerating agent after the war. We didn't walk in it. We laid in it ...

There are lots of mild deficiencies here [Quantico], but with the shiny goal in sight, all's well. This is so much like civilization too. Carolina, perish thy memory.

They're always telling you here not to trust your memory, but always to check the chamber of a weapon to see if it's loaded. So every-now-and-then a boy strips and reassembles a weapon and then during a break between classes one of the instructors puts a blank cartridge in the rifle. So the class reconvenes and they tell the boys to pull the trigger of their weapons. Last month one passed out he was so surprised. It's pretty amusing. Once the gunny pulling the trick left his watch on the table. The fire from the blank blew the watch into the wall, so that time the student had the chuckle.

Yesterday we stripped & reassembled the BAR [Browning Automatic Rifle] in 10 minutes, blindfolded. I put my identification bracelet in instead of the recoil spring, so I had to start over.

We have a test on the BAR tomorrow so I have to study on it some.

I love you, darling,

Your Clinton

P.S. I almost forgot, darling! Guess what. The day we left Lejeune, about an hour before departure, we had a mail call and I got some pralines. Aren't I lucky? Thank you so much, Jane. They didn't last ten minutes, or there were several U of T boys within two bunks of mine, who knew of Lammes. I got some though, you know. I surely am glad they came before I left, too. Good timing, I understand. I do love you so; there's no one as sweet as my little Janeson. Goodbye for now; I'll be thinking of you every minute, and missing you more than ever before. I want to be with you so.

Love always,

Clinton

Chapter Three
Thanks for the Memories

"He could say more in a sentence than some could get in a book. A good thing, too, because his notes grew shorter as time passed."
–Kenneth Swanson

With his talents for terseness and the *bon mot*, and if he hadn't empires to run and fame to achieve, Clint Murchison, Jr., might have gone on to become a wag—one of those professionally anonymous observers with something pithy to say about any subject. He started young. He committed his first known pun, on his own name, when he wrote a story for the Country Day School newspaper, describing a grey day with the phrase *murky sun*. World War II short-changed his generation of the luxury of sophomoric humor; his letters home from the officers' training program at Duke University show a drollness and a sense of irony several cuts above what most of us face, flinchingly, when forced to read what we have written home from school. His spelling of Duke as Dook probably said more about his irreverence than his sense of slapstick.

One of his oldest friends was Kenneth Swanson, who began as one of his youngest, in their boyhood days of barefoot summers and innocent, habitual mischief; an era when a traffic jam was a special event in Dallas, and North Dallas was much farther south of Oklahoma than it would soon be. Clint, Sr., and his boys lived among the wild acreages of Addison, north of Dallas. To people down in Dallas it might as well have been Kenya.

Kenneth Swanson remembers: "Clint was one of my first friends. We were classmates at University Park Grade School. He lived 10 miles north of our house, and in those days that put you in the country. His father had purchased a polo club, and the family home was the renovated clubhouse—complete with a roulette wheel and other casino amusements. The grounds had a tennis court, the club's swimming pool and lanai, and a large, terraced garden around a cement replica of a wrecked pirate ship. The developed portion of the property was surrounded by woods through which White Rock Creek flowed (on rare occasions flowing right on in to the swimming pool). Clint's younger brother Burk ran a trap line into the woods. Could there be a more exciting place for young boys to grow up?

"During those grade-school years Clint and I often walked the few blocks to my house and spent every afternoon playing after school. We spent several weeks each summer on Matagorda Island down off the South Texas coast. It was under long-term lease to Clint, Sr., except for a bombing range on the northeast end used by the then Army Air Corps. Fishing, boating, hunting, exploring, working the cattle and small herd of buffalo—every day was a new adventure. John and Clint, Jr., could each invite two friends to spend time on the island. Delo Castleberry, who lived in Rockport, was the manager and looked after us. There was a cook borrowed from the Murchison home, and two mechanics who kept all the equipment running and doubled as hunting and fishing guides. After we'd reached our middle teens, sometimes in the winter we'd make short trips to the island for quail, deer, goose, and duck hunting.

"We hunted quail from topless 1936 and 1937 Ford sedans equipped with gun boots and bucket seats bolted to the front fenders. The birds often hid under large cactus clumps. You'd hunt them by quietly driving up within range and then gunning the motor to flush them into flight. It was tough shooting because they often left cover only after the motor had been gunned several times, and by the time you'd done that, the car was rocking considerably. Your reputation as a marksman depended on the behavior of the driver. An abundance of rattlesnakes made conventional hunting inadvisable; it was too dangerous to walk the birds up behind bird dogs. Duck and goose hunting was done from barrels sunk into the sand near fresh-water ponds. This worked fine except that rains washed out the sand around the barrels, causing them to float and raising them above ground level. The hunter's weight would lower them enough to provide a good hiding place, but every time you fired a shot the recoil would tip the rim of the barrel backwards, dipping a copious sluice of icy water down your backside. The island was unique in many ways.

"One year Clint invited Toddie Lee Wynne, Jr., to join us regulars. I didn't know him, other than that he was the son of one of Mr. Murchison's close friends. When we were down at the island, all of us were anxious to get started early every morning, but Toddie Lee would sleep an hour or two later than the rest of us. After about a week we were all pretty tired of it, and somebody had an idea. That morning we were having hotcakes for breakfast. When Toddie Lee finally got up and came to the table, we all sat down with him and watched while he doused his hotcakes with the motor oil we'd substituted for the maple syrup in the pitcher. He took a bite, chewed briefly, looked each of us in the eye in turn, picked up the pitcher, poured more motor oil on his hotcakes, and then systematically ate every bite on his plate. We were impressed. And he kept sleeping late."

It is Kenneth Swanson's contention that those idyllic days on Matagorda Island in the thirties played a part in a minute but significant change in the design of America's automobiles.

"The starters on those old Fords were located on the floorboard, next to where the light dimmers were. Much of the driving was done on the beach, and it had to be done near the water line, where the sand was wet and solid; dry sand would trap a car in a minute. The prolonged exposure to the salt spray from driving on the beach would short out the starters in a hurry. Not only was it inconvenient to replace the parts frequently, but you were liable to be stranded with a drowned starter miles from the house. So Mr. Murchison instructed the mechanics to replace the floorboard starters with pushbuttons mounted on the dashboard to protect them from the spray. It worked, of course, and later, some executives from Ford Motor Company were guests on the island. They asked about the novel dashboard buttons. When it was explained to them, they said it sounded like a good idea. They made the change in Ford's next model year, and a year after that the whole car industry followed suit."

As the years passed, the island chums' paths diverged. "Clint enrolled in Country Day School and Lawrenceville and then MIT. I completed high school and junior college at Kemper, then entered the University of Texas. He became a Marine; I enlisted in the naval flight-training program. We both lived in Dallas after our marriages, but I soon moved to Midland. Inexorably, we were together less frequently as our lives took different paths. But the feeling that he was a good and close friend never diminished. He was often in my mind. Sometimes, my mail would bring something from Clint—perhaps enlargements of snapshots of us he had run across from years ago at the island, or a terse comment when he was reminded by a current event of something we had done together as kids.

"There was little about Clint's physical aspect to mark his true stature—until one looked into his warm, intelligent, laughing eyes. He was made a small man, but he was agile, quick, and fast, both physically and mentally. He outran us all.

"What made him a giant? His lineage? It certainly played a major part. His father's business success is widely known, but the bequests he left his children included much more than wealth. There was enterprise, hard work, industry, consideration of others (even those who were *not* less fortunate), personal accountability; they were among the many qualities he possessed and insisted upon from his children and demonstrated to us, their friends. He never had to discipline us; we could tell if he disapproved of something we had done and would forthwith resolve not to repeat that mistake again. He believed that if someone in his employ made him money, that employee should share in the rewards. He did not waste time investigating people's honesty or reliability in advance. If it later proved that his confidence had been misplaced, that was the time to sever the relationship. These qualities, and many others, he passed on to his sons.

"All the Murchisons were private people. In Clint, especially, this quality approached shyness. Those who did not know him well often misread this trait as coldness, but they couldn't have been more wrong. They were caring people whose natures were to give rather than to receive. Clint and John's record of social service was largely unknown, other than John's election as president of the Boy Scouts of America and Clint's sponsorship of the annual Salesmanship Club Cowboys game and his work for the Boys' Clubs.

"Clint had the common touch with people. Nothing in his appearance or demeanor gave any clue that he was a wealthy man. He was always willing to share a friend's troubles or problems, and to help where he could. He was a man of intelligence, warmth and wit. His friends, from all walks of life, were myriad. I can't recall anyone who didn't like him.

"His last words to me were 'I'll be seein' you.' It is a marvelous promise. After all, Clint never misled me."

Kenneth Swanson died on February 22, 1991.

First Impressions

Joshua Muss was the second generation of his Chicago and Washington, D.C. investment family to do business and pleasure with Clint Murchison, Jr. "In the early fifties," he recalls, "my Dad and Clint put together a company, Texas Management Company, by combining some 20,000 military housing units which they owned, either together or separately. The interests in the company were allocated based on the values of the properties each had contributed. It required an elaborate computation, which Clint did on the back of an envelope while he and Dad had lunch one day at '21' in New York. About eight years later, when the last of the properties was sold, Clint sent Dad a note that said simply,

Not bad for calculations on the back of an envelope.

"That note was accompanied by a schedule prepared by Gene Hewitt, showing that 30 million dollars in equities had been produced by the properties, and it correlated very closely to the values they had originally estimated on the back of that envelope."

Joshua Muss's favorite Clint story "Goes back to the first time I met him, in Chicago, in January of 1960. It was a cold, blustery day, and I had just dropped my Dad off at Midway Airport to catch a plane to New York. As Dad got out of the car, I noticed him stop to talk to a slight young man with a crewcut and glasses; he was standing, shivering slightly, on the curb outside the terminal, wearing what looked like a lightweight brown suit. It was probably OK for Dallas weather, but this was Chicago in January.

"They visited for a few minutes, and then Dad introduced me to Clint and asked if I would drop him off downtown. Coincidentally, he was staying at the Centex apartment, which was in the same building where I lived. While we drove downtown, Clint mentioned he was in Chicago to make the final arrangements to get an NFL franchise for a Dallas team. After we'd driven for a few minutes, I kept noticing that despite the bitter cold weather, Clint didn't seem to have a topcoat.

"'Did you leave your coat at the airport?' I asked him.

"He said, 'No, I don't own a coat. They're always getting in the way, or you're sitting on them, or you're checking them in checkrooms and having to buy them back. Really, you don't use them much. You're in a cab, then on the street for a moment, then back indoors. The whole time I was at school in Boston, I was only really cold once. Heck, that doesn't justify owning a coat!'

"I'd never looked at it that way before, and while I must admit I still own a topcoat, ever since then I've followed Clint's thinking and seldom worn one."

How To Spot a Smart Millionaire

Bill Georges has forgotten the year, but not the first impression:

"There were three of us working on a deal, and we had left Dallas on a plane for New York. I didn't know then who Clint was, but I could see he was a young guy. On the plane I started trying to work a crossword puzzle, and after awhile I gave up on it.

"He said, 'Are you through with that?'

"I gave it to him and in four or five minutes he had the thing finished. So, already I knew the guy was smart. When we got to New York City, we got a cab and we dropped Ray Smith off somewhere. When we got in to the Drake Hotel, Clint said, 'I don't have any money. Would you pick up the cab?' So then I knew he was rich, too, because really rich people don't pick up the tab. Or carry much money."

Thanks for the Memories

Another time, Georges flew to Los Angeles with Clint and Spinny Martin.

"We got into a limo and headed south. After about an hour and a half we stopped at some roadside place and had a beer. Then we got back in the limo and took another highway, and we finally got to a kind of bluff overlook, and we're looking at a really pastoral scene.

"I said, 'What is this place?' and Clint said 'It's the land my father bought a long time ago. And one day it's going to be worth a whole lot.'

"Later we're back at the first stop, having another beer, and Spinny is in a reflective mood. Spinny said, 'You know, Clint, if I went to my banker and told him I wanted to borrow a couple million dollars to buy some land that *might* develop two light years from now, he'd throw me out of the bank. But because the Murchisons bought it, you make 20 million dollars in 20 years, and so you're an *astute* thinker.'

"Clint was a legend in his time," Bill Georges would later say at a posthumous birthday party with Murchison friends, "and one of the greatest guys who ever came out of Texas. I know bad things happened to him, but he should be Mister Dallas, and I'd love to see that stadium out there named Murchison Stadium. He was kind, he was considerate, he was compassionate, he was mischievous, and sort of impish. The best way to describe him, in my mind, would be that if he could've reduced his problems and everything to a mathematical equation, he'd have it all solved."

The Murchisons do not like to invest in a business that will require close, active, personal management on their part. When they buy control of an entity, they want to acquire good management that will stay on under the new ownership. "They insist on a passive role in management," is the way one knowledgeable Dallasite put it.
—New York Times
June 20, 1971

Classic Clint

"For more than 30 years," says Gene Hewett, "I enjoyed Clint's sense of humor on a number of occasions. Sometimes I was the object of it."

Hewett often was the management equivalent of a utility infielder in running some of Clint's interests. Versatile managers like Hewett used to be called troubleshooter, or liaison. Either sounds like a more interesting job than interface, the grand yuppie word for it. "During the 1960s," Hewett recalls, "Tecon Construction was very much involved in the heavy construction business. Some of our jobs made money and some lost money, but it seems that on balance we lost money in this business. Clint never visited a job site and had no personal experience or expertise in heavy construction, but it became an obsession with him. And the more we lost, the more determined he became to be a success in heavy construction."

Although it was Clint who had been the Marine, it was Gene Hewett who had to take the role of drill instructor at certain times.

"One day I went to see him in his office in what was then the First National Bank building. I told him we were losing money on a number of the construction jobs. Our people, I told him, were aggressively looking for more work. I suggested that we either get out of the construction business of else limit our participation to joint ventures where we were a nonsponsor and our partners had a reputation for being successful.

"'Clint,' I said, 'look at the companies that are successful—J.A. Jones, H.B. Zachry, Brown and Root. They're all managed on a day-to-day basis by the people who own them. Dedicated construction people!'

"I told him that any yardbird who could make bond could get into this business, and if there were any professional managers around who were good enough that we would want them, they'd already be in business for themselves, not working for us. In short," I told him, "'our big problem is absentee ownership.'

"That was about as far as I got. Clint held up his left hand, like a traffic cop, opened the middle drawer on the right side of his desk, and said:

"'Gene, just a minute; let me save you some time. You're getting ready to give Gene Hewett Lecture Number 12. I have it recorded right here. Let me play it for you . . .'

"Clint had made his point, and in the future, I always tried to think of a fresh approach."

For at least 12 Hewett lectures before that, Tecon had been worrisome to a Murchison. Hewett has in his files a series of memos from Clint, Senior, which make a case for the hereditary aspects of acerbic wit and terseness. One was dated Jan. 1, 1959, the day of the Castro revolution in Cuba. Fulgencio Batista had fled to Florida.

> **Dear Gene:**
>
> Thanks a lot for your breakdown on the Tecon estimates of receipts from jobs now under construction; this is about the only manner in which I can in a vague way keep up with the activities of Clint W. and Bob <Thompson>. I hope you are not going to lose too much money on Batista. He has done what I have tried to get them to do—fly the coop.
>
> Best wishes for the New Year.
>
> Sincerely, C.W. Murchison

His worries were well-founded. The Castro regime eventually expropriated Tecon equipment and materials from jobs in progress.

Hewett also saved another memo from the elder Murchison from 1959, the year Clint, Jr., was urgently flying around the country to meetings that would land him a football franchise. The father's memo suggests that the idea of the Dallas Cowboys was not universally enchanting.

> Mr. Gene W. Hewett
> Vice President-Treasurer
> Tecon Corporation
> Davis Building
> Dallas, Texas
>
> **Dear Gene:**
>
> I did not take the trouble to check your invoices on the tractor I purchased from you, but I am taking the trouble to tell you to charge it to Clint W. as part of the $65,000 note of mine he is using against C____ H_____. I hope this is satisfactory to you.
>
> Of course, since Clint W. is buying jet airplanes and football franchises, I am sure this will be satisfactory to Clint W.
>
> Best regards,
>
> C.W. MURCHISON

Classic Clint

Clint wasn't intimidated by his father's grousing over his quest for a football franchise, nor even his purchase of Spanish Cay, the exquisite island northeast of Abaco in the Bahamas. Spanish Cay generated a legend that is recalled by Clint, Jr.'s longtime friend Hugh Bradford:

"Shortly after Clint had acquired Spanish Cay. Bob Thompson had been up in Clint, Senior's office and mentioned to him that Clint, Junior, had bought the island.

"'Well,' Murchison Sr. had grumbled, 'I guess the next thing the little s.o.b. will want is a string of racehorses and a mistress.'

"After the meeting was over, Thompson went down to Clint, Junior's office and related what his Dad had said. Clint immediately picked up the phone, dialed his Dad, and when the old man answered, Clint said, 'Do you know where I can get a string of racehorses?'"

That's one of Bradford's favorite Clint stories, which he refers to as "anticdotes." If the word didn't exist before, it probably should now. Another Bradford anticdote echoes Gene Hewett's doubts whether Clint should have gotten into construction.

"Shortly after Clint and Bob Thompson had started Centex, they were feeling pretty cocky about being able to take on any kind of contracting job. These were two ex-Marines and Texans to boot, you know. One day they were having some drinks with Bob Madden, who owned one of those fine houses over near Inwood and Northwest Highway. Madden mentioned that he had decided to put in a tennis court and was going to put the job out for bids.

"I already mentioned they were having some drinks, didn't I? Well, Clint and Bob said there was no need for him to put out bids; now that they had this big construction firm, Centex could do a dinky job like a tennis court in its spare time. They mentioned some ridiculous figure, somewhere between $1,000 and $2,000. Bob Madden recognized their figure for what it was, absurd, and he immediately accepted.

"Somewhere between six months and a year later, several substantial cracks appeared in the courts, along with a profusion of grass growing out of them. Madden, most distraught, called Clint and told him about the problem.

"'I've got cracks all over the courts and grass growing up. What the hell can be done about it?'

"Clint said, 'Mow it.'"

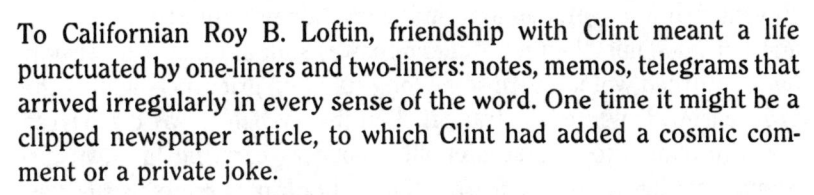

To Californian Roy B. Loftin, friendship with Clint meant a life punctuated by one-liners and two-liners: notes, memos, telegrams that arrived irregularly in every sense of the word. One time it might be a clipped newspaper article, to which Clint had added a cosmic comment or a private joke.

At Christmas of 1963 Loftin received a postcard that had originally been postmarked "BLACKFOOT, IDAHO." On it was a photograph of the homeliest woman Loftin had ever seen, inscribed to Clint: "Love, Opal."

Even when sending gags, Clint unfailingly sent them typed, never handwritten. Loftin says this one required a two-liner for Clint to get the joke across:

> ROY: Next time you go to Blackfoot, please check this out for me.

A few days later there was a follow-up telegram:

> D LLM306=FAX DALLAS TEX 13 354P CST
> ROY B LOFTIN
> 1573 SUNSET PLAZA DR LOSA
> HURRY. THE RACE GOES TO THE SWIFT=
> CLINT MURCHISON JR=

Later in 1964 Loftin had proposed a business deal. He says he no longer remembers what the deal even was, but he has saved Clint's reply:

> Dear Roy:
> I certainly want to go into this deal, but please don't make me read about it or eat it.

That philosophy is reminiscent of Clint's (and Loftin's) friend Gordon McLendon, the legendary broadcaster who mesmerized the nation in the fifties with his recreated baseball broadcasts as The Old Scotchman. McLendon later ran a chain of radio stations, and is considered to be the creator of the playlist format in pop radio.

Classic Clint

McLendon's rule for financial well-being was, "Never invest in anything that eats or needs painting."

In 1964 McLendon had been a candidate in the Democratic primary, running for the U.S. Senate seat of the incumbent, Ralph Yarborough. It was a bitter and flamboyant campaign, spiced by the showmanship of McLendon and sensationally interrupted when another man, mistaken for McLendon, was shot at Love Field airport by a disturbed woman with some long-standing grievance against the broadcaster. It was even stranger than that. When it was discovered that the man who was accidentally shot was carrying his own girl friend's panties in his briefcase, Clint told Loftin, "I guess justice was served after all, because you can't let a crazy man like that go walking around in public places."

When the woman was later charged in the shooting, Clint sent a letter to Dallas District Attorney Henry Wade:

> February 21, 1964
>
> Dear Henry:
>
> I am sure that in the case of the state vs. Mary Elizabeth S_____, the defense will plead insanity. However, in an effort to help your case, I would like to point out that any woman who attempts to shoot McLendon can't be completely nuts.

McLendon figured, probably quite culpably, in one of Clint's most elaborate practical jokes. The victim was Roy Loftin.

"I came to Dallas to conduct the auction for the Planned Parenthood fund raiser that Gordon (McLendon) was holding at his ranch, Cielo. I played it fairly straight at the auction and said I'd do anything, travel any length, for Planned Parenthood.

"But Clint knew the truth, and the truth was that Gordon and I had arranged to be leaving from Dallas for a week in Paris the next day. We would be staying at the George V, which would give us a convenient base for our cultural tours and other pursuits befitting men of our temperament. Gordon and I were both single in those days.

"When we arrived at the hotel, we discovered good old Clint had arranged for two beauties to join us for dinner. Not only that, but, months earlier I had mentioned to Clint that I'd always wanted to have dinner at Maxim's. Lo and behold, Clint had arranged for us to dine at Maxim's, with our two companions.

"'Gee, what a beautiful gesture,' I was thinking. What I didn't know was that my date was a female impersonator.

"Later that night I stumbled back into the room where Gordon was. I was shaken, tears in my eyes, telling him to get rid of her—it—for me because I didn't trust myself.

"Gordon played the role of the distressed friend to the point of nausea, saying what a shame it was in the luck of the draw that he got the real girl, when all the time the trip had been my idea. Hell, he was in on it.

"The next morning, early, I was awakened by one of those liveried George V bellmen, carrying a magnificent silver tray. On it was a cablegram. From Clint, of course. It said:

THIS IS CARRYING PLANNED PARENTHOOD TOO FAR. CLINT.

"Those were great years," said Roy B. Loftin.

A Couple of Hell Razers

One of Clint's occasional venture partners was the late Paul Trousdale, who had developed Trousdale Estates, perhaps the most prestigious of all the exclusive Beverly Hills residential developments. One of the first property owners in Trousdale Estates was Danny Thomas.

Hollywood music producer Snuff Garrett, a longtime friend of Clint's from Dallas, had rejected a three-million-dollar offer for his own Beverly Hills home in the early eighties. "Trousdale Estates?" he said once. "Now you're *really* talkin' high cotton."

Trousdale and Clint collaborated on several projects. One of Trousdale's favorite stories was about their purchase of the Mills Estate in Mill Gray, California.

"It was 1,200 acres," he said. "Mill Gray was a short way down the peninsula from San Francisco. Odgen Mills, for whom it was named, was a famous early Californian, a successful miner and industrialist. Six or seven men of that caliber, men like Stanford, Crocker, Flood,

Classic Clint

etc., each built enormous mansions there. When Clint and I closed the deal for purchase of the property, Clint agreed to meet with the starchy, old Mills attorney at his office on Wall Street. Each of us was to give him a cashier's check for $1,750,000.

"Clint was 20 minutes late and the attorney was getting not only impatient, but suspicious. About then Clint dashed into the office, which was on the 27th floor, and said to me, 'Give me a dollar, Paul, I've got to go pay the cab.'

"By the time he ran out of the office, the Eastern attorney, who was fusty enough to belong in a Dickens novel, was sure he was dealing with screwballs. When we finally finished closing the deal, we had to listen to the lawyer's lecture about how famous and revered the old Mills Estate was, and his admonitions to us was to be sure and take good care of it.

"As it happened, the house was a hideous Victorian monstrosity with about 80 rooms. We had plans for a hundred feet of dirt fill all over the house site. The cheapest and quickest way to get rid of the house was to set it afire one night.

"The newspapers came to take pictures of the previously announced inferno. Clint immediately sent pictures of the blaze to the old lawyer on Wall Street. His caption on the pictures was:

"'We are taking good care of the house.'"

Wine with the Proper Turkey

"We had another venture near San Francisco," Paul Trousdale recalled. "We bought a thousand-acre ranch in Marin County, at the bargain price of one million dollars, from the California wine magnate Louis Petri. The next time Clint came to San Francisco, I took him out and showed him the property.

"'It's a little far out, isn't it?'" Clint had said. It was his only comment about the property.

"That night, Petri and his wife gave a beautiful, formal dinner party for us, celebrating the deal, in their beautiful two-story penthouse 27 stories up on a hill with a breathtaking view of the city.

"When Clint arrived, he was greeted by Petri at the door.

"Clint handed him a live turkey.
'I'm reciprocating that turkey you sold us,' Clint told him.

"The turkey immediately started careening around the room, very excited, flapping its wings and knocking over crystal and vases and drinks on tables. He was also leaving his calling card just about every place, including the hostess's chair in the dining room.

"Finally, someone caught the turkey and gave it to Petri.

"'What am I supposed to do with this thing?' he said, trying to hold down its wings while his wife stood and screamed. Petri finally walked over and tossed it off the balcony. Its wings hadn't been clipped, so our last view of it was it wheeling down to the ground, something like a helicopter making a forced landing."

The North Dallas Ship Channel

Trousdale was visiting Clint in Dallas one summer when Clint enlisted him as one of an elaborate wrecking crew in one of his most grandiose practical jokes.

"Bob Thompson, his partner in Centex, had been visiting in Hawaii and got to spend a month on a friend's yacht. It had been a typical Dallas summer month, too hot, and Bob had irked everyone in his circle, especially Clint, with a barrage of post cards from exotic Pacific ports, telling about what a wonderful time he was having and how much more pleasant it was than suffering through the Dallas heat.

"A couple of days before Thompson was due back home, Clint got a bunch of us, together with some real workers and a winch, and we went out to Thompson's house. They dismantled his stone garden wall, brought in a 24-foot cruiser and hoisted it into the swimming pool. That boat didn't leave much free room in the swimming pool. Then they replaced the wall and fixed the damage to the garden.

"He put a sign on the cruiser that said, 'Just so you won't miss your boat.'

"So far as I know, Clint never did own up to Bob about who was the instigator of that prank. He had had all the bills—the charges for removing and rebuilding a garden wall, the purchase of the boat, and the resodding and planting of the garden—sent to Thompson."

Clint of Arabia

Clint's travels, and sometimes the lack of them, through the Middle East are the stuff of many remembrances.

New York investments manager Bruce Jacobi:

"Shortly after the energy crunch when we had gas lines all over the country, I think it was the one in 1979, Clint told me was chartering one of Harding Lawrence's Braniff jets to fly over to Saudi Arabia. He said he was planning to be gone about five or six days and that he was going over to negotiate for oil.

"A couple of days after his departure, I got a phone call from him. I told him his voice was coming through amazingly well and clear, even though he was calling from across the world in Saudi Arabia.

"'I'm not in Saudi Arabia,' Clint said. 'I'm in Dallas.'
'What happened to the trip?' I asked him.
'Oh, I took the trip. But when we finally got to Saudi Arabia, I stepped off the plane, looked around the airport, and saw all of my neighbors from Dallas. So I came back.'"

Clint's longtime friend from the airline business, Walter Hagan, could think only of Clint during the first days of the crisis in Kuwait, Iraq, and Saudi Arabia that would lead to the Persian Gulf War.

"I was thinking about a couple of the times we went over there together. When I was with Braniff, Clint had called Ed Acker to charter a jet, and Ed told me I'd better go along and look after things. It turned out to be a good move on Ed's part.

"Clint was trying to work on a deal to build some airfields for the Saudis, I think. So we stopped in Kuwait City, and I left the hotel to go out to the market and buy us some Arab outfits. They measured me down in the native quarter and for 26 bucks I got the whole deal. I wanted to get one for Clint, but he wasn't with me for the guy to measure. I was trying to explain to the tailor about Clint's size, and I wasn't getting through to him. Finally, I looked out the door and this little Arab fellow was walking past the shop along the alley, and I just pointed to him.

"The merchant went outside, brought this strange Arab back inside the shop, and fitted him up. It didn't take long for the guy to finish the outfit, so I took it back to the hotel and handed it to Clint. It was a perfect fit. He really got a kick out of it. I didn't tell him who the model was. First thing he wanted to do was have our pictures made.

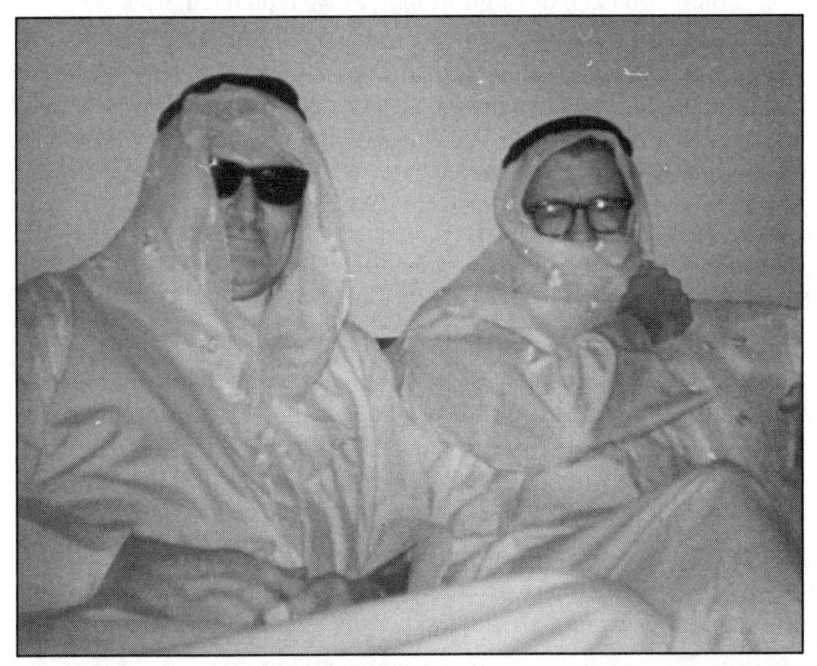

Clint of Arabia; Walter Hagan on left. On the trip when Turks didn't accept credit cards. —photo courtesy of Walter Hagan

"The night before we were leaving for Riyadh, we were in a restaurant and Clint ran into a guy he knew, a banker from New York. He'd missed his flight that morning going down to one of the emirates. I think it was Dubai.

"So Clint said, 'Well, we're going down to Riyadh—we'll just drop you off on the way.'

Classic Clint

"Clint was a mathematical genius, but he didn't know much about geography. Look at a map and see where Riyadh is from Dubai? Clint was in the Mideast and so he thinks everything's next door. Going from Kuwait to Riyadh by way of Dubai is about like going from Chicago to Dallas and telling a guy, 'Well, we'll drop you off in Puerto Rico on the way.'

"We got to Dubai and the plane broke down at that point. It was chaotic, but Clint could always roll with the punches. On the way back we couldn't go back through Athens, as we'd planned, because of the political situation or something, so we went through Ankara, Turkey. The plane's captain had two credit cards for fuel, but since we hadn't planned to go through Turkey, they weren't the right credit cards. I scrambled around trying to get some cash together. I had a little cash, and the captain had a little cash. So I went up to Clint and I asked him, 'I don't suppose you have any cash, do you?'

"He gave me that look, like why should I even ask. Clint never carried a dime. But the rest of us chipped in, and we got enough fuel to get us from there to Brussels."

In 1981 Clint hosted one of the triumphal benchmarks of his business career in New Orleans. Pete Kleifgen was there, in a ballroom of the Royal Orleans Hotel, for the closing dinner for Clint's massive acquisition of 28,000 acres of real estate, all inside the city of New Orleans, for the development known as New Orleans East. He was celebrating the sale of a one-half interest in 5,000 of those acres to two Kuwaiti families. The Kuwaitis were there to formalize their investment of 25 million dollars in the venture.

Kleifgen recalls: "During the cocktail hour before dinner, Barton Higgs, the project manager for New Orleans East and an Australian, had arranged for a formal signing of the documents officially closing the purchase by the Kuwaitis. Adjacent to the cocktail room was a rotunda-shaped vestibule lined with royal blue curtains, with indirect lighting across a gold-domed ceiling.

"There was a pedestal in the center of the room, and resting atop the pedestal were the volumes to be executed by Clint and each of the representatives of the Kuwaiti families. About half an hour before dinner, Higgs called all of the participants into the vestibule for the official signing. While the guests lined the circular walls, he described to all present in reverential tones what was about to happen.

"The atmosphere grew hushed as the first dignitary, Mohammed Al Yagout, was invited to the podium to sign on behalf of one of the families.

"Al Yagout crossed the room importantly, and slowly, and spoke in English with a heavy accent:

'I will sign in Arabic.'

"Then he picked up the pen and signed three documents in his native script. Then Higgs stepped to the podium and invited Dr. Mohammed Diab to execute the other family's documents.

"Dr. Diab, too, walked solemnly to the podium and intoned,

'I will sign in Arabic also.'

"Next Higgs came to the podium and announced Clint Murchison, Junior.

"Clint, dwarfed by the two larger Arabs, stepped up with a slow, erect pace, lifted the pen and said, in that shy, quiet voice:

'I will sign . . . in Apache.'

"After the roar of the crowd had subsided, Higgs invited the throng into the ballroom for a seven-course dinner. After dinner, Higgs again rose to thank everyone who had worked on the project. This led to some round-robin tributes, with the principals and their lawyers all taking turns saying something nice about their counterparts.

"This went on for about 45 minutes," Kleifgen said. "Then Higgs asked Clint to say something, since he was the most distinguished person present. As Clint rose to his feet, a hush fell over the crowd.

"'I want to welcome all of you to New Orleans,' he said, 'and I particularly want to congratulate my Kuwaiti partners on their purchase of 2,500 acres of my interest in New Orleans East for a price slightly in excess of the entire Louisiana Purchase.'

"The Kuwaitis' astonishment was lost in the roar of the crowd."

Bloody Noses & Broken Fingers

In his Scotch-and-water days, Clint was a member of the "Moveable Feast" school of drinking. If it was time to leave and he wasn't finished with the drink, he would take it with him to the next stop. It is frowned upon now. Then it was just inadvisable. "Roadies" are more illegal than ever in most states, but in the sixties and seventies American society wasn't as sensitized; there was no M.A.D.D., the giddy were objects of giggles more than ostracism, and a man named Foster Brooks made a good living in show business by playing a guy who was always in the bag. As it happened, though, Clint's fondness for roadies caused problems for other people, not him.

"Usually, Clint would just walk out of a place with his drink under his jacket or stuck in his pocket," says stockbroker Bob Foley. "He used to do that at George Ellson's club downtown, and George must've known about it but never said anything about it. One Christmas season, Clint walked into George's place with two huge boxes, elaborately gift wrapped. Inside it were all the glasses Clint had taken drinks home in."

Another of Clint's Dallas cronies, Pat Cashman, recalls an incident on the opening night of Carlos and Pepe's, a North Dallas nightspot. "It was one of the first restaurants in Dallas that had valet parking," Cashman said. "We walked out the door together, each of us taking a drink with us. Clint stood out in the driveway holding his drink and waited for the attendant to bring his car. When his car came, he tipped the guy, got in the car, and drove away.

"Now, my car is next, and I'm standing there, holding my drink, and the parking guy stops me and says, 'You can't leave with that drink.'

"'But Clint just took *his* drink with him,' I told the guy.

"'Yessir,' the parker said, 'but you're not Clint Murchison.'"

A Chicago friend, Jimmy Martin, tells the story of the time Clint and Spinney Martin were at Danny's Hideaway, the famed New York saloon, feeling no pain in the "whee" hours.

"Clint walked out the door carrying his unfinished drink. A very large, Mediterranean-looking doorman gruffly informed Clint that he was not allowed to leave with a drink in hand. Clint promptly, and wisely, turned around and went back inside.

"Spinney was still inside. When he saw Clint come back in, he asked him what the problem was.
'Guy out there told me I can't take the drink with me,' Clint said. Spinney said, 'Hell, he can't do that. Gimme that drink.'

"Spinney walked out to the doorman with Clint's drink in his hand and started talking to him. In a few moments, Clint heard a loud commotion over by the door and he ran outside to see what was happening.

"Spinney was lying in the gutter with blood pouring from his nose.

"Clint leaned over him, looked down, and politely asked Spinney, 'What happened to my drink?'"

Martin says he was present with Clint at another famous New York bar, Jilly's, owned by Jilly Rizzo and Frank Sinatra. It was a hangout for a wide range of Sportsmen. "A lot of tough guys used to hang out there," Jimmy Martin said.

"The telephone was located down by the men's room. On one of the team trips, I think it was, Craig Morton, the Cowboy quarterback, got in an argument with a couple of these wise guys. They whacked him around. They broke his finger.

"Clint heard about it and called some people in Chicago, 'You know, I don't like this, you know, breakin' my quarterback's finger, and I'm madder than hell. I want something done about it.' He was serious.

"So a couple days go by and Clint got a call from New York this time, and the guy said, 'Well, Clint, I'm sorry about what happened. But the next time you're in New York with Craig, the guy that broke his finger, Craig can break TWO of his fingers. Is that good enough?'

"Hey, Clint can tell the guy is serious, so he says, 'Well, we don't really, you know, need THAT, but let's just have'em show a little more respect for people in that club. Especially Texans.'

"About six months later, I was back in there with Clint, there in Jilly's, and we just happened to walk down the steps to the washroom together. There was a couple fellows on the telephone—I'd forgotten all about what happened before, you know, previously—and they was cursin' and swearin', and Clint happened to sort of bump into one of them on his way past. They wheeled around and started to glare at Clint, and then they recognized him, I guess. They quick hung up the phone and ran up the stairs.

"Clint looked at me and he said, 'I guess they got the message, Jimmy.'"

Ahead of the Times

No one had much success in one-upping him. One who tried was Jack O'Connell, who with Clint's help started United Exposition Service, Inc., in Houston in 1978.

"On Clint's birthdays, I'm always mindful of his 60th, on Sept. 12, 1983, when I sent him a facsimile front-page of the *New York Times* for his actual birthday, Sept. 12, 1923. I pointed out that even the *Times* seemed to have missed noting the birth of the future owner of such eminent organizations as the Dallas Cowboys, Tony Roma's, and Calorific Reclamation Anerobic Process (C.R.A.P.). 'Too bad you didn't make the front page,' I told him.

"His reply was, 'Thanks for the newspaper. You obviously got an early edition.'"

The Daily Double

It's curious how so many of his pals and associates say that there are a couple of things that really stand out in the memories of Clint, and how these are always different couples of things. Here is insurance executive Kenneth Tapley's pair:

"1. If Clint received a telephone message that the caller said was 'very important,' when Clint returned the call he would invariably ask, 'Is this important to you, or to me?'

"2. I'll never forget the time in a meeting he said that we must all remember in dealing with a certain man: 'He has all the attributes of a dog, except loyalty.'"

Thanks for the Memories

"I always buy my doubleknits at THE GARMENT DISTRICT."

St. Patty's Day Fashion Plate

Pat Cashman, a distinguished-looking Dallas haberdasher who sported an eye patch, didn't approve of Clint's taste in clothes. Over the years he was unrelenting in his efforts to sell the ever evasive Clint at least one pair of then stylish double-knit pants. Clint made light of the situation by creating a mock ad for his friend's store in which he posed wearing a green derby and a shamrock embroidered eye patch and an over-sized pair of double-knits. He surprised Pat with it in 1973 at a St. Patrick's Day party before a crowded room full of their mutual friends.

Ever the salesman, Pat ran the ad in The Griddle, the Press Club of Dallas' prank publication dedicated to its annual Gridiron Show, and it earned an award for originality. —photo courtesy of Pat Cashman

Classic Clint

Best Whooshes on Your Birthday

Along with Ted and Annette Strauss, Stuart and Jeanne Hunt were neighbors of Clint and Jane in their early married years in the house on Wateka.

"It was John Murchison's birthday, and Jane had had a large cake made by a Mrs. Stallings, who was famous for her layer cakes and thick frostings. Jeanne and I were there along with John and his wife Lupe, Clint's aunt Duce, and Clint and Jane. Jane brought in the cake with a flourish, all the candles glittering on it, and placed it on the coffee table in front of the couch where Jeanne and John were sitting. Clint said, 'Wait a minute,' and left the room. Duce said, 'Isn't that sweet! He's gone to get a camera!'

"Clint came back into the room, not with a camera, but with a fire extinguisher. He popped it open and blew the cake, frosting, and candles all over Jeanne and John. The end of another birthday!"

Cut to the Chase

"Everyone knew him as a man of few words," said William Seiden, "but it was always amazing to realize *how* few." Seiden, too, joined United Exposition Service Co. and is executive vice president and treasurer in the Chicago office. "Clint and I first started talking about my going to work for him in 1977. One day I got a call from his secretary, Ruth Woodard. She said Clint wanted to speak to me.

"I went out to a public phone so that I would have privacy and dialed his number. Ruth said she'd put him right on. I expected Clint to come on and say 'Hello' or 'How are you?' or 'How's it going,' but it was none of the above. All he said when he picked up the phone was, 'When are you available?' I guess that is vintage Clint.

"Shortly after Janie and I moved to Dallas," Bill Seiden recalled, "apparently some tax people from one of the law firms and, I believe, Pete Kleifgen, were meeting at Clint's house and were talking about some tax planning. Clint wanted some input from me, so he called my apartment. My son, Bill, answered the phone.

"Clint said, 'Bill?'
"Bill said, 'Yes.'

"Clint immediately went into a long explanation of the problem, with a dissertation about cash flow and contingency reserves and such. He'd been talking for a couple of minutes when finally my son Billy said, 'Excuse me, but I think you have the wrong Bill.'

"I think most people would've been peeved over the wasted time and breath. Not Clint. All he did was laugh and tell Billy how everyone used to mistake him for *his* Dad."

Reach Out and Touch Someone

Clint and his Centex partner Bob Thompson were close for years with Tom Lively, a Dallas homebuilder who was killed in a boating accident at Lake Texoma. The death hit Thompson especially hard. Walter Hagan remembers the day of Lively's funeral, when he went with Clint and Thompson.

"Bob kept brushing tears out of his eyes and saying, 'Gee, he was a good little sonofabitch.' We had filed by the casket to view the body and we were walking out when suddenly Bob snaps his fingers and starts heading back to the body.

"Bob was remembering this thing Lively did with a hundred-dollar bill. Lively would be at a party, and he'd roll up a hundred-dollar bill, stick it in his mouth and say, 'OK, who wants it?'

"At the funeral home Bob reached in his pocket, pulled out a wad of bills, and peeled off one of the hundreds. He gently put it in Lively's hand and patted him on the head.

"Well, I knew that hundred wasn't going to last five minutes in there, in that crowd, so I took it out and put a dime there instead.

"'What the hell are you doing?' Bob said to me.

"I told him, 'Hey, we don't know where he's going, but if he gets there and needs the money, all he has to do is call us.'"

The Deviled Egg War

"Clint loved lawyers," said Marshall Simmons, who is one. "He especially liked giving them pain. We had this big law suit, the biggest one that I'd ever worked on for the Murchison brothers. I had kept trying to pin Clint down for a deposition that had to be taken, and he finally agreed to let me come out to his house on a Saturday. I'd warned him it was liable to take most of the day.

"We started at 9:30 in the morning, and it got to be 12, and then 12:30, and 1 o'clock. There had been no sign of anything to eat. I finally said, 'Clint, I know what you're trying to do. You think we're going to give up and leave to go eat, but it's not going to work. So you might as well go in the kitchen and bring us out something to eat.'

"So he gets that grin, you know. I only know one way to describe that grin, and I can't use those words in polite company. The second word is 'eating.' He goes off into the kitchen and I figure, well, the servant will come out with this big spread. Wrong. Clint comes out with one of those trays, like you served deviled eggs on, except the eggs are half gone and beginning to wither. It's obviously left over from some party. There's a chunk of rat cheese, also half gone, and a box of saltine crackers.

"There were four of us there. He set it down and said, 'Help yourself.' We ate everything but the box. We worked until a little after four, and when I left I went up to a store on Forest Lane and I bought some rat cheese and a box of crackers. I went back to Clint's house and rang the bell. Anne came to the door, and I said, 'Give these to Clint and tell him I didn't want him to be short, and I was sorry I couldn't get any deviled eggs.'

"I felt really good about that. I'd put one over on Clint! The next week I expected something to happen, and nothing happened.

"Months later, I had some business with him and he told me on the phone, 'Well, I can see you during the lunch hour.' I said 'great, I'll bring the lunch.'

"About five minutes later my phone rang, and it was his secretary Ruth. She said, 'Mr. Murchison said if you're bringing cheese, he likes his with a *lot* more eggs.'"

Priorities

"Once he got involved in a deal with all them Libyans," Bobby Jack Kennamer said. "I was working for Clint, and he told me to squire these guys around. The first two that had come over were some guys with titles like Minister of Hydraulic Resources and Minister of the Interior. I took 'em out to Vegas and all that stuff, and on the way out the airline lost their luggage. We stayed out there a couple days and they're having too much fun to stop and buy clothes.

"We came back to Dallas and got out there to the house. I told 'em, 'Clint's got some money in an envelope for you.' There were two envelopes. One was marked '300' and one was marked '500.'

"I asked Clint, 'What's the one with 300 dollars in it for?'
He said, 'Buy 'em some clothes.'
'OK. How about the *five* hundred?'
'Buy 'em some deodorant,' he said."

Vanity Gag

One of Clint's favorite lunch spots was at the old Statler Hilton Hotel on the east end of downtown Dallas: not the well-appointed public restaurant, but the spartan barbecue stand located off the basement arcade. At the Hilton, Clint had gotten to know Joe Cavagnaro, first the food and beverage manager and later front office manager. Clint arranged for Cavagnaro to be hired as manager of Texas Stadium.

"Clint was famous for always giving Tom Landry a free hand at coaching the Cowboys," Cavagnaro recalls, "but that didn't mean Landry was immune to Clint's gags.

"This happened right after Ralph Neely, the Cowboys' all-pro tackle, had broken his leg on a motorcycle. Landry got out a memo to all the players that nobody under contract to the Cowboys could even get *on* a motorcycle.

"Clint saw the memo and it started him thinking, of course. This was also right at the time when they had just signed Tony Dorsett, and he'd posed with that number '33' Cowboys jersey, the same number he'd worn in college at Pittsburgh. So Clint called a friend of his in

Classic Clint

Austin and somehow got them to make one of those miniature motorcycle license tags. It said 'TD-33.'

"Then he got a Dallas policeman, who was a friend of his, to drive a motorcycle out to the practice field with that tag on it. He had him park right in the middle of Landry's reserved parking spot."

Clint with Ralph Neely, one of his favorite Cowboys.

Is that you, Clint?

"He was always hearing about episodes all over the country where some guy had done things, or *charged* things, while claiming to be him," says Clint's son Robert.

"He was on a trip once to Cleveland for a Cowboys game. I've forgotten how the game ended but it must have been back in the days when the Browns were annihilating us a lot. Dad had had to stay over in Cleveland after the game, and next morning he was checking out of the hotel. When he signed the charge slip, the clerk peered at him and said, 'Wait a minute. You can't be Clint Murchison. He's a great big guy with a big 10-gallon hat and cowboy boots.'

"Dad just looked up at the guy and said, 'Well, is his credit good?'"

Counterfeit Memories

The lengths to which some impostors went impressed him, though he was chagrined when decent people were caught in the scam. Sometimes he didn't hear about it for years:

> Physics Department
> U.S. Naval Academy
> Annapolis, Maryland
> 29 October 1971
>
> Dear Mr. Murchison:
>
> In the fall of 1957, while a Lieutenant (jg) in the Navy, I met you in the Mapes Hotel in Reno, Nevada. During the course of the evening I had the pleasure of being invited to join your party. Being a Naval aviator and also owning my own plane, we had something in common; in fact you offered to let me fly your Cessna 310 the following day, which regrettably I was unable to do. If I remember correctly, you gave me your card with the words 'My guest—anything' written on the back. (I wish I could find it). That particular evening, I'm sure, has been forgotten by you, but was memorable to me. If I could have a few minutes of your time I would like to explain the purpose of this letter.
>
> Since 1957 I have continued my career in the Navy and am now a commander on duty at the Naval Academy. As of May 1972 I will have completed 20 years of duty and am considering retirement. In order to prepare myself for this eventuality I have been working part-time

for an engineering consulting firm. Since I have a multi-faceted aviation, engineering and management background, including Master's degrees in Oceanography and Systems Management, this type of enterprise is where I believe my talents and experience could best be utilized. Trident Engineering Associates, Inc., is a small company ($300,000 gross) with outstanding potential in the technical investigation field as well as consulting in areas such as Oceanography, Systems Safety and all engineering disciplines. Primarily due to the efforts of its vice president, Mr. Robert Shepard, the company has managed to maintain a status-quo condition during the past three years . . .

What I need is a way to have the majority of the stock owned by forward-looking shareholders who believe in an approach that would require ownership of 76,500 out of 150,000 shares. The first step to acquire the necessary stock would be the acquisition of 45,000 shares held by American Export Isbrandtsen Lines who are willing to sell. The remainder of the necessary shares are presently held or available to persons in sympathy with an aggressive business posture. The cost to pick up these 45,000 shares, making the buyer a majority stock holder, should not exceed $100,000. Although the Corporation has first option to buy back this stock, it does not possess the assets to do so. To preclude a power struggle which would undoubtedly ruin the corporation, the purchase of the stock would have to be consummated quickly and without affording the incumbent president time to establish a consortium to buy it himself and thus maintain control.

I realize that this proposition is bold, but I see no other way to save Trident and give myself an opportunity to fulfill my ambitions. I am convinced of the potential of this company if directed wisely and believe that Mr. Shepard and myself, with an interested and experienced board, can make it grow. If this proposal interests you, Mr. Shepard and myself would be happy to brief you on the complete financial and business aspects of the corporation. We possess no qualms about our goals and capabilities; we lack only the major ingredient which you could supply. We would be pleased to tell you of our plans, and listen to what you think of them. Not only would you be doing me a great personal favor, you might find the venture profitable.

Sincerely
DONALD W. STEVENSON
CDR USN

p.s. Could I convert the fifty dollars you borrowed that evening in Reno into a bit of your time?

November 2, 1971
Commander Donald W. Stevenson
Physics Department
U.S. Naval Academy
Annapolis, Maryland 21402

Dear Commander Stevenson:

For reasons of policy, I would not be interested in investments such as Trident Engineering Associates, but I do appreciate your calling the opportunity to my attention.

Incidentally, I am sorry about your fifty bucks, since I have never been in Reno. I have had people use my name before, but the character whom you met was the first one I have heard of who was enterprising enough to have cards printed. I hope that I at least picked up the dinner check.

Sincerely,
CLINT MURCHISON JR.

Stories of Innfluence

"Sometimes it seemed Clint just kept forgetting he was rich, famous, and powerful," said a friend who ran various Murchison ventures in southern California. "One year there was going to be an NFL meeting in Palm Springs, and Clint called me just before the meeting. He said, 'I hate to ask at the last minute like this, but is there any place out there where you could get me a place to stay?'

"I told him, 'Clint, remember? You *own* the Palm Springs Racquet Club.'

"He said, 'Oh, that's right. I do, don't I.'"

He learned from the experience, though. In 1971 Joe Bailey was the 24-year-old business manager for the Cowboys, and a call from Clint Murchison could be lump-in-the-throat time.

"My secretary said, 'Mr. Murchison on line 50,' and as usual panic set in. That year one of my responsibilities was to make all road trip arrangement for the football team. The day was a Friday before our

Saturday departure for St. Louis to play the Cardinals. Everything was in order—buses and trucks, team meals, rooming lists, etc. All was smooth except that we were staying at a new hotel across from Busch Stadium. I had selected it myself and was determined to have a great stay. To me, it was a bold move because the hotel was brand new. It was so bold that I never even told our president and general manager, Tex Schramm.

"But I'd run into one hitch earlier in the week. A bowling convention had taken up all the extra rooms in the hotel, but with some wheeling and dealing I was able to scrounge just enough rooms for everyone.

"When I picked up the phone, I heard Clint say, 'I'll be coming up to St. Louis Saturday night. Can you get me a room?'

"'Holy ____', I thought. To this day I can remember stuttering, 'I'll try my best, but boy, it's going to be a little tough because of these bowlers.' (Why did I say *that*?) 'But of course I'll try my very best.' ('What am I going to do,' I thought, 'tell Tex and Tom they have to room together?')

"Clint just said, 'Call me back.' The phone went dead.

"Ten minutes later I heard it again. 'Mr Murchison on line 50.' Very reluctantly I picked it up.

"'I just remembered something that might help,' Clint told me. '. . . I think I own the hotel.'"

Angles of Ideas

"Dad didn't think like other people," Robert Murchison said. "We were at a going-away party for a friend who was leaving for law school in England. While some people would say, 'Pip pip' or 'Cheerio, Ol' Chap,' or whatever, Dad's parting words to him were, 'Now remember, over there you say 'Tally Ho, the fox!,' not 'Yonder goes the sonofabitch.'"

The annual fall Peppermint Stick Tournament was the biggest event of the year for Clint and his golfing pals at the Brook Hollow Golf Club. "We'd talk about the Peppermint Stick a lot," remembers Jack Jones, an insuranceman and victim of more than one of Clint's capers.

The inspiration came during an outing to Spanish Cay, the Murchison island off the Bahamas. "We had a party on our last night there," Jones said, "and during the dancing somebody bumped into me just as I was taking a sip of my martini. It jolted me so hard, it broke off a cap on my front tooth. We were leaving to come back to Dallas the next day, and Clint told me, 'You'd better make an appointment with Bledsoe to get that fixed.' Bledsoe was Dr. Jim Bledsoe, who was also the Cowboys' dentist.

When Jones went back to have the permanent cap fitted, Dr. Bledsoe showed it to him, all pearly and gleaming, and Jones nodded his approval. The dentist took back the cap and then he took the mirror and tucked it away in a drawer. Then he turned back around and attached the cap.

"In a few minutes I was back out on the expressway, driving to work, when I looked up into the rearview mirror and smiled to admire my new tooth. It was peppermint striped.

"But I may have gotten even with Clint. I liked it so much I wore it for about a week. I'd go around, smiling at people as broadly as I could, and they'd all give me this funny look, not quite like I had a piece of spinach caught up there, but close."

Coup deVille

Another Brook Hollow gag scenario involved a color scheme. The victim was Dudley Ramsden, the longtime manager of the Neiman-Marcus fine jewelry department. Ramsden was enamored of a new Cadillac he was driving. (The most monumental of Clint's jokes on Dudley and his cars came after Dudley had switched to a Rolls Royce, cited in the chapter on Inspirations & Other Outrages).

Clint, Dudley, Bobby Stewart, and Jack Jones were the usual Brook Hollow Saturday morning golf foursome. They would customarily tee off at 7:30, play a round of 18, and be back in the club house for drinks, lunch, and a card game.

Classic Clint

This episode took place on one of those warm December days with which Dallas golfers are blessed, and which help make up for the hellishly hot ones that stretch from May through September.

Dudley had arrived at the club in a new black Cadillac. The other three had often heard Dudley's feelings about the color; an elegant car should likewise be of an elegant and aggressively understated hue, i.e., prudently, tastefully, and blindingly black.

The foursome went off on the round, and a couple of hours later when they holed out on No. 9, they began walking toward the clubhouse to see Dudley's beloved car parked athwart the steps. Clint had hired a couple of off-duty caddies to paint Dudley's Caddy in festive colors of the season, half red and half green, with an advertising slogan promoting Richard Eiseman, a competitor for Dallas society's fine-jewelry trade.

"The boys had really gotten into the spirit of the assignment," Jack Jones said, "slapping that paint on there as fast as they could do it with both hands. As a result, it wasn't real neat, but it was impressive just the same." Jones' role in the gag was to make sure the paint was water based and would eventually wash off.

"It's the closest I ever saw Dudley come to fainting."

Ramsden eventually held his own in the car gags, however. More than once, Clint would return to the club parking lot after a round of golf and would have that head-scratching feeling that something was wrong. His car wasn't where he thought he had left it. Sometimes it had mysteriously seemed to move a few yards one way or another or was facing a different direction. At other times it was at the remotest reaches of the lot. Ramsden had arranged once to get Clint's car keys from the club locker, had had copies made, and would have someone move the car whenever the mood struck him.

Chapter Four
A Funny Thing Happened On the Way to the N.F.L.

(The Washington Redskin Fight-Song Caper according to Clint)

One afternoon in 1958, Barnee Breskin, a Washington, D.C. bandleader, called Tom Webb, an associate of mine living in the same city. Barnee, it seems, had written the music to "Hail to the Redskins," the official song of that team, and the late George Preston Marshall, owner of the team, wished to obtain legal title to the song. Now this was no idle request on Marshall's part; there were some who claimed that he cared more for the song and its halftime presentation than about the football team. Morrie Siegel, a Washington columnist, observed that taking "Hail to the Redskins" from Marshall would be like denying "Dixie" to the South, "Anchors Aweigh" to the Navy, or "Blue Suede Shoes" to Elvis. In any event, even though Barnee and George were longtime friends, music was Barnee's profession, and he felt he should be recompensed. He was afraid, he told Tom, that Marshall, a pretty good salesman, would sweet-talk him into giving away the song, as opposed to selling it. Why, Barnee asked, didn't Tom buy the song, then sell it to Marshall? Tom wouldn't have to pay Barnee anything until the subsequent sale, at which time Tom would turn over to Barnee whatever Marshall had paid. Tom, seeking to help a friend from his dilemma, agreed.

Tom didn't realize it then, but this bit of innocent fun, or chicanery if you were on Marshall's side (fortunately for Tom, nobody was), gave a big assist to the great rivalry that has prospered between the Redskins and the Cowboys. It also put me in the soup.

The Wages of Sin

'Bout a year later, I applied for a franchise with the National Football League. My negotiations were with George Halas, then head of the League's Expansion Committee. Everything went swimmingly for me until well into the 1959 season; the League meeting was set for the following January, but that was a mere formality. Then one evening Halas called me. What was this about my stealing Marshall's song? Song? Song? What song? It seems that Marshall, from our nation's capital, was preparing to employ a tactic sometimes used by a senator when he wishes to block a presidential appointment of a particularly loathsome adversary. He was going to declare to the world in general and to his fellow owners in particular that I was to him "personally obnoxious." Now when a senator says this of an appointee, that appointee is washed up. This particular ploy has been used by senators only seven or eight times in history and it has never failed. Huey Long even successfully invoked it against a Roosevelt appointee in 1933 and Roosevelt wasn't exactly a political novice. The other members of the league were not, however, so easily intimidated; they introduced a constitutional amendment to the effect that the granting of a new franchise would not require a unanimous vote. By the end of the 1959 football season, Marshall was stalemated but smouldering, Tom had the song, Barnee wanted some money, and I was confused. At this point I had never met Marshall, and I wondered, "If he thinks I'm obnoxious now, how will he feel when he meets me?"

Dueling Accordions

This set the scene for the league meeting in Miami Beach. The night before it began, Marshall spied George Halas, Jr., sitting across the lounge in the Kenilworth Hotel. He summoned a strolling accordion player and directed him to Halas' table to serenade George with "Hail to the Redskins." Halas sent the musician back to Marshall, where he played "The Eyes of Texas." I wandered through, but no one had sufficient courage to introduce me to Marshall. The plot was thickening.

A Funny Thing Happened On the Way to the N.F.L.

It was getting so thick, in fact, that I couldn't stand it. The next morning, the meeting was to start at 10 o'clock. At eight, I decided that enough was enough and went to the hotel suite of George Marshall and his attorney, Leo DeOrsey. George answered my knock. "No one else would introduce us, so here I am," I stated. George couldn't have been nicer. We chatted for about 10 minutes, at which point George's brow furrowed. "Say, Clint," he began, "there's a fellow working for you who has MY song, and he won't give it to me."

"You're kidding," I replied. "Who in the world is that?"

"Tom Webb."

"Heck, George, I can take care of that in a minute. Where's the phone?" I grabbed the telephone to call Tom in Washington, while George walked over to continue his interrupted discussion with Leo. "Operator, I want to make a credit card call," I said, giving her my card number. George, overhearing, assumed a shocked expression. "See, Leo, I told you we couldn't trust that guy. He can even remember his credit card number."

It was a nice meeting. Tom gave George the song; George gave me his vote for my admission into the NFL, and I gave Barnee two thousand bucks.

The Little Big Horn wasn't the only Indian victory. Hail to the Redskins!

More than 30 years after the whipsawing of George Preston Marshall, Tom Webb can't restrain the chuckles as he recalls that fight song morning. Retired now to the splendor of Jackson Hole, Wyoming, Webb had worked first for Clint's father and then with Clint, Jr., in an intriguing career as the Washington-based troubleshooter for the Murchisons and their interests. There was a lot of trouble to shoot over the years—the Bobby Baker and Watergate hearings, in which the Senate probed Murchison companies' involvement in political and party-time contributions; globetrotting trips to negotiate construction, oil, and electronics concessions; the smoothing of waters and the mending of fences, and on one occasion, Webb reasoned with

Classic Clint

a startled Washington cop who was curious why Clint, Webb, and Bob Thompson were leading a Tennessee Walking Horse bearing a Dallas Cowboy blanket through the front door of Duke Zeibert's restaurant. "I guess you could describe my years with Clint as his friend, attorney, lobbyist, and facilitator," Webb says. "I saw that sonofabitch do some wonderful things."

It isn't often that boy's horseplay gets to involve a real horse. It was Bob Thompson's champion Tennessee Walker, being led through Duke Zeibert's Washington, D.C. restaurant on a bet, as a dazzled and impressed clientele watched. Thompson is at the horse's immediate right, back to camera; the smiling face on the far right belongs to Tom Webb, Clint's longtime Washington lobbyist. Clint himself, the loser of the bet, is nowhere to be seen. —photo courtesy of Tom Webb

There is a Rest of the Story to Clint's version of the fight song caper, Tom Webb says.

"It was a serious situation, Marshall wanting to blackball Clint. In those days one guy like that could keep an expansion owner out. We'd discussed the song strategy, of course, and before he went over to the meeting with Marshall, Clint told me, "Stay in your office and wait for my phone call. We're gonna have some fun with this son of a bitch."

"Sure enough, he called me from Miami Beach. But he'd told me not to say anything on the phone, to let him do all the talking. So he called and said, 'Tom, I'm here in the room with George Marshall and Leo DeOrsey, and George told me that if you'll agree to let him have the rights to that song, he'll give us the vote . . .'

"I'm still not saying a word and Clint goes on, 'Yeah, I know, Tom, I know you think he's a no-good sonofabitch, but this franchise means a lot to me and I hope you'll consider that so we can get this thing settled . . .'

"I'm still not saying a word, and Clint says, 'Come on, Tom, be reasonable. I don't know what he's ever done to you, but, please—after all, you work for me, and I'd appreciate your doing this. Tom? Will you at least think about it?'

Webb recalls: "Then he hung up the phone. Clint told me later Marshall said, 'What'd he say? What'd he say?' Clint told him, 'He thinks you're a no-good bastard, apparently, and he's just not going to let you have the song.'

"Then Marshall pleaded with him to call me back. He called me back, went on like before for about a minute and a half, and then finally he said, 'Oh, good, Tom. I really appreciate your doing this. I really want to get into pro football!'

Webb says, "DeOrsey, Marshall's lawyer, was a good friend of mine and smart enough to know it was some kind of gag. He told me later he enjoyed listening to Clint's performance, too.

"I really miss Clint," says his longtime power broker. "I had a lot of fun working with him. He'd give you something to do and then leave you alone and let you do it. It put you in a position where you weren't going to let him down. That's what I don't like about all this micro-management going on today. Feelings of sentimentality don't mean anything any longer, and that's what makes deals go."

Classic Clint

In Pittsburgh in the early 1960s, for a Cowboy-Steeler match-up, Clint and Bedford Wynne ended up inside a police paddy wagon, but the service was special delivery. Clint's other Washington lawyer-lobbist, Irv Davidson, had arranged with Pittsburgh Police Chief Larry Maloney to let their Saturday night pre-game party saloon stay open past curfew. The next day, the paddy wagon showed up at the William Penn Hotel; Clint and Bedford were told they were under arrest. The wagon took them to the game site at the University of Pittsburgh stadium, then out onto the field, and let them out on the 50-yard line.

Chapter Five
The Creation of the Dallas Whatsits

"From day one until the day he sold the team he never declared a dividend for himself or took any money from the team."
—Tex Schramm

Time can erode the facts of football history as it does the memories of its players. A deed gets traded for a myth to be named later. Students of Dallas Cowboys lore are lucky that Clint wrote a series of columns for the team's Insiders Newsletter during the 1970 season. Even then there was a growing swirl of popular and erratic myth about the origins of the team. As a reluctant sportswriter, Clint was cogent, honest, and droll. As history's first Cowboy fan, he was also the only person who had been present throughout the creation.

He began the story with his tongue in his cheek: "Most people think that when you organize a football team, such as we did with the Cowboys back in 1960, the first thing you do is hire a coach and sign players; then, presumably, you're in business. Well, that's not so. There are some other very important items that must be taken care of first. Such as determining the name for the team. And the team colors. And the design for the windshield decals. Because I have been through this and am possibly an expert in this field, let me tell you how I handled those problems.

"The first thing I did when the NFL awarded Dallas a franchise was to employ Tex Schramm, and I told Tex that he could take care of getting the coach and the players, and that I wouldn't bother him, but that I was going to assume charge of the really tough problems. Because I had been attempting to land an NFL franchise since 1952, I obviously had the edge in experience here, anyway."

The beginning of the dynasty: Clint stood with his youthful cohorts Tom Landry, Bedford Wynne, and Tex Schramm.

(In 1983, in a note to Blackie Sherrod, Clint would expand on the Schramm choice with a remembrance of Chicago Bears owner George Halas' effect on the seminal franchise: "Halas had another interesting contribution ... After we completed all the details, George asked me, 'What are your plans for running the team?' I mentioned that I viewed someone (whom I named) as being an excellent candidate and that I might entice him by offering him some stock. George frowned and said, 'I don't think you have to go that strong; there are some pretty good men around. Why don't you talk to a young fellow with CBS Sports who has a good head for football; his name is Tex Schramm.'")

The Creation of the Dallas Whatsits

Clint's version of Genesis continued: "I guess it was this experience that made naming the team easy for me; it came to me right away, like a bolt from the blue: THE DALLAS RANGERS. Now there, I declared, was a name for a football team if ever there was one. Its connotations were historical, proud, tough. My grandfather, who was one, would have loved it.

"At least he would have loved it more than Tex did. Schramm, who was still floundering around with the veterans' draft, started hollering that there already was a team in Dallas called the Rangers. Even worse, allowed Tex, it was a baseball team. The media would confuse the two. It would be an impossible situation, particularly in view of the impending competition with that other football team, the Dallas Texans."

(Lamar Hunt, cofounder of the competing American Football League and owner of the Texans, later the Kansas City Chiefs, says he had been invited by Murchison in 1959 to be a partner in the NFL franchise. "We both wanted pro football in Dallas. I had been turned away by the NFL, and by the time Clint had approached me it was too late; I felt obligated to remain with the league I helped form.")

"I diplomatically pointed out to Tex," Clint wrote, "that New York had two Giants, that St. Louis had two Cardinals, and that Dallas was surely big enough to hold two Rangers. Besides, why didn't he read his contract?

"Common sense finally prevailed, and our first press release read THE DALLAS RANGERS. Unfortunately, however, Tex had apparently viewed our entire discussion as an attack upon his journalistic acumen. Booby traps were carefully planted. Late night phone calls, whispered needles, raised eyebrows became the order of the day. Finally it became apparent that to preserve any semblance of peace, we must compromise.

"But what? The only good name was being abandoned, all the animals, at least all the good ones (Tigers, Bears, Lions) were used up. Lamar Hunt had preempted the entire state of Texas. (The Dallas Texans of the new American Football League.) If you don't think I got even for that, drive out to Irving and check the name of the stadium.

Classic Clint

"We sifted names like Sutter sifted sand, but no nuggets were to be found. In desperation, we compiled a list of some 12 names, and then for one reason or another eliminated all but three; but deciding among these was just about impossible, like choosing between an Edsel, a Frazier, and a Tucker Torpedo.

"After a fruitless day of indecision, I went to the airport one morning, preparing to leave town for about a week; there, I received an urgent call from Tex. The decision could not be delayed until my return, he stated, hinting that the only alternative to decision would be to move the franchise to Corpus Christi.

"'Okay, Tex, let's have those three names again,' I replied. Not that I didn't know them by heart; I just couldn't believe that our entire franchise had dwindled to this.

"Three times he uttered a name, three times I winced. The door to my plane was about to close. 'Okay, let's go with Cowboys . . .'

"Well, you know the rest. Gradually, the name became accepted, and even admired. The name Dallas Cowboys became a name of which to be proud. Thinking about it one evening in the winter of 1965, as we prepared for our first winning season, I called Tex, the old journalist, and suggested an idea for some offseason p.r. Why didn't we propose changing the name back to Rangers? Maybe we could stir up something. Tex released the story.

"The next day an enterprising reporter suggested in his column that any interested fan might give me a call to express his preference. As a convenience, my office telephone number was included. At 9:45 the next morning, I received a stack of messages from my telephone operator, on the top of which was a message of her own: 'I give up.' I advised the newspaper as follows:

> First let me say I was somewhat disappointed with the pulling power of the unsolicited ad for Southwestern Bell which your paper carried last Sunday. So far, I have received only 1,148 calls. These break down as follows:
>
> Keep the name Cowboys 1,138
> Change the name to Rangers 2
> Murchison is stupid 8

The Creation of the Dallas Whatsits

> The vote on this latter category is somewhat encouraging because five years ago when we originally changed the name there were 16 such votes. Under the circumstance, I think it is safe to say that sentiment is overwhelming that the team retain its present name, regardless of what the fellows think at Apache Pass.

"After the name, the rest was easy. The team color was a cinch. Lamar had red, so we took blue. It took me eight years to finish the decal design, but you will eventually become used to it, even as I have to the name. One of these days, I'll even finish up with the team blazer."

The 1960-62 seasons were antic times in Dallas football. The Cowboys and the Texans were playing home games in the Cotton Bowl on alternate Sundays, ignoring each other's existence publicly, their players and front-office staffers determinedly avoiding the other side at appearances and in interviews. They were fighting a grim public relations and promotional war on the sports pages.

The Cowboys were playing established teams with name stars; on the other hand the Texans were winning games. Hal Lewis, then the

Face in the crowd: Clint at the Cotton Bowl, surrounded by Cowboy fans including his wife Jane, at left. —photo courtesy of Dallas Cowboys Newsletter

managing editor of the *Dallas Times Herald*, grew so weary of the gimmickry and marketing stunts that he threw up his hands in the newsroom one day and grumbled that neither team should get any free coverage in the sports pages; they should have to buy ads.

Before the season began, the Cowboys had drawn first blood by managing to sign Don Meredith, already a local hero as the Southern Methodist University quarterback. He was originally signed not as a Cowboy player but to a personal services contract for Clint himself. The Chicago Bears actually drafted him first; years later, Clint would recall that part of the negotiations with George Halas, shortly before the franchise had been awarded.

I agreed to the various details of the Dallas franchise, such as price, etc., with George, not as a "power broker of the NFL" but as head of the expansion committee; Walter Wolfner, the other member, was also present. Anyway, subsequently George agreed that we (the Cowboys) should have the draft rights to Meredith and (Don) Perkins—the latter because of Sen. Anderson. (Perkins played for the University of New Mexico; Clinton Anderson, an old friend of Clint's father, was the New Mexico senator and, perhaps, part-time power broker on Clint's behalf.) Later, during the draft, a rumor floated around that George Preston Marshall, forever the malcontent, was going to draft Meredith in the fourth round (before the Cowboys could draft him), and so George called me and suggested that he, the Bears, draft him in the *third* round. I agreed and we subsequently gave Chicago the third-round draft choice the next year for Meredith. A month or so after the draft, I was at home watching the East-West Shrine game on television. Don Meredith was spectacular. The TV commentator signed off with "I can summarize this game in two words—Don Meredith." Just then my phone rang. It was Halas calling from his office in Chicago: "How do you like *our* quarterback?"

One of the Dallas public's first glimpses of Clint's scalpel humor came in a Q. & A. interview with the *Times Herald* during the Cowboys' and Texans' third season of fighting it out for Dallas' favor.

Q. Printed estimates claim your team has lost about $1,000,000 in each of your first two years here. How accurate is this figure?

The Creation of the Dallas Whatsits

A. There was a printed report that Dewey beat Truman in 1948. As was that one, this estimate is quite wide of the mark. We have not made a profit, but I think we have an excellent chance of doing so next year.

(Clint later would say of those early seasons: "The first game I really enjoyed was a Saturday night affair between Pittsburgh and Philadelphia before our 1961 game with Cleveland. It was the only game I'd seen since joining the NFL that hadn't cost me $50,000.")

Q. Will two teams continue to exist here, and if so, how much longer will two be here?

A. As long as the Texans are here, there will be two teams.

Q. Will you ever move from Dallas? If so, under what circumstances?

A. When we have won five consecutive world championships, we may put the team up for bids; however, I am sure that Bedford (Wynne), being a real fan, will be high bidder. He says he will stay here if he can't get the Austin stadium; he has a travel problem during football season, you know.

Q. When asked which team in Dallas would win the two-team battle, John Breem (an official of the AFL Houston Oilers) said, "The first one that leaves town." How do you feel about this?

A. At least I will agree that Breem is certainly familiar with Dallas because he hasn't been too proud to build a championship team using some good ex-Cowboys who were not quite good enough for the NFL.

Q. In the eyes of the public, which do you think would create the better image—to stay here and continue to fight and lose money, or move the team to another city?

A. To stay here and make money, which we will do.

Q. If you decide to move the team to another city, would you retain ownership or get out of football completely?

A. Have you stopped beating your wife?

Q. Two years ago there was a well-founded rumor that you met with the owner of the other team to discuss a merger. Did this meeting take place, and what was said?

Classic Clint

A. There were several meetings, and I think the subject matter was completely covered in the (antitrust suit) testimony in Baltimore last year.

Q. Is there any chance of a merger of the two Dallas teams in the future?

A. Apparently not.

Q. Do you feel your team has gained any advantage over the other team in the three years? Has it lost? Remained the same?

A. At the one game during which the Cowboys were a contender, we drew over 45,000 spectators. This was considerably in excess of any crowd drawn by the Texans with their championship team. The conclusion that must be drawn from this is obvious.

Q. In respect to winning or losing the battle of Dallas, what game was the big test this year, and how do you interpret the outcome?

A. We have never felt that our success depended upon what the Texans did, but rather upon what we did. We were most gratified to see this opinion supported when, at the one home game this season in which we were in contention, we drew over 45,000 people. It is apparent that as we continue to improve in the standings, we will continue to improve at the box office.

Despite their loss to Vince Lombardi's Green Bay Packers in the NFL championship game, Clint was proud of his '66 squad. (Clint's the one in the business suit.)

The Creation of the Dallas Whatsits

Q. If the other team were not here, and there was no television conflict with home games, how much increase do you believe your team would have experienced?
A. I think that we would have at least one additional fan; I refer, of course, to Bunker Hunt.
Q. We realize this is purely conjecture, but please predict the winning team and score if the two teams were to play right now.
A. I would love to, but Coach Landry is using my IBM right now.
Q. When will they play?
A. When Bedford gets his lease on the Austin stadium.

"In between lawsuits," Clint wrote four years after the Q&A interview, "Lamar and I are really quite friendly. During his final Spur Club meeting of 1960, I slipped into the luncheon wearing a Texan blazer and wished all a hearty Merry Christmas. The following week, I was entertaining at my home one evening when a couple of friends carried in a huge box, gift wrapped. I pulled the ribbon and out popped Lamar. I have received some unusual gifts from time to time, but that topped them."

(In 1982, on Lamar Hunt's 50th birthday, his wife and friends played for him a surprise video with appearances and testimonials by Howard Cosell, Pete Rozelle, former Patriots owner Billy Sullivan, and other football celebrities. In the finale of the video, the camera approaches a large, gift-wrapped box. The contents of the box can be heard asking a muffled "Ready? Now?"

Up and out pops Clint, squinting into the sun, smiling tightly, and wearing a bright red Dallas Texans blazer. "Hey, Lamar, when are y'all movin' out to Texas Stadium? Happy birthday!")

Big D Wasn't Big Enough for the Two of Them

(Clint's column from the 1970 Cowboys Newsletter about his friendship with his implacable corporate rival Lamar Hunt.)

Early Lamar

Back in 1956, Jane and I were invited to dinner by our aging and somewhat corpulent neighbor, Stuart Hunt, and his pretty wife, Jeanne. The only other guest that evening was Stuart's nephew,

Classic Clint

Lamar, a nice looking young man, then a student at SMU, and already exhibiting a precocious interest in professional sports promotion as the proprietor of the Zima Bat establishment located at what proved to be a rather fateful corner on North Central Expressway. That was the only time I was to meet Lamar before we declared war on each other.

Even if Lamar hadn't been personable, it would have been difficult for me not to like him, if for no other reason than that so many people mistook the two of us. That in itself was flattering to me, since I spotted Lamar a good ten years, and besides, who wants to dislike his alter ego? Once at a luncheon club in Dallas, I remember being introduced by a mutual friend of our fathers to a group of men, all of whom knew me. They didn't know Lamar, however, and before I realized what was happening, I was being introduced around as Lamar. Everyone present just smiled and said hello, but the gentleman making the introductions had no reason (in those confusing days) to be embarrassed. Several years later, during merger negotiations between the two leagues, a young man entered the Cowboys offices and asked for Tex Schramm. The receptionist eyed him quizzically for about ten seconds and asked, "Mr. Murchison?" "Lamar Hunt," replied Lamar. I sent the young lady two photographs captioned, "This is Clint" and "This is Lamar."

In 1960 Lamar leased the Zima Bat location once again, this time for use as the Dallas Texans' practice field. Naturally I bought the land to build a building to house the offices of the Cowboys, and Lamar had to move his locker room to the adjacent lot. Subsequently, when the Texans transferred to Kansas City, the Cowboys' practice area at Rebel Stadium was no longer available to us, so we bought Lamar's empty locker room and pulled it back onto our property.

That's got to be some kind of travel record for a locker room.

At a party in my home in 1960, a few days before Christmas, a similar moving job occurred. With great tugging and pulling, several friends brought in the biggest Christmas present I'd ever seen, beautifully gift wrapped. I expectantly pulled the ribbon to open it. You guessed it: out popped Lamar. As I've commented before, it was the perfect present for the football owner who has everything.

And now it's ten years later. In less than a month, the once inconceivable will happen: the Dallas Cowboys will meet the Kansas City Chiefs in the Cotton Bowl. Lamar and I will meet in the pressbox, shake hands, and make some small talk. Then we will see a great battle on the field, one that everybody has been anticipating for ten years. But it won't be a fight like in the good old days. I hope, however, that the wags from those times were wrong. Remember? The way they had it, it was the WINNER that got to leave Dallas.

Where is Anybody?

The two-team years generated grim stories that would be more amusing later, when they could be viewed as nostalgic anecdotes. In the summer of 1967 Clint wrote a remembrance in the *Dallas Times Herald* of those early years of battling with the Texans for Dallas fans' attention, and attendance:

". . . I remember a season-ticket holder wanting to change his seat location because someone was sitting in front of him. That same year, I went to the press box at halftime during the San Francisco game, looked down and saw not a soul; it was drizzling and the few spectators were sitting invisible beneath the stadium overhang. I didn't go back to the press box for two more years . . ."

In those early and losing years, Tom Landry was introducing a series of offensive shifts that would later become standard in the league, but at the time merely seemed to be wasted motion in games the team invariably lost. Once again it was time for Clint to hear from his Pen Pal from Hell:

September 25, 1964

Mr. Clint Murchison
1201 Main Street
Dallas, Texas

RE: Shifts

Dear Clunk:

When it comes to football, I have no peer. Your Cowgirls think they are putting one over on me, but I recognize the new formations —particularly the disguised audibles being used to make "shifts."

Who would have ever thought of using the animal kingdom to designate shifts!! I particularly like the end-around pitch-out option, where Dandy Don retains the ball. I understand this is called the "Chicken Shift." I know this is correct, because in the Cardinal game when Dandy looked back for Amos Marsh and he wasn't there, he said in a loud voice, "Chicken Shift."

Classic Clint

Apparently, this play was called again last week when Dandy Don came out of the game and talked to Landry about his hurt ankle—hoping to get back on telephone duty—but Tom sent him back to the meat grinder instead. As Dandy Don stumbled back on the field, he mumbled to himself, "Chicken Shift."

Another "shift" which came to light last week was the quick opener where Dandy sent Amos into the line. Unfortunately, Sam Huff was reading this play and met Marsh head-on, on two or three occasions, with devastating tackles. As time wore on in the game and Dandy Don called this play, Amos Marsh would indignantly respond with "Bull Shift." This type of audible apparently is not restricted to the Cowgirls, for when Mitchell had Cornell beat for a cinch touchdown and the pass slithered through his fingers, the Washington coach was heard clearly to yell, "Horse Shift."

To show you that I am not the only one who has deciphered your audible calls, at one point in the game last week the man next to me said in a low voice, "Here comes the Big Shift." You were walking up the aisle at the time.

Helpfully,

COTTONTAIL SCHNEIDER

Multitude To Be Named Later

Probably no story of the slim attendance legends illustrated the problem as stunningly as Clint's ticket trade with New York restauranteur Toots Shor in 1962. The Cowboys had met the Giants in New York early in the season, and Shor had obtained four extra box seat tickets for Clint's party. To repay him when the Giants were due to return to the Cotton Bowl for their second game in November, Clint shipped a large carton to Shor.

November 7, 1962

Mr. Toots Shor
Toots Shor Restaurant
1270 Sixth Avenue
New York, New York

Dear Toots:

Enclosed are the box seats for the New York-Dallas game Sunday about which I spoke to you Friday night. And in case you want to

The Creation of the Dallas Whatsits

bring any of your friends with you, I am also sending you Sections 1, 2, 3 and 4.

Sincerely,

CLINT

There were 10,000 unsold tickets in the carton.

Shooting the Messenger

The early Cowboys teams veered between being inept and just being overmatched. The Cowboys lost, and Hunt's Texans won. The drumfire from fans for one or the other to leave town continued in the city's papers until, in the third season of the two-team town, Clint cut out the jokes in a private letter to Sherrod, the *Times Herald's* principal columnist and executive sports editor.

> December 19, 1962
> **PERSONAL**
> Dear Blackie:
>
> I am sure that (drama and music critic) Gene Lewis has, from time to time, criticized certain performances of the State Fair Musicals; however, I am also sure that as a result of these poor performances, it was never suggested that the Musicals be moved from Dallas. With respect to football here, although I may disagree on occasion, I can certainly take no exception to criticism of team performances, at least as long as the criticism is not ridiculous, or to fans indicating a strong team preference. However, I think that the Times Herald, in repeatedly printing letters demanding that either the Cowboys or the Texans leave town, is unintentionally giving editorial support to an opinion it does not hold. It appears to me that this is not in the best interests of either of the football teams, your newspaper, or our city.
>
> Sincerely,
>
> CLINT

The Purist

Clint always held to the opinion that the NFL was the authentic league and the AFL just a bunch of clownish usurpers. Part of the Other league's appeal was its flamboyant style of play, enhanced by

Classic Clint

the pizzazz of ABC's gimmicky television techniques. By 1965 CBS announcer Chris Schenkel had moved over to ABC.

> August 31, 1965
>
> Mr. William McPhail
> Vice President-Sports
> Columbia Broadcasting System, TV
> 51 West 52 Street
> New York, New York
>
> Dear Bill:
>
> For several years past during football telecasts, ABC has had the clever habit of switching camera angles just as the ball was snapped. Their personnel handled this very adroitly, completely camouflaging the play, with the obvious intent of concealing from the viewing public the fact that it was really watching the AFL, not a football game.
>
> It is now apparent that in the Chris Schenkel trade CBS obtained several of these cameramen, at least one Sports Director, and an undisclosed amount of cash. I would appreciate your advising these people that most of the NFL fans really prefer to watch football, and that no camera tricks, derricks, or other such impedimenta are necessary.
>
> Sincerely,
> CLINT

Coach Clint

The element of Clint's ownership of the team that is most often mentioned is his policy of never meddling with the team's management, nor especially with Tom Landry's coaching.

"The fact is," says Clint's son Robert, "Dad fancied himself a pretty good coach. Through the 1950s and into the sixties, we kids all played football in the Town North YMCA program, and Dad always coached our team. We were all fourth, fifth, and sixth graders. While Landry was sending in plays for the Cowboys with alternating guards or quarterbacks, Dad was sending us hand signals from the sidelines. It wasn't allowed, of course. One day I looked up from the huddle —another kid was the quarterback—and I saw Dad beginning to make some signals when he saw Jack Semones, the director of the league, approaching him. Dad had been waving arms, fists, fingers, etc., but,

The Creation of the Dallas Whatsits

when he saw Jack, quickly turned aside and switched from those signals to just scratching his elbow and other motions.

"Our team never finished worse than second under Dad. Something else he did back then, on Saturday afternoons after the game he'd call Landry at home and tell him how good his coaching had been that morning."

Clint, famous for never having meddled in the coaching of the Cowboys, took a more active hand with his sons' YMCA six-man football teams. His 1963 season playbook was sketched on a legal pad by son Robert.

The 1958 4th grade YMCA champions, St. Mark's Lions, with coaches Clint and John Rauscher, Jr. Son Burk is front row, third from left; Robert, holding the sign, was the team mascot. —photo courtesy of David Laney

Classic Clint

No-Coaching Zone

A note to Tom Landry, who had just taken the team to Florida to prepare for the Cowboys' first Super Bowl appearance, against Baltimore:

> January 6, 1971
>
> Mr. Thomas W. Landry
> Galt Ocean Mile Hotel
> 3200 Galt Ocean Drive
> Fort Lauderdale, Florida
>
> Dear Tom:
>
> I have taught you all I can. From now on, you're on your own.
>
> Sincerely,
>
> CLINT

Word to the Wise

Maybe it wasn't an official Meddle, but Clint sent a cautionary note to Landry just before the Cowboys were to play a preseason game in Tulsa. Tulsa was where the Cowboys' new quarterback Jerry Rhome had played college football, and Landry had indicated that Rhome might not get to play before the home crowd.

> September 8, 1965
>
> Dear Tom:
>
> I understand that after (Los Angeles Rams Coach Harlan) Svare elected not to play Baker in the preseason game last year in Portland, the Rams are no longer welcome in Portland. *(Ed. note: Terry Baker was a Heisman Trophy quarterback from the University of Oregon, drafted by the Rams.)*
>
> I own a $3,000,000 rock quarry in Tulsa, and a frightening thought has just occurred to me.
>
> Have you ever tried to move a rock quarry?
>
> Sincerely,
>
> CLINT

The Creation of the Dallas Whatsits

The Female Franchise

Clint could sympathize with the identity crisis of Rankin Smith, owner of the new Atlanta franchise, when it was time for Smith to name his team. But as something of a wordsmith, linguist, and crossword buff himself, Clint knew some obscurities of the language that other people didn't. He also may have answered a question that would be asked later by thousands of Toyota owners.

> August 31, 1965
>
> Mr. Jesse Outlar
> Sports Editor
> Atlanta Constitution
> Atlanta, Georgia
>
> Dear Mr. Outlar:
>
> I ran into Rankin Smith about a week ago and he told me that he had selected the name FALCONS for the Atlanta football team. I pointed out to him that the falcon is a female peregrine. I certainly don't have anything against females, but I have never seen one play football. Accordingly, I suggested to Rankin that he change the name to the TERCELS. He didn't give me a definite answer, but I think you had better check into this right away; for all I know, Rankin may have his scouts up at Wellesley, Vassar, and Sweet Briar right now.

Heil, Murchison

Fans who remember the Cowboys' difficulties with the Green Bay Packers at the championship level may have forgotten that first, their nemesis was the Cleveland Browns. Meeting Cleveland in the early years, Clint's team would usually come down with a severe case of the 48-to-7s. Later, as the Cowboys improved to the point that they might almost be favored in a match with the Browns, a lesser Cleveland team would upset them.

Thus the stage was set for Clint's letter to some Cleveland friends on Oct. 21, 1966:

> Dear Becky and Russ,
>
> I appreciate the apples which were here when I returned from Cleveland, via New York. Aside from the good fun, this is about the only thing we have been able to get out of Cleveland in the six years we have been in the league.

Classic Clint

> I enjoyed our visit and hope I will see you again soon. Be sure and watch the television in November.

Clint's sly mention of the Thanksgiving night game in the Cotton Bowl against the Browns referred to an event that would revolutionize not only the televising of NFL games, but many of the league's images as well.

The crowd of 80,000 in the Cotton Bowl that evening gave a collective gasp when it first saw what had been done. So did millions of television viewers. Much of the new look of the field had been conceived by Clint in his eager role as set decorator and psychology consultant. First of all, the barren, November-bleak turf had been painted a rich emerald green. The end zones looked different. The sidelines looked different. Midfield looked different. The next day's *Dallas Times Herald* reported on page one:

"It was New Year's, the Fourth of July, and Thanksgiving all rolled up in one package... The Cotton Bowl was dressed in its finest for nationwide colorcast on television via CBS. Yard strip numerals alternated in ochre and blue—and would you believe they even painted the Cowboy benches a baby blue? A big 'D' was encircled in color right in the slap-dab middle of the 50-yard line and each end zone proclaimed in 20-foot letters the name of the Cowboys... It was made to order for the color cameras."

That night, too, saw the debut of Clint's idea of the national anthem played by trumpet soloist Tommy Loy, who would thus begin every home game for as long as Clint owned the team.

Tattoos of drums reverberated across the stadium, the lights were brilliant and the crowd's incessant, fevered rumbling voice gave the night a sort of benign Nuremberg Rally quality—if you were a Cowboy fan. Clint and the Cowboys beat Cleveland that night, 26-14. It was a preview of the way the NFL's fields eventually would look.

Squeaky Wheel Time

Clint had another complaint for CBS Television.

During the sixties and seventies, the opening video montages of the network's intro to NFL games included a few seconds of Tom Landry's face distorted in a rictus of anguish. It was all the more

The Creation of the Dallas Whatsits

dramatic for involving the man famous for never showing emotion. The shot had been made during a league championship game against Green Bay, at the moment Landry had learned that Cowboy lineman Jim Boeke had been called offside, stalling a last-minute Cowboy goal-line drive. The Cowboys lost the game by a touchdown.

November 28, 1967

Mr. William McPhail
Vice President-Sports
Columbia Broadcasting System, TV
51 West 52 Street
New York, New York

Dear Bill:

During the television introduction to the NFL games, I wish you would quit using so frequently that clip of Tom Landry wincing; I am afraid it will give him a complex, like Kuharich.

Besides, as everyone knows, that scene was staged.

(Joe Kuharich was the hyper-excitable coach of the Philadelphia Eagles, the emotional opposite of the stoic Landry.)

Tom Landry's grimace was a featured part of the opening montage of NFL broadcasts for nearly a decade. —photo courtesy of NFL Films

Classic Clint

An Inter-Office memo to Tex Schramm:

> January 31
>
> Tex:
>
> I heard on the news last night that a basketball coach had been fired because he punched the owner in the jaw. To prevent any future misunderstanding, I think we should alert our personnel to the fact that a similar regulation is in effect with respect to the Dallas Cowboys.

Knowing mathematics, and money, as well as he did, he couldn't help sharing a captivating statistic with Arthur Modell, owner of the Cleveland Browns:

> To: Arthur Modell
>
> **HOME GAME SUMMARY—1968**
>
> | EASTERN CONFERENCE | RECEIPTS |
> |---|---|
> | Dallas | $2,446,722 |
> | Cleveland | $2,446,262 |

And Clint's casual talents as a pro-football scholar were impressive:

> August 18, 1969
>
> Mr. Frank Glieber
> KRLD
> Dallas, Texas
>
> Dear Frank:
>
> Yesterday was not, as you reported on the radio this morning, the first time that a rookie ever received the game ball in his first outing.
>
> George Halas did the same thing when the Staley A.C.'s opened against the Massillon Tigers in 1923.

Scattershooting

To Lou Spadia, owner of the San Francisco 49ers, about a situation that remains a mystery in the files:

> March 3, 1970
>
> Dear Lou:

The Creation of the Dallas Whatsits

If I knew what the hell I was doing, Lamar would still be in Dallas and I would be banking $500,000 a year.

Sincerely,

CLINT

To a complainant who apparently had written Clint with advice on how to run the team:

January 12, 1970

Dear Mr. Rosales:

I agree that you are no "uneducated hothead who knows nothing about football." You are obviously an educated hothead who knows nothing about football.

Yours truly,

A reply to a fan who had written to complain about the policy of home game television blackouts:

December 23, 1970

Dear Timothy:

"Instead of cursing the darkness, light a candle."

Or buy a season ticket.

A television systems company had filed suit against the National Football League and the three TV networks over broadcasting and blackout policies.

It was an awkward time for the company's president to write to Clint:

Management Television Systems, Inc.
277 Park Avenue
New York, N.Y. 10017

June 25, 1970

Dear Mr. Murchison:

MTS is seeking to negotiate with individual teams of the National Football League for the large screen, color closed circuit telecasting of each team's regular season home games. Though MTS's lawsuit against the league and the three networks is still pending, I believe we can meet at this time on a business basis only, without prejudice to any party's rights.

Classic Clint

We are in the process of preparing some material to illustrate the MeTaVision process, which provides large screen color television of the highest quality. We also want to describe to you our experience in the fields of football, basketball, soccer, prize fighting, automobile racing and many other successful programs. We believe this medium will be a prime source of substantial additional revenue for the football clubs, beginning with the 1970 season, and have developed a formula which will not interfere with stadium attendance.

I know you and the Dallas Cowboys will find our proposal interesting, and I hope to hear from you at your early convenience, so that we may arrange a meeting at a mutually convenient date.

Sincerely,

E. WILLIAM HENRY   **signed in Mr. Henry's absence**
Chairman of the Board

Perhaps it was the "Signed in Mr. Henry's absence" touch that drove Clint over the edge. He answered the letter on July 6:

DALLAS COWBOYS FOOTBALL CLUB
1111 EXPRESSWAY TOWER
6116 NORTH CENTRAL EXPRESSWAY
Dallas, Texas 75206

July 6, 1970

Mr. E. William Henry
Chairman of the Board
Management Television Systems, Inc.
277 Park Avenue
New York, New York

Dear Mr. Henry:

You must be out of your goddamned mind.

Sincerely,
CLINT MURCHISON, JR.
Chairman of the Board   **Signed in Mr. Murchison's Absence**

The Creation of the Dallas Whatsits

The Adjective Avalanche

Before the Cowboys were America's Team, they were Destiny's. The 1970 club, humiliated at midseason 38-0 on Monday Night Football by the St. Louis Cardinals, went on to win seven straight regular season games and the playoffs that took them into their first Super Bowl.

In a *Dallas Times Herald* column a few days before the Super Bowl, Blackie Sherrod had pondered over a term to describe the team. Clint wrote to help him out:

> January 6, 1971
>
> Dear Blackie:
>
> In yesterday's column, you were looking for words to describe this year's team. I've got several. How about analytic, aloof, bland, balanced, cold, computerized, distant, deliberate, eclectic, emotionless, flinty, factual, grave, geometric, haughty, hermetic, impassionate, imperturbable, and maybe jejune?

Happy Trails: the Cowboys had just won their first NFC championship against the 49ers at San Francisco's Kezar Stadium. Lurking behind Clint is an unidentified son, who surely stuck out that day in the 49er partisan crowd, but who now desires to remain anonymous. —photo courtesy of Robert F. Murchison

Classic Clint

Rubble Trouble

Charlie Waters, the team's defensive back, was not many of those adjectives. His sleek piledriver elegance, though, was a hallmark of that team. He remembers a story about Clint from that season.

"The Saturday practice before a Sunday game is always loose—well, looser than a typical Tom Landry regimented practice. With the game plan set and the fine-tuned details ironed out earlier, Saturday was just a fun reminder of what we had worked on for the last week. In the training facility after the brief, spirited workout, Dave Manders, a seven-year veteran and starting center, and I got into a 'grab-ass' competition. Pushing and shoving ensued, and somehow I blasted into Dave at just the right angle and sent all 260 pounds of him crashing into, and through, the plaster wall. He was lodged between the studs and joists with sheetrock and plaster crumbling everywhere. Everyone stared, and then laughed. Me, too.

"I was still laughing when I noticed a hush had fallen over the rest of the room. I turned and found myself face-to-face not only with Tom Landry, but Clint Murchison as they were observing our pregame state of mind. Clint's reaction was impossible to read, as always, but predictably, Coach Landry's was not. He was displeased over our lack of seriousness and the chance of two key players being injured by horseplay.

"I cringed, pulled Dave from the rubble, and crawled back to my locker. I knew pro football was a serious business, and it was different from college in that you don't have to have the 'Win one for the Gipper' attitude at all times; but was I going to be punished?

"The day passed with no repercussions and Sunday, the game was on us before we knew it.

"The Cowboys won and clinched a playoff berth. I intercepted a pass near the end that iced the victory. I was pleased, but I was also still haunted by the retribution from my wrestling match, and the demolition of a wall section at the practice field, and my lack of professionalism the day before a big game—all in front of not only the coach, but the *owner of the team.*

The Creation of the Dallas Whatsits

"As I sat in the locker room afterward cutting off tape from joints, a ballboy came running up to me with a scared look on his face. 'Mr. Murchison is looking for you—he's on his way over here now.'

"My thoughts then were: (1) God, I know they'll deduct the cost of that wall from my check, that way I'll get off easy, (2) No, they're gonna fine me, (3) No, I'm traded for sure . . .

"As all these scenarios entered my mind, the little man in the crew cut stopped in front of me with a two-foot-square piece of torn-up plaster, wrapped with a blue satin ribbon that was tied in a bow. I took the offering from Mr. Murchison with puzzlement, and slowly looked up from my seat until I had eye contact with him. He just gave me a deadpan 'Good game,' and then he walked off. I untied the bow from the oblong slab of plaster and sheetrock and blew away the dust to read:

"'Charlie, tear up the opponents and not my practice field.
Clint Murchison.'"

Squeaky Wheel (cont'd)

Schramm ran the club and Landry was the coach, and Clint, being just the owner, took advantage of his position to complain like any other irate fan, if they knew Mark Duncan was the supervisor of NFL officials.

> September 22, 1970
>
> Mr. Mark Duncan
> National Football League
> 410 Park Avenue
> New York, New York
>
> Dear Mark:
>
> Nutty things seem to happen to us in Philadelphia. Remember a couple of years ago when I offered to design an electronic whistle? That was when Dan Reeves, nonchalantly returning to the huddle after a play, was accosted by a defensive back who grabbed the ball from Danny, and it was ruled a fumble.

> Last Sunday, we got fifteen when Hill spiked the ball. Then Monday night, I saw the Detroit highlights; three spikes in three plays shown, one being at the end of Gregg Landry's 47-yard sneak.
>
> Anyway, I'm glad you got rid of that slow whistle in Philadelphia.
>
> Sincerely,
> CLINT

Setting the Record Straight

The Colts won that Super Bowl on a field goal literally in the last seconds, 16-13. Yet through the off-season and the beginning of the next, the Cowboys, with their mystique and their mischief, were the sensation of the league and its fans.

Miami Herald columnist Edwin Pope wrote a wry piece on "The Cowboys, Football's Peyton Place. They've got everything: sex scandals, player-management bitterness, bankruptcies, divorces; plus a Super Bowl football team . . .

"All the inner strife doesn't sound like the kind of organization that would be put together by a 130-pound former halfback at Massachusetts Institute of Technology, which is what owner Clint Murchison happens to be . . ."

Pope went on with a detailed list of scandalous events. So Clint replied:

> Mr. Edwin Pope
> Sports Editor
> Miami Herald
> Miami, Florida
>
> Dear Ed:
>
> With reference to your recent column about the Dallas Cowboys, you're full of shit. I weigh 142 pounds.

Over several seasons, Tom Landry and Tex Schramm had chatty "Dear Tom" and "Dear Tex" columns in the Cowboys Insiders Newsletter in which they answered fans' curiosities about running the team. Clint seemed to delight in commenting privately to Schramm about his answers, especially when they involved Clint.

The Creation of the Dallas Whatsits

Fight, Beavers, Fight?

Clint persuaded Tom Landry to pose crimson-clad for a large full-color poster that he reproduced in mass and presented as gifts to his friends and fellow Trustees at M.I.T., whose mascot is the Beaver. —photo courtesy of Robert F. Murchison

One exchange in the newsletter went:

> Clint Murchison is one of the most behind-the-scenes owners in pro football. How important was he in the initial phases of growth? It doesn't appear that he interfered with the machinery of the club.

Schramm's answer:

> One of the greatest assets we had in the beginning was Clint Murchison. He had taken a great deal of interest in the development of the team, and he was in contact with me a great deal because I sought his counsel on a lot of matters . . .

Clint underlined the *in the beginning* phrase and sent the clipping on to Tex, signing Landry's initials to a comment written beneath:

> But what has he done lately?

Another time, a fan had written Tex to rhapsodize about the Cowboy Way:

> There have been many theories as to why the Dallas Cowboys have become so popular worldwide . . . The primary reason I think they are so popular is the way the individual fan is allowed to feel personal involvement in the Cowboys organization . . . The daily publicity is about an individual player or how the team can provide better exciting entertainment. This is what the fans can identify with—not what some millionaire owner did yesterday . . .
>
> TEX: Our fans are our greatest strength and we sincerely thank you.

Clint sent that one back to Schramm, too, adding a line at the bottom:

> Tex: What are you, some kind of communist nut?

Clint also sent to Tex a marked clipping he had found in another newspaper:

> There's talk about the National Football League adopting the extra large Cowboy first-down markers next season. Dallas loaned the markers to Minnesota for the NFL title game and they were also used at the Super Bowl . . . Another Tex Schramm innovation—the white border around the field—was adopted by the NFL two years ago.

Clint's comment in that case was:

> Tex, I don't mind your getting credit for merging the leagues, or Leonard Woodhull the credit for inventing my radio-control clock, but you guys stay away from my first-down markers.

The Creation of the Dallas Whatsits

Schramm, as a CBS executive, had glimpsed the linked futures of computers and sports in the 1960 Squaw Valley Winter Olympics. Clint, with his M.I.T. background, understood their potential. The Cowboys thus would be pioneers in computerized talent-scouting. Their first venture was a cost-sharing consortium with the 49ers and Rams. Clint wrote a learnedly playful column about computers:

Science and the Super Bowl

"Some models are cute, but mathematical models are exact."
—W.C. Fields

Computerized football according to Clint (Cowboys Newsletter column, 1970).

> Pierre de Fermat was a brilliant 17th Century French mathematician given, perhaps more than some of his colleagues, to the scientific secrecy prevalent during the Renaissance. It was his habit to scribble in the margin of his copy of Diophantus notes of interest and profundity. On one such occasion, in reference to what is now called Fermat's Last Theorem, he stated, "I have found for this a truly wonderful proof, but the margin is too small to hold it." Such was his repute that mathematicians have over the succeeding three centuries not really doubted his proof, but, unfortunately, they have been unable to duplicate it.
>
> One spring evening in the year 1631, Fermat was enjoying an after-dinner cordial with an equally accomplished mathematician, Blaise Pascal, when they were joined by a noted French gambler. Quite naturally, the gambler began to discuss games of chance, and, as gamblers are wont to do, volunteered his opinions thereupon.
>
> Little did these three realize that they were taking a first step toward the victory of the Dallas Cowboys in the Super Bowl. Not even, at that point, did Gil Brandt know.
>
> Not that football is a game of chance; far from it. That fact is the very point of my story, as you shall see. But this meeting led to the orderly investigation of games of chance, an investigation which subsequently resulted in mathematical methods called probability. Meaningful application of these studies to biological, social, political, and economic problems were not, of course, immediate. But in the early part of this century, Karl Pearson and Sir Ronald Fisher initiated such applications and built the general structure of knowledge which is called statistics. And you are undoubtedly aware of the importance of

statistics to a sport. In the early 1960s, the Dallas Cowboys initiated a program to investigate the feasibility of statistical applications to the game of football. Our efforts were amply rewarded; by 1965 the Player Selection System was developed. Its objective is to rank potential professional football players; this ranking serves as an important guide to us at the time of the National Football League Player Draft.

Each year there are over 500 potential ball players who graduate from colleges and vie for positions in professional football. Since the capabilities of a football player are described by a multitude of factors, one of the first steps in the development of our Player Selection System was to find a small, representative set of these factors. This was accomplished using Factor Analysis, a technique introduced by Spearman in 1904. Factor Analysis came into being specifically to provide mathematical models for the explanation of psychological theories of human ability.

The first step in this analysis is the identification of the characteristics which have an effect on the 'value' of a person as a football player. The second is to establish a scale of measurement for each of these characteristics. Thirdly, to establish quantitative relationships between the characteristics and the **value** and impute a scale for the measurement of **value**. Fourthly, to evaluate the potential player on the scale of each characteristic. Finally, to use the relationships so derived to calculate the **value** for each player and subsequently to obtain an ordered ranking of all potential players.

After an exhaustive study, five nonphysical characteristics were found to be relevant to the **value**— Character, Quickness, Competitiveness, Mental Ability, and Strength. These are general categories, each including a few subcategories. For example, one subcategory of Competitiveness was the term, "He would hit his mother if she were on the other side." The two physical characteristics are Size and Speed. Also for each position there are two other categories, Specifics and Hands, the latter being relevant in certain positions such as a flanker.

Each of these characteristics is graded according to a scale ranging from one to nine; scientists since Fermat have determined that the human mind cannot distinguish more than nine classifications.

The third step involves the determination of relative weights for each characteristic. This is accomplished by interviewing various coaches, scouts, and psychologists. Mathematical methods such as linear programming are then used to determine the weighting. The mathematics involved in deriving this set of factors is quite intricate. For example, a typical equation employed in these procedures is:

$$\frac{\partial T}{\partial^a j p} = \delta_1 p^j j_1 - \sum_{k=1}^{n} M_j k^a j_1^2 k_p = 0 \quad (j = 1, 2, \ldots n;\ p = 1, 2, \ldots, m)$$

The final step of assimilation, analysis, and ranking is performed by an IBM 360 Model 65 computer, a necessity caused by our vast accumulation of data and calculations.

The point of all this is to reduce the occurrence in player selection of subjective errors. And to win—which accomplishment, I assure those of you faint of heart, will not take the three centuries required to develop our mathematical system.

Ruffles & Flourishes

"He wanted to present a Dallas team in a winning way—that was number one—and with class," Tex Schramm would write in 1987. "First class all the way, in everything."

Some think Clint's devotion to class was never better shown than in the way the national anthem was presented at home games, another of the innovations that began with the benchmark pageantry of that "Nuremberg-night" Thanksgiving game against the Browns.

In the pregame according to Clint, as the color guard marched to midfield, a slight, balding man in a blue blazer and grey slacks, trumpet tucked and reversed under his arm, marched onto the field. His name was Tommy Loy, a musician Clint had met long before on the Dixieland club circuit.

Loy played *The Star-Spangled Banner* with no other accompaniment. The sweet, clear notes of the trumpet solo soared across the gridiron and beyond the stands, the final fading notes lingering in the inevitable hush that gripped the crowd. Loy's and Clint's national anthem was a patriotic equivalent to the architect's adage that less is more.

Clint enjoyed orchestrating special pregame ceremonies. His instructions for the color ceremonies before the Texas Stadium game on December 21, 1980 were specific:

Anthem introduction—no words prior to these.

> (This announcement should be made after the teams line up on the sidelines and as the color guard marches on to the field position. The announcement should be finished *before* the color guard reaches its final position so that the guards' final 8-10 steps are made in silence.)

Beneath those directions, he wrote his own ecumenical prayer:

> In this joyous season as we celebrate the birthday of our Lord, we should remember that one of His gifts to us is the gift of freedom, the greatness of the United States, one nation under God.

Other musical trademarks of Cowboy home games were Clint's, too, notably the adoption of Jerry Jeff Walker's "Redneck Mother" as an unofficial fight song, and occasionally playing a recording of Don Meredith singing "Turn Out the Lights, the Party's Over," famous from ABC Monday Night Football.

In a Nutshell

Despite his mythic reluctance to meddle in team affairs, Clint made the exception that proved the rule with his milestone gesture on behalf of Tom Landry in 1964. As the team floundered through another season and critics called for the remainder of Landry's scalp, Clint backed his coach by handing him a 10-year contract. It was a decision that led, among other things, to the biggest broadcasting cliche of all: "Tom Landry, the only coach the Cowboys ever had..."

When Landry's hometown of Mission, Texas, held a Tom Landry Day in 1984, planners wrote to Clint asking for a capsule comment on Landry's effect upon football and the Cowboys.

> Mr. Harlan Woods
> Director of Public Information
> Mission Independent School District
> 1116 Conway Avenue
> Mission, Texas
>
> Dear Mr. Woods:
>
> I think an unknown Tom Landry fan put it best in 1960 as he introduced Tom to the Salesmanship Club on his arrival in Dallas when he said, "I was talking to a friend about Tom recently and he said that Tom Landry was the next Paul Brown; I said 'No, he is the first Tom Landry.'"
>
> And he still is.

The Creation of the Dallas Whatsits

Memo to Mimi

In the summer of 1984 Mimi Lay, widow of corn chips millionaire Herman Lay, became a minority shareholder in the team. Clint welcomed her to ownerdom with some advice:

> July 19, 1984
>
> Dear Mimi:
>
> Congratulations on joining the Cowboys family! But I should give you two tips:
>
> 1) If we win, don't **say** anything but leave the impression that you were responsible; I would suggest wandering around the room with an enigmatic smile.
>
> 2) Don't worry about losses; they're Landry's fault.
>
> Good luck! Herman would have loved it!
>
> Sincerely,
>
> CLINT

After the 1970 NFC championship victory over San Francisco: Clint and Bullet Bob Hayes from the rear, which is the same view of Hays that defenders usually saw. —photo courtesy of Dallas Cowboys Newsletter

The Bear Facts

When Mike Ditka, the former Cowboys player and assistant coach, was named head coach by the Chicago Bears, Clint chose an oblique message of congratulations:

> March 29, 1982
>
> Coach Mike Ditka
> Chicago Bears Football Club, Inc.
> 250 N. Washington Road
> Lake Forest, Illinois 60045
>
> Dear Mike:
>
> One of my companies bought a sky box at Soldier's Field. I am counting on you to make it a good investment.
>
> Sincerely,

> **CHICAGO BEARS**
>
> April 13, 1982
>
> Dear Clint:
>
> The sky box that your company bought will end up being one of your wisest investments.
>
> The Bears are going to return to the top of the Central Division with good, hard aggressive type of play.
>
> I would like to thank you for the great opportunity afforded me while working for the Dallas Cowboys. Those years will never be forgotten and my appreciation to you and the Cowboy organization will never diminish.
>
> Sincerely,
> MIKE

The Pete Papers

Clint and Commissioner Pete Rozelle came into the National Football League at about the same time. They were allies on many league issues and adversaries on others, but through it all they maintained an easy and usually bantering friendship, perhaps all the stronger for their counterbalancing personal traits—Rozelle the public extrovert, Clint the private enigma. Many of Clint's impulsive messages to

The Creation of the Dallas Whatsits

Rozelle were his trademark bolts-from-the-blue; and Rozelle often gave as good he got.

> November 15, 1978
>
> Dear Pete:
>
> I'm getting tired of these anti-Cowboys decisions and I'm going to SUE. Sue the officials, the applauding sportscasters and you, you SOB. This will not be a $5 million suit but one of $50 million (Texas Stadium bonds, you know).
>
> Now I'm not suing in federal court; Ralph Neely can explain why that won't work. I'm suing in the Justice of the Peace court in IRVING, TEXAS, where we can all get a fair trial (except maybe some of those goddamn officials, and maybe you).
>
> My principal complaint will be that ABSOLUTELY IDIOTIC call when Heintz claimed Andy Cverko was holding on Gene Lipscomb in the Dallas-Pittsburgh game of 1962. The instant replay clearly shows that Andy wasn't holding, he was saving his life. Boy!
>
> If you think I'm kidding, call one of those dumb lawyers of yours who have gotten us unionized, anti-trusted, compulsory-televised and, finally, price-controlled.

Rozelle's answer:

> Dear Clint:
>
> Some years ago Warren Beatty told me he had played freshman football at Northwestern. He said he realized the game wasn't for him and quit when his roommate came home ill late one night and threw up a whole pork chop.
>
> I haven't been able to tell this amusing little story because of forgetting the name of the roommate. Your thoughtful note has corrected this and I am most grateful.
>
> It was Andy Cverko.
>
> Cheers, PETE

> October 31, 1967
>
> Dear Pete:
>
> I recently ran across some definitions which are, I believe, pertinent to the vicissitude of one of our member clubs, herewith listed alphabetically:
>
> BACK: That part of your friend which it is your privilege to contemplate in your adversity.

> **FIDELITY:** A virtue peculiar to those who are about to be betrayed.
>
> **FRIENDSHIP:** A big enough boat to carry two in fair weather, but only one in foul.
>
> **MINE:** Belonging to me if I can hold or seize it.
>
> **SUCCESS:** The one unpardonable sin against one's fellows.

The otherwise all-powerful commissioner could never tell when he might open his mail to find a Murchison heckle in it. Clint once sent him a newspaper clipping about Rozelle's inspection of the under-construction Seattle KingDome:

> Although delays in construction cost the county more than the $40 million bond issue specified, NFL Commissioner Pete Rozelle recently inspected the stadium and said, "Seattle got more for its money than any other city I've seen."

Clint may have been miffed at Rozelle's slighting of the deal Clint thought he had gotten on Texas Stadium. Whatever the reason, he added a note to the clipping:

> **Pete:**
>
> Speaking of bargains, when Joe Foss was commissioner his salary was only $50,000.

Between the peacemaking and the actual merger of the leagues, NFL owners enjoyed bragging rights with Green Bay's lopsided victories over the AFL in the first two Super Bowls. The Nationals' pride was devastated when Joe Namath's upstart AFL New York Jets upset the Baltimore Colts in the 1969 Super Bowl.

It gave Clint the chance to mix football and politics when he sent Rozelle a clipping about the current Vietnam peace talks. It contained a timely typographical error involving the Viet Cong's National Liberation Front (NLF). But instead it had come out:

> . . . South Vietnam President Nguyen Van Thieu's government has vowed never to recognize the NFL, though some leaders have indicated a willingness to do so.

Clint added to the clipping his sour comment on the Super Bowl of the day before.

> **Pete:**
>
> After yesterday, I don't blame them.

The Creation of the Dallas Whatsits

Testimonial, Sort Of

Namath's resulting super-stardom was a problem for the commissioner that summer, when he ordered America's new idol to sell his interest in Bachelors III, a New York restaurant suspected of being a gamblers-and-Mafia hangout. Namath responded by quitting football. An eventual compromise was announced when Namath hired James J. Lynch, a former FBI agent, to police Bachelors III.

Clint wrote the commissioner:

> Dear Pete:
>
> Jim Lynch, Broadway Joe's new employee, worked for me during the Alleghany proxy fight.
>
> In the midst of the battle, I had a very hush-hush meeting with him in Gordon McLendon's hotel suite to obtain a progress report on the security machinations. Later that evening, as Gordon was checking out, he saw some papers on the table: Jim had forgotten his counterspy notes and his plane ticket to Chicago.
>
> All kidding aside, Jim is a very competent and trustworthy individual, although I doubt that he can single-handedly stamp out the mafiosa.

Clint thought of ways to express gratitude that Rozelle wouldn't hear from other NFL owners. Soon after Rozelle's controversial OK of the use of a snow plow to clear the field for teeing up a winning Patriots' field goal against Miami, he wrote:

> December 16, 1982
>
> Dear Pete:
>
> A couple of days ago we had a high school playoff game in Texas Stadium between Dallas Carter and L. D. Bell. Carter's mascot is a pony, and before the game he romped up and down the field with the cheerleaders, during which time the pony had an accident on about the 20-yard line.
>
> In the first quarter, Bell made a significant penetration but was held on third down, and so they prepared to kick a field goal. Suddenly the holder noticed that they would have to place the ball at the precise point of the accident. Bell objected, and through the groundskeeper, who was prepared for the removal, Joe Cavagnaro (the stadium manager) was asked to arbitrate. Joe thought a minute and then said, "Pete Rozelle says in the NFL it's okay to remove snow before placing

the ball down for a kick, so it's okay with me to remove the accident," which was done

Thank you for helping us clean up the game.

Sincerely,

CLINT

p.s. The kid missed the kick—wide to the right. I won't repeat what he said.

The Texas Stadium scoreboard message noting his friend John "Smelly" Taylor's 1983 wedding engagement. In an exchange of notes afterwards when Taylor pointed out that "Congratulations" was misspelled, Clint promised to get the scoreboard manager "a dictshunary." —photo courtesy of John Taylor

Chapter Six
The Hole in the Roof Gang

If I had any guts I would tell you that you are stupid. However, since I don't, I will merely thank you for your comment.

Looming high-tech grey, forbidding, and famous in the prairie angle between three freeways, since 1971 Texas Stadium has been home to the space-age image of the Dallas Cowboys. It began as a scandalous civic revolt and continues to bear out the worst nightmare of surviving Dallas oldtimers every time a Cowboys telecast begins with the words, "Good afternoon from Irving, Texas . . ."

Clint Murchison, Jr., was the reluctant rebel in the stadium revolt episode. He was pitted almost single-handed against the massed clout of the Dallas establishment, a civic force that had gone undefeated through several decades in the oligarchy league.

The city leadership, long and tightly knit in what author George Sessions Perry described as a "benevolent despotism," had no tolerance for boat-rockers in the midsixties, when Clint first made public his dissatisfaction with the declining Cotton Bowl as a home for the Cowboys. He confided to a friend that he'd been thrown off a Chamber of Commerce committee in 1955 for advocating "the heretical idea of a regional airport to be shared by Dallas and Fort Worth."

Instant landmark on the North Texas prairie: Texas Stadium rises from the confluence of three freeways. —photo courtesy of Joe Cavagnaro

The Cowboys' first home, the Cotton Bowl, was a legend and a landmark and very nearly a Dallas shrine. Since its completion in 1936, in time for TCU to beat Marquette 16-6 in the 1937 New Year's classic, it had put Dallas into the big leagues, bowlwise, with Pasadena, New Orleans, and Miami. In the reverential view of the people who were running the city, it was the closest thing Big D had to an Alamo with yard markers; now here was this guy Murchison, who after all had gone off to school back East somewhere, trying to reject the Grand Lady, saying it was no longer good enough for his Cowboys; more specifically, it was no longer good enough for their fans.

The Cotton Bowl had probably stood up about as well as anything with 1930s technology would have, through three decades of blistering summers and frigid winters and waterspout springtimes, with up to 76,000 people coming in to sit on it frequently. The Cotton Bowl of 1960-65 bore little resemblance to the one of later years—which, incidentally, by 1991 was once again deemed in need of major refurbishing, at an estimated cost of $32 million, greater than the original cost of Texas Stadium or the Astrodome.

As a centerpiece for the controversy, the suddenly imperiled stadium was only a part of what concerned the Dallas leadership of the time. It sat amid the several hundred acres of the State Fair of Texas fairgrounds, a pseudo-Greco, art-nouveau collection of museums, exhibit halls, esplanades, and midway games that had brought Dallas the role of hosting the Texas Centennial of 1936. Three decades later it was an enclave of decline, decay, insufficient parking, and soaring crime on its perimeter streets and parking lots. The city wanted to improve it. Clint wanted to abandon it for a new stadium to be built downtown.

The opening of the Astrodome in Houston in 1964 had topped off Clint's disenchantment with the Cotton Bowl. It also revolutionized sports stadia and their profit centers by introducing the idea of the luxury suite.

Clint's main adversary in what he would come to call the civic "cold war" was J. Erik Jonsson, brilliant entrepreneur, cofounder of Texas Instruments, *eminence grise* of D-FW Airport, and patron saint of the I. M. Pei-designed City Hall. Jonsson was probably the most intellectual of all of Dallas' mayors, but not much of a sports fan, especially amid such burgeoning municipal agendas as a massive new city hall and the need for a gigantic regional airport, whose idea had finally come.

Clint never challenged the importance of those kinds of projects— well, at least not the regional airport—but his contention throughout the stadium flap was that, sports fandom aside, any of his stadium options made more sense, financially, to an ever-strained Dallas taxpayer than the expensive half-measures that would keep things the way they used to be.

Nobody in authority wanted to hear Clint's kind of talk. They also didn't want Clint comparing their view of progress with the kind of mindset that produced the eternally congested North Central Expressway and the "new" Dallas Love Field, already obsolescent on the day it was dedicated in 1957.

The five-year Stadium War was not so much a set-piece battle as a series of sniper incidents. The patrician Jonsson stayed out of the trenches, appearing occasionally to announce that his mind was still made up. Other, lesser functionaries from the Cotton Bowl and State

Classic Clint

Fair committees, civic figures, city council members, and loyal private citizens hurled allegations of Murchison greed, profiteering, negativism, ingratitude, and wrongheadedness. Clint hired consultants, wrote letters to the editors, appeared before boards and business groups to argue his points. He also commissioned an imaginative report that tried to quantify the public-relations value to Dallas of having its name in 'x' number of sports-page datelines around the world, every time someone wrote or spoke or televised something about the Cowboys and Dallas. Since the Dallas image was spending those years in the world's penalty box over its role as the site of the Kennedy assassination, it was a compelling idea for a study.

It's arguable that the ensuing years of the Cowboys' swashbuckling successes on the gridiron, their eventual corporate persona as cleancut winners, sleek human beings, and the darlinghood of being America's Team did more than any other single factor to rehabilitate the image of Dallas from that of a nest of assassins and nuts to a city of champions. But because of the city leadership's passionate recalcitrance in the face of Clint's cool and bemused logic, the Dallas Cowboys would be doing it from the city of Irving.

During the cold war, Clint also took occasional licks from people who otherwise wished him well. When the architect's rendering of Texas Stadium, with that startling hole in the roof, first appeared in the Dallas papers, I'm afraid I was the columnist who called it the Half-Astrodome. I couldn't help myself.

On one occasion early in the battle, Mayor Jonsson had shrugged off Clint's campaign in an interview in the *Dallas Morning News* with a remark about this whole flap being the fault of the Astrodome. Clint wrote to the mayor at his home:

> **Dear Erik:**
> I noted in the morning paper your comment that until the Astrodome was built, everyone thought the Cotton Bowl was pretty good.
>
> Of course, until the transistor was developed, people thought the vacuum tube was pretty good.

Since the mayor's personal, and considerable, fortune stemmed from Texas Instruments' developmental work with the transistor and semiconductors, it was an engaging observation to make.

The Hole in the Roof Gang

On April 12, 1965, Clint wrote personal letters to each member of the State Fair of Texas' Athletic Committee, which was the ruling body in Cotton Bowl management. The letters were mailed to their home addresses, but Clint had thoughtfully provided copies to the sports editors and editorial pages of the Dallas and Fort Worth papers. The recipients included Robert B. Cullum, a diminutive scrapper who had founded the Tom Thumb grocery chain and was chairman of the committee; and C. A. Tatum, a powerful civic figure in addition to his job as president of Dallas Power & Light. Some of the group's public statements had suggested that Clint was an ingrate because of the cheap rental he was getting from the Cotton Bowl.

> There is a misconception concerning the Dallas Cowboys Football Club which I wish to call to your attention.
>
> It is that the Dallas Cowboys enjoy one of the cheapest stadium rentals among professional football teams. The enclosed schedule shows to the contrary that we pay the fourth highest rental among *all* teams in professional football. Actually, based upon attendance last year, the percentage we paid was the third highest, but since our percentage declines as the attendance increases, I have computed the attached schedule based upon an average game gross of $150,000; I feel that this is a reasonable assumption as to what we might expect to gross in the next year or two. Note that two of the three teams which pay a percentage in excess of that which Dallas pays are teams which rent from privately owned baseball parks and are therefore partially competitive with their landlords. This, obviously, affected their rental negotiations. The third team rents a new 25-million-dollar stadium which assures a virtual sellout at every game.
>
> A much fairer comparison, however, would be to compare our rent to the rent of other teams in professional football which have been granted franchises since 1960. In most cases, these newer franchises have negotiated rentals which have taken into account the large collateral benefits of professional sports to a community. Among this group of teams, which includes Minnesota and Dallas in the National Football League and all teams of the American Football League, you will note that the rental paid by Dallas *is in excess of 300%* of the average rental paid by the other young teams.
>
> Since 1960 our football club has paid the State Fair almost $400,000 in rentals; last year we paid over $130,000. Soon we will be paying much more. This income received by the Fair does not include

Classic Clint

supplementary income received from other sources. I do not feel that this rental would be justified for any adequate facilities, let alone for those available. Cities, no less than football teams, must be competitive.

I am sending a letter identical to this to the other members of the Athletic Committee of the State Fair of Texas.

The accompanying stadium-rental chart Clint had compiled was a sports-page revelation upon its release. The figures had been individually available in franchise cities, but apparently no one in the sports media had bothered to compile or correlate them in a comparative overview.

Stadium Rentals Paid by Professional Football Franchises

Team	Rental (% of gross)	Comments
Detroit Lions	18%	
New York Giants	15.5%	
Washington Redskins	14.5%	New super-stadium under construction
DALLAS COWBOYS	13.5%	
Pittsburgh Steelers	12.5%	New super-stadium being built in immediate future
San Francisco 49ers	11%	
Green Bay Packers	10.5%	Major recent renovations
Chicago Bears	10.5%	New stadium under discussion
Los Angeles Rams	10%	Major recent renovations
St. Louis Cardinals	10%	New super-stadium under construction
Boston Patriots	10%	Team owns concessions
Philadelphia Eagles	9%	New super-stadium being built in immediate future
Baltimore Colts	8.5%	
New York Jets	8.5%	New super-stadium under construction
Cleveland Browns	8%	Team owns concessions
Minnesota Vikings	8%	New stadium
Oakland Raiders	4%	New super-stadium under construction
San Diego Chargers	3.5%	New stadium
Kansas City Chiefs	2.5%	Major recent renovations; team owns concessions; rent-free offices

The Hole in the Roof Gang

In the Spring of 1965 there would be options presented on both sides for a renovation of the Cotton Bowl, and for the construction of a stadium in downtown Dallas. Clint already had commissioned an architect to draw up preliminary plans for the downtown stadium. At the same time, the Philadelphia Eagles were at similar loggerheads with the City of Brotherly Love over the stadium facilities and scheduling conflicts with the Phillies baseball club. The Eagles were asking for a bond-financed stadium and had mentioned the possibility of the team's guaranteeing the bonds. Otherwise the Eagles would be looking for a new home.

The subsequent letter Clint wrote to the Eagles' president reveals the shape his own plans for the stadium had begun to take. Clint knew a treacherous precedent when he saw one.

> May 13, 1965
>
> Mr. Jerry Wolman, President
> The Philadelphia Eagles Football Club
> 13th and Market Streets
> Philadelphia, Pennsylvania
>
> Dear Jerry:
>
> I agree with the stand you are taking in your negotiations for a stadium lease. I feel very strongly that all of our franchise teams should be provided an adequate stadium at a reasonable rental. I have something of the same problem here, although we are not faced with the problem of exclusiveness; our problem is that the existing stadium is inadequate. In my negotiations, I am going to take the same position which you are taking.
>
> There is one point in your proposal, however, on which I would like to comment. You mentioned the possibility of the Eagles guaranteeing the payment of the bonds. I don't know exactly how you propose to do this, or if you were serious, but I feel that it would be a mistake for any of our franchises to be obligated for such payments. I think that in this day and age these financial obligations should be borne by the city, although, of course, under certain very restricted conditions it might be necessary to commit to stay in the stadium as a tenant for some limited period of years.
>
> I am presently having Welton Becket prepare plans for a stadium meeting the following specifications:
>
> a. Capacity: 50,000
> b. All seats sideline

c. All seats covered (but, for aesthetic reasons, an open field.)
d. Designed for football use only—to decrease cost and to improve sight lines)
e. Cost, exclusive of land: $7,000,000.

The capacity could be increased an additional 15,000 for perhaps less than a million by the addition of end zone seats, although my present thinking is that it would be better to increase the average seat price than to increase the capacity. A great deal of thought is being given to crowd control, concessions, restroom locations, and the general exterior and interior appearance of the stadium. I think that this project could result in the best football stadium in the country. The preliminary plans should be completed within six weeks. If you think it will help you in your cold war, I will be happy to send additional information at that time.

Sincerely

Clint

cc: Mr. Pete Rozelle

Clint's "cold war" with the establishment continued through the midsixties. His opponents had other plans for his downtown stadium site—a new convention center complex. Clint went to Irving. Once the designer's rendering of Texas Stadium was released to the media. Clint frequently pointed out that even with the hole in the roof, the stadium would be more comfortable in temperature extremes than the open-air Cotton Bowl. As strongly as he felt about the aesthetics of the open roof, Clint didn't mind the added bonus of saving the estimated $30,000 a month cost of enclosing and air-conditioning Texas Stadium. On Sept. 8, 1965, a few days before the Cowboys' season opener at the steamy Cotton Bowl, Clint dropped a line to Tatum, the Dallas Power & Light president, meticulously typed, as always, on the Murchison office's customary IBM typeface:

Dear C.A.:

It sure is going to be hot out there a week from Sunday.

Sincerely,

Clint

(Texas Stadium, as it turned out, would be just about as hot as the Cotton Bowl for those not in Circle Suites.)

The Hole in the Roof Gang

The city leaders, going ahead with plans to upgrade the Cotton Bowl and adjoining State Fair facilities even though the Cowboys were leaving, announced plans to give the Fairgrounds' Livestock Coliseum ice-rink facilities for hockey games. After these plans appeared in the *Times Herald*, Clint wrote to sportswriter Steve Perkins, who earlier had moved to Dallas from Houston to become the Cowboys' beat writer.

> **Dear Steve:**
>
> I think that it is marvelous that the State Fair people have apparently agreed to spend $45,000 for pipes and a scoreboard to turn the Livestock Coliseum into an ice arena. This is apparently Dallas' answer to Houston's proposal to put a dome over the entire downtown area of that city. Please don't think I am knocking the Dallas approach. I think that it is indicative of that traditional Midwestern conservatism which we all admire and for which we here can be so proud. It is just unfortunate that occasionally this attitude results in such oddities as Sapulpa, Oklahoma, being connected by direct barge canal to the Gulf of Mexico, 40 years or so before our city has gotten around to it.

Clint was referring to Dallas' historic inability to do anything about making the Trinity River navigable. Dallas' founder John Neely Bryan had built his first campsite on the banks of a fork of the Trinity, whose water even the Indians of the time must have found undrinkable; they left. The Trinity is muddy, snaggly, sluggish, mostly nonnavigable, and something of a mediocrity among Texas rivers for much of its 550-mile length. But it has in its valley more large cities, greater population, and more industrial development than any other river basin in Texas. Around Houston it is drained off to flood rice fields. Fort Worth leaches it to fill four reservoirs from its waters; it makes a major lake near Lewisville and another east of Dallas at Lake Lavon, plus Lakes Ray Hubbard and Joe Pool. Its three forks meet near Dallas. No wonder it's turgid. Most of the boating on the Trinity is done by South Dallas householders escaping every spring when the river floods them out of their homes.

Classic Clint

Meanwhile Sapulpa, as Clint pointed out, even though it was hundreds of miles north, had been linked to Gulf barge traffic by the Corps of Engineers' Arkansas River project.

By early 1968 the plans for Texas Stadium were announced and underway. The Cowboys and the city of Irving would finance Texas Stadium through revenue bonds, maturing in the year 2008. The bonds were in denominations of $250, $500, and $1,000. One bond gave the buyer the right to purchase a season ticket in a general reserved section at the stadium. $50,000 entitled the owner to purchase a Circle Suite luxury box. When the bonds went on sale, the proud owner of a chain of hamburger restaurants went to lunch and showed friends his new Circle Suite bonds—200 $250 certificates stacked in a shoe box, looking like a ream of new stationery.

Clint bristled at the opposition's frequent claims of elitism in the concept of the Circle Suites and the belief that everyone else would have to buy either a bond or a season ticket even to attend one Cowboy game in the new stadium. Stadium seats not reserved by bondholders would go on public sale. He replied to one citizen who had written a letter to the editor complaining about the arrangement.

> **Mr. David H. Claborn**
> **14220 Haymeadow Drive**
> **Dallas, Texas**
>
> **Dear Mr. Claborn:**
>
> **There will be thousands of tickets available on a game-by-game basis at Texas Stadium for those not wishing to purchase season tickets. And all those seats will be protected from sun and rain, will have backs and arm rests, and will have adequate parking available for their occupants.**
>
> **I hope to see you there.**
>
> **Yours very truly,**

(During the stadium crisis, there would be no respite from the Pen Pal from Hell:)

The Hole in the Roof Gang

STEPHEN W. SCHNEIDER
740 Hartford Building
Dallas, Texas 75201

February 7, 1968
Mr. Clint Murchison Jr.
First National Bank Building
Dallas, Texas

Dear King:

The "Free Stadium" Committee keeps stating that your bond plan is unfair to the loyal fan, that the bonds you buy will pay off before the rest of ours, and that you are, in short, taking advantage of the public.

You will be pleased to know that I have defended you, that I have told these people of your faultless honor and your flawless integrity, and that I know your foremost interest in this stadium endeavor is to enrich the community and its citizens.

I am for you 100%.

p.s. Are you screwing the public pretty bad on this deal?

Another letter to the editor had stirred a reply about the Cowboys' problems with their winding-down years in the Cotton Bowl.

August 30, 1968

Editor

The Dallas Morning News

Mr. J.H. Thompson has written you suggesting that I am a crybaby because the State Fair won't give the Cowboys free rent this year. Just to keep the record straight, some facts:

Since 1960 the State Fair has realized a profit of approximately $1,350,000 from Cowboys games. Since 1960 the Cowboys, on the other hand, have realized a TOTAL profit of $381,000. I have never complained about this.

Want more? Last year, the Cowboys paid the State Fair more total stadium rent than rent paid by any other team in the NFL or AFL, with the sole exception of one team which rents a magnificent new 24-million-dollar stadium. So what happens? This year the Fair suggests raising our rent $40,000.

Fortunately, Bob Cullum has apparently agreed that instead we can pay according to the SMU formula; while this will probably result in an increased rent, the increase wouldn't be $40,000; the Fair would realize over $300,000 from our games. No matter how Mr. Thompson

> figures it, over $300,000 ain't hay, and it surely isn't "free." It is, however, a fair price, as I have agreed.
>
> As to my being a crybaby, I admit that I have been known to break into tears upon losing a $2 press playing golf. But when it comes to losing $40,000, I don't cry. I go into shock.
>
> Very truly yours,

It may help to remember the texture of 1966, the year of Vietnam buildups, Lyndon Johnson's War on Poverty, and movies such as the James Bond *Thunderball* and Oscar-winner *A Man For All Seasons*. Not so long ago, maybe, but the prices of things in 1966 today seems prehistoric. A Mercedes Benz 230S was $5,700. Several members of the West Point graduating class of 1966 bought Corvettes at fleet prices for under $3,800 apiece. In Dallas the Seven Seas restaurant offered all-you-can-eat fish fries with trimmings for a dollar. A sirloin strip at the Colonial was $1.24. McDonald's hamburgers were 15 cents, soon to be raised to 18 cents after the chain's sole TV-network sponsorship of Super Bowl I in 1967. At the S.A.G.E. superstore chain, a giant tube of Ipana toothpaste was 17 cents; four six-oz. cans of Minute Maid orange juice cost 77 cents. Titche's camera department sold Nikon F 35-mm cameras with 28mm lenses for $113.30. Domestic housemaids want ads offered $30 for a five-day week.

On another occasion, Clint clipped a piece of an article from the *Times Herald*, pasted it on a sheet, and sent it to publisher Jim Chambers with his acerbic and rhetorical comment:

> Quizzed on a similar "communications gap" between the Fair board of directors and the press, Clullum said he could not speak for the board on a change in policy of "closed" board meetings.
>
> He questioned the propriety of the "voluntary, nonprofit civic body, which is working for the public good, acknowledging an obligation to invite the press to its meetings."

Clint's comment on the margin of the clipping was:

> Jim:
>
> Exactly what is the obligation of a "voluntary, nonprofit civic body, which is working for the public good?"

During the years of the campaigning to keep the team within the city limits of Dallas, the Cotton Bowl faction's arguments generally

The Hole in the Roof Gang

appealed to plain hometown loyalty. The argument, in which Clint was the villain-of-the-decade, went: we need to keep our assets in Dallas, and quit diluting the city's strength by supporting so many projects in the suburbs. Projects like a new home for the Dallas Cowboys. *Dallas Morning News* sports columnist Roy Edwards had written a column recapping these civic laments and implying that Clint had avoided responding to Edwards' queries about them. In its news and editorial pages, the *News* had shown a customary anti-Clint, pro-Dallas feeling. The sports section, having long covered the Cowboys as an institution rather than an issue, was generally more tolerant of Clint's dilemma. Thus Clint's opening puzzlement in his answer to Edwards' unsympathetic column:

> I was mildly surprised by your column this morning. I won't bother to comment on the several gross inaccuracies—my telephone number is RI 1-6031, and I never refuse a call from a journalist . . . Fortunately, the chauvinism which has been apparent in the stadium argument has not prevented this city from supporting other outlying civic undertakings such as The University of Texas at Dallas (in Richardson), and the Dallas-Fort Worth Regional Airport (in Irving). Or even Southern Methodist University (in University Park).

Two of the examples Clint had chosen—UT-D and D-FW Airport—happened to be ideas that had long enjoyed the warm and active support of Mayor Jonsson. SMU's location in the privileged and municipally sovereign enclave of University Park hindered its spiritual adoption by the entire city of Dallas.

A few months earlier in 1969, Clint had hardly controlled his indignation over a Dallas stockbroker's written complaint (on the brokerage's letterhead) about Cowboy ticket increases and the general stadium controversy. The broker had contrasted the Cowboys' ticket hikes with the stability of ticket prices offered by their nemesis, the Green Bay Packers. The broker had also made the common, but to Clint, unfathomable, error of spelling Tex Schramm's name with only one 'm'. Clint's reply to the broker was to become known as the Perplexity-Amazement-Astonishment message.

> Dear Mr. E_____:
>
> I am perplexed that anyone who sells common stocks at 50 times next year's earnings would complain that the Dallas Cowboys has raised its ticket price by a total of 16% in the last three years, during which

period, according to a report issued last week by the Department of Labor, the cost of "All Services" (a category which includes entertainment) has risen by 21%; over this same period, the total cost of operations of the Cowboys has risen by 39%. It costs money to build a championship team from scratch, something Green Bay has not recently been required to do.

I am amazed that anyone should complain that I have committed over $9,000,000 of my own money to see that this community acquires a modern sports stadium rivaling the Astrodome, to be built at no cost to the taxpayers. People so desiring can purchase bonds to reserve seats; those not so desiring may attend the games without any such purchase requirement. Since you have recently moved to Dallas, you may not realize that the major expansion of the Cotton Bowl, which occurred in 1948 and 1950, was financed in precisely this manner; specifically, your (Cotton Bowl) seats in section 108 were financed by a bond purchaser who received far fewer emoluments than a bond purchaser at Texas Stadium.

Finally, I am astounded that you should have the presumption not only to outline your complaints on the stationery of your employer, but to place the name of that employer as signatory of your letter, thereby implying that your obvious personal opinions are those of _____ Corporation, an implication which I have cause to doubt.

Yours truly,

p.s. Tex Schramm's name is spelled "Schramm."

He was considerably briefer with his reply to the letter of another critic:

Dear Mr. L_____:

If I had any guts I would tell you that you are stupid. However, since I don't, I will merely thank you for your comment.

Very truly yours,

Clint W. Murchison Jr.

The bitter stadium disputes had escalated into some personal and extracurricular areas, too. On Sept. 27, 1967, Clint wrote to grocer-Cotton Bowl patron Cullum, whose chain had recently acquired the upscale gourmet food store, Simon David. The Murchisons and many of their friends shopped there.

The Hole in the Roof Gang

Mr. Robert B. Cullum
Tom Thumb Stores, Inc.
3300 West Mockingbird Lane
Dallas, Texas

Dear Bob:

In the Tom Thumb store which you purchased from Simon David, there is on one of the cash registers a sign in full view of your customers and my friends saying, "Don't charge to Murchison Jr."

Now I wonder, is this another gambit in the cold war, or is Jane really slow pay?

Sincerely,

Clint Murchison Jr.

When the Cowboys became a civic football: Clint's shocking decision to abandon the Cotton Bowl for Texas Stadium led Dallas Morning News *cartoonist Bill McClanahan to depict him heading out against the traffic.*

Classic Clint

In the spring of that year there was a city election, with Mayor Jonsson once again heading the establishment slate officially known as the Citizens Charter Association (CCA). Leaving for a lengthy business trip in March, Clint couldn't resist dropping a note to the mayor:

> The Honorable J. Erik Jonsson
> 4831 Shadywood Lane
> Dallas, Texas
>
> Dear Erik:
>
> I think you will be happy to learn that I am leaving town tomorrow and won't return until shortly before the April 4 election, at which time I intend to vote for the entire CCA slate.
>
> Sincerely,

That summer the Dallas leadership and CCA announced a referendum for the biggest single bond improvements program in the city's history, called the Crossroads Program. It included massive upgrading of the Cotton Bowl and other State Fair facilities, including land acquisition and displacement of families living in the Fair Park area, as well as convention and cultural facilities. A carefully chosen citizens' committee, characterized as nonpartisan and demographically diverse, was appointed to promote the bond election.

One of the members was an acquaintance of Clint's, attorney and Democratic Party figure Robert Strauss, who would become National Democratic Chairman and advisor to Presidents Lyndon Johnson and Jimmy Carter.

> Mr. Robert S. Strauss
> Republic National Bank
> Dallas, Texas
>
> Dear Bob:
>
> I noted with interest that you have been selected as a member of the Crossroads Committee.
>
> In your capacity of informing the public concerning the proposed bond election, do you intend to inform them that the proposed auditorium expansion was a compromise resulting from a disagreement by a competitive private-interest group, and that as a result of this compromise, the proposed convention facility will be

The Hole in the Roof Gang

typically unimaginative and not place Dallas in the forefront of this type enterprise? Perhaps in your publicity, this approach should be likened to that taken during the planning of Central Expressway or of Love Field ten years ago.

Will you advise the electorate that no study concerning the cultural facilities of this city recommends any expansion, improvement, or even use of the State Fair Music Hall? Or that the firm which made the report to the State Fair recommending the renovation of the Music Hall admitted that it would remain a second-class facility even after the expenditure of several millions?

Will you explain to the voters that the land being acquired for parking at the State Fair will perhaps not be required since the Dallas Cowboys have stated definitely that it had no intention of playing at the State Fair location on a long-term basis?

Should the people be told that if a stadium is built in Irving, as will probably be the case, it is doubtful that **any** games will be played at the Cotton Bowl after the next several years, so that the proposed bond expenditure for improvement of that facility is, in fact, a monument to obstinacy?

Should the voters be advised that the suggested $12,600,000 expenditure for the State Fair is merely the table ante and that the Fair Board's actual intention is to spend ultimately in excess of $50,000,000 at that location?

What will the people be told concerning the residents displaced by the acquisition of land in the Fair Park area? Since no funds are recommended for providing housing for these unfortunate people, is it your intention to send them also across the Jordan?

Do you realize that the mayor proposes to spend ten million dollars for five acres of park and garage land—erroneously referred to as "cultural facilities" in the City Hall publicity releases—when for the same sum **forty** acres of land could be purchased two blocks away, also fronting on Young street, an equal distance from the Main and Akard intersection, adjacent to the Municipal Auditorium, and therefore offering the city an opportunity to have a vastly superior convention and cultural facilities actually at a lesser total cost?

I hate to appear negative, but you have apparently agreed to lend your good name to a controversial municipal project of doubtful value without first checking with Annette.

Sincerely,

Classic Clint

(Annette was Mrs. Ted Strauss, Robert Strauss's sister-in-law and onetime Greenway Park next-door neighbor of the Murchisons. She was involved in civic activism and would become a city councilwoman and later, in 1987, mayor of the Dallas that would spend a further 80 million dollars for a cultural center replacing the facilities in the Fair Park of 1967.)

In 1970, during the Cowboys' last full season at the Cotton Bowl, Clint wrote his cold-war memoirs, an ironic recap of the stadium battles, in one of his columns for the team's weekly fans' tabloid, the Dallas Cowboys Insiders Newsletter. His choice of a title for the piece, "Xanadu," was a subtle and typically obscure literary reference to Kubla Khan's "stately pleasure dome" in the epic poem by Coleridge. It was also the name Orson Welles gave to the Byzantine Hearstian estate in the film "Citizen Kane."

The Cowboys would christen "Xanadu" on October 24, 1971, with a 44-21 victory over the New England Patriots. —photo courtesy of Joe Cavagnaro

The stadium battles were mostly over; in the real-time of 1970 the catalyst for his memoir was Mayor Jonsson's continuing struggles with the financing of the new Dallas City Hall.

Xanadu

Well, I see that Mayor (J. Erik) Jonsson has finally succumbed to the inexorable pressures of common sense; he has suggested the postponement of his controversial City Hall project. This is no mean accomplishment; the history of the Citizens Charter-dominated administrations of this city is replete with fixations. In progress toward their announced goals, they are, like Caesar

> "... *constant as the Northern Star,*
> *Of whose true fix'd and resting quality*
> *There is no fellow in the firmament."*

This discipline, this singleness of purpose, is great if the pot of gold happens to lie in a northward direction, but at times I'm sure even Caesar found it expedient to veer from Polaris, perhaps even toward the setting sun.

You may recall the years these administrations battled the concept of a regional airport until one day the Federal Aviation Agency (then headed by a former Dallas resident who recognized mulishness when he saw it) said, "No regional airport, no federal funds for Love Field." Thus, overnight, was the Dallas-Fort Worth Regional Airport invented by our leadership. Where, they now wanted to know, had everybody been when they were seeking support for this great new project? Where? Out reading last year's political speeches, that's where.

When I first began talking with these people about a stadium, I should have recognized the symptoms of what my ophthalmologist calls tunnel vision, but my enthusiasm and the synergistic effect of the enthusiasm of those with whom I consulted led, I now must admit, to touches of this same affliction. Anyway, the stadium story is long and involved, one that has never been told in toto, and one to which those of you interested in the genesis of new concepts, and the difficulties attendant thereto, should be exposed.

By 1964 it had become obvious that the Cotton Bowl, a grand lady in her day, suffered from terminal illness. That year I had to resort to mild trickery to have the restrooms whitewashed; later a high-school band member was to suffer heatstroke before water fountains were installed; and on, and on, and on. The question soon arose as to whether the Cotton Bowl should be repaired, or a new stadium built;

Classic Clint

and if the latter, where. The State Fair answered the first question; it employed a California research firm to study the problem; this study indicated that it would cost more to renovate satisfactorily the old stadium than to build a new one; the Fair accepted this report and it was Bob Cullum's decision (ed. note: then the chairman of the State Fair Board of Directors) to build a new stadium.

Meanwhile, I employed a national polling firm to determine if the people attending football games preferred the State Fair location to another then undetermined site. The poll was revealing: by a 4-to-1 vote, football fans preferred a location other than the Fairgrounds.

But where? A friend suggested Irving. Mayor (Tom) Vandergriff of Arlington proposed the expansion of Turnpike Stadium (ed. note: later enlarged and known as Arlington Stadium). Then one day a downtown stadium was suggested. Silly, I sez; the land is too expensive, and there's not enough parking area. Don't be hardheaded, Clint; check it out. And so I checked it out. What I learned startled me; there was a location available, at a price much cheaper than I had supposed, and it would provide parking for 8,000 cars. Within five blocks (the distance from the present Cotton Bowl to the gates of the fairgrounds) there were already available 14,000 additional parking spaces. The project could be financed without cost to taxpayers (and without requiring present season-ticket holders to purchase option bonds). Finally, as an added dividend, the city would obtain 10 acres of land adjacent to the stadium as a location for an art museum and a music hall. I exposed the plan to civic leaders. Great, they said. Merchants liked it; hotel operators liked it; restaurateurs liked it; convention promoters liked it; the president of the Dallas Citizens Council liked it so much he even proposed expanding the concept; both newspapers loved it.

Erik Jonsson hated it.

He never told me why; in fact, he didn't tell me anything for over a year; I read in the paper that he felt a downtown stadium would create traffic congestion (on Sunday afternoons?).

But that was it; when Erik made up his mind, he, like Caesar, did not deviate. Not yet anyway. I made one last effort; Bob Cullum and I met with the mayor at lunch to present our opposing views—a new stadium at State Fair, or one downtown. The arguments lasted over two hours without comment from the judge. I even agreed to commit the Cowboys to play at the Fairgrounds location if a new stadium were built there, provided the taxpayers were informed as to the extravagance of this alternative. (For reasons too involved to set forth here, the stadium proposed by the State Fair would have cost the taxpayers at least fifteen million dollars more than one downtown.) Finally, the verdict came, as sure and swift as a Turk's scimitar. "There is no stadium in my plans for the foreseeable future," intoned the mayor, "because of other more pressing requirements (the City Hall?). And thus was born Texas Stadium.

The denouement you know, and it is too dreary to discuss except in précise. AFTER I had legally contracted for the move to Irving, the City Council voted to include over 13 million dollars for stadium improvements and attendant parking in the Crossroads bond issue. AFTER the City of Irving had sold 20 million dollars of bonds to build Texas Stadium, the Dallas Council approved the expenditure for the Cotton Bowl improvements and for parking. Jonsson even chided a fellow councilman for having the temerity to request from the Fair officials figures relating to the economic feasibility of their project.

The mayor had come full circle; from no expenditure by the taxpayers (an opinion with which I agreed) to the unsupported expenditure of millions upon millions of dollars; from no land purchase downtown to the condemnation of homes in South Dallas; from soup, in short, to nuts.

And where does all this leave you, the taxpayer? Footing the bill for over 13 million dollars for stadium improvements, without offsetting revenues, which can be likened to purchasing three-and-a-half million dollars worth of blueprints for a 'postponed' City Hall. Ah, well; it's only money. And we can still look forward to the expenditure by these people of five million dollars to improve the unimprovable Music Hall. At least they haven't yet proposed air-conditioning the John Neely Bryan log cabin.

Such is progress. Keep your eye on the North Star.

Classic Clint

The stadium's Circle Suites, with their wet bars, decorator furnishings, climate control, corporate tax deductibility, and seating for 12, were an immediate status sensation in the Dallas football culture. Still, at $50,000 a suite, it took awhile for a complete sellout of the suites. By the midseventies, there was a frenzied market among speculators; a Dallas car dealer who had paid the original $50,000 for his suite would later sell it for $500,000.

But in the Cowboys' second season at the stadium, 1972, some of the suites around the end zone arcs still remained unsold. A Fort Worth financial agent sent a form letter to owners of the more desirably located suites, offering to buy one. Clint himself somehow ended up on the mailing list.

ROY T. RIMMER, JR.
Summit Center
1330 Summit Avenue
Fort Worth, Texas

November 10, 1972

Mr. Clint W. Murchison Jr.
1st National Bank Building
Dallas, Texas

Dear Mr. Murchison:

At the request of a client, I am contacting you regarding your present ownership of a Texas Stadium Circle Suite.

My client's main interest is whether you might be interested in selling at this time, and at what price.

Should you have any interest, please do not hesitate to contact me. All replies will, of course, be held in strictest confidence.

Sincerely yours,

ROY T. RIMMER JR.

CLINT MURCHISON JR.
Dallas, Texas

November 14, 1972

Dear Mr. Rimmer:

At the present time, I have several Texas Stadium Circle Suites, nineteen to be exact, priced at $50,000 each.

I would love to sell them.

Very truly yours,

The Hole in the Roof Gang

Clint and Bert Rose, the first manager of Texas Stadium, cut into Texas Stadium's 5th birthday cake. —photo courtesy of Dallas Cowboys Newsletter

Having become an instant landmark from opening day, Texas Stadium by 1972 was being pictured in promotional publications sent out by the Dallas leadership to tout its tourist and convention assets. In his *Times Herald* column, Blackie Sherrod took note of this irony. Clint's note in response:

> Blackie,
>
> ... In 1950 I was kicked off a subcommittee of the Chamber of Commerce for advocating the desirability and inevitability of the Regional Airport. I checked back with the Chamber sixteen years later, and they were all for it. Now, as your column pointed out, the administration has reversed its position on Texas Stadium in only a year. That's progress.

There was one more chapter of the cold war waiting to vex the stewards of Fair Park and the Cotton Bowl. By 1974 there was a movement to get the Cotton Bowl's sole remaining football tenant, Southern Methodist University, out of the stadium. SMU had been playing its home games at the big bowl since the late 1940s, when the Doak Walker-era teams had brought the Mustangs into the collegiate bigtime. Their original on-campus field, Ownby Stadium, was too small and too charming to accommodate the crowds that wanted to watch SMU.

Even with its bond-election refurbishing and the installation of 76,504 seats with backs and armrests (which Clint pointed out were too cramped and close together), the Cotton Bowl still had, in too many minds, the three cardinal flaws of location, location, and location.

The study on whether to move, and where, was being conducted by SMU athletic director N.R. (Dick) Davis. Quite oddly, the alternatives he was given included a *further* improved Cotton Bowl, an enlarged Ownby Stadium, and even a new stadium somewhere. What was missing from this picture? Texas Stadium? Wasn't that out in Irving somewhere? Clint wrote Davis on April 1, 1974:

> Dear Dick:
>
> I am aware that there are some people at SMU who are apparently placing the interests of the State Fair above those of the Southern Methodist athletic program. I am also aware that these few have influenced the feelings of others to the extent that it makes it most

difficult for you to make an impartial decision. Finally, I am aware that you recently took a poll of SMU season ticket purchasers as to their preference for a playing site; here, I only wish to point out that such a poll would be meaningless if the respondent had not in fact attended a game at Texas Stadium, as many have not.

I would like to suggest therefore that before you make a final determination as to where SMU plays its games you do the following (which is something I did a number of years ago and which precipitated my actions in seeking that the city or some other entity build a stadium at another location.

(1) Drive to the game about 10 minutes prior to the kickoff without the use of a parking permit. The purpose of this late arrival is to assure that you have to park either outside the fairgrounds or at a remote location therein. Note that the parking within the fairgrounds accommodates only approximately 15,000 spectators (6,000 cars). Do this before a night game and pick a game which you feel will be reasonably well attended. Take your wife. I think I should caution you that in the last two years of the Cowboys' stay at the Cotton Bowl there were reported to me (and not carried in the newspapers) at least six cases of muggings and purse snatchings and one extremely frightening case of terrorism perpetrated upon the employee of a friend of mine. I am certain that countless similar incidents were not reported to me.

(2) On another occasion, park wherever you want but go to a daylight game and sit again with your wife in the upper deck of the east stands (opposite the press box).

(3) On both occasions, take with you a friend at least 6'2" tall. I have here a double purpose: First, I want you to be able to hear his comments concerning the conflict between his knees and the back of the seats in front of him, and second, at the night game you and your wife will feel more comfortable as you walk back after the game to retrieve your car.

After you have followed this procedure, I believe you will agree with me that progress is wonderful and that SMU should certainly participate in it. Should any continue to dispute this fact, you might suggest that they too go through this exercise, which is no worse an experience than the average fan is subjected to at every game.

Sincerely,

Clint.

The reference in paragraph (2) was to the blinding sunlight faced during day games by fans in the east stands.

(Texas Stadium had been sited so as to minimize the effect of sunlight spilling in through the roof gap, although there are sections in Texas Stadium where fans can expect a last chance for a seasonal suntan during games in September and October.)

By the late seventies, not only was SMU playing its home games in Texas Stadium, but it also had become, for thousands of high school football players, the memorable neutral site for state championship playoff games of teams from all over the state.

With its endemic facelifts making it the structural equivalent of the Gabor Sisters, the Cotton Bowl has endured as the annual home of the Texas-Oklahoma football rivalry and the Cotton Bowl New Year's Classic. It competes with Texas Stadium for rock concerts and mammoth religious rallies.

There continue to be suggestions for its improvements. It was outfitted with an expanse of expensive Astroturf in the 1970s refurbishment; in 1988 a civic group asked that the artificial turf be torn up and replaced with natural grass in order for Dallas, Fair Park, and the Cotton Bowl to host the 1994 soccer World Cup. In early 1991 consultants said the Cotton Bowl could be made eminently competitive with one more $32 million improvement project.

To Clint's eye, there would be one more postscript to the stadium cold war. On a brilliant spring day in 1974, Clint and Boys Club executive Ralph Pahel called on Jonsson in the latter's downtown high-rise office to solicit a contribution. As Pahel recalls the day, "From the office, one could see for miles north and west of downtown Dallas. After we left, we were in the elevator, and out of the blue Clint turned to me and said, 'Did you notice the great view Erik has of Texas Stadium?'"

Chapter Seven
Almost Strictly Business

"Expanding in real estate doesn't bring you notoriety; it's owning a football team and having your butt kicked three times in a row by Cleveland."

In the mass of correspondence on the mountains (and valleys) of deals in which Clint was involved, or in which others devoutly hoped he would be involved, there is a common denominator in his notes and letters: the impish urge to leave 'em laughing. Even in the dreary literature of profit and loss, he could summon up the punchline, or the putdown.

His delight in being the owner of the Dallas Cowboys was usually evident, too, although it was out of all proportion to the profits the Cowboys actually brought into the fold.

His files contain a note to "A.N.," undated but apparently as the team was escaping the lean seasons of the early sixties:

"Expanding in real estate doesn't bring you notoriety; it's owning a football team and having your butt kicked three times in a row by Cleveland."

Clint and Houston entrepreneur Oscar Wyatt were associated in a company that was having a rocky period. It was also almost time for the opening of the Cowboys' regular season:

August 24

Oscar,

Enclosed is a waiver to the OSI auditor which I would appreciate your signing and returning to Arthur Young & Company.

I have not meant to keep you in the dark, but we have been involved in an elaborate refinancing plan, first with respect to the common stock, which should be complete within the next month or two. As part of this, the shareholders are agreeing to a substantial change in the price of the warrants attached to the debenture issue. There are also two most substantial contracts upon which we hope to have resolution within the next 90 days. I will be in a position to discuss these matters with you before year end.

Meanwhile, the company is losing approximately $100,000 a month, and Staubach will be out until December with a separated shoulder.

Intensity on the Cowboy bench during a long-ago November's fog: from left, Larry Stephens, Clint, Bedford Wynne and Dan Reeves. —photo courtesy of Dallas Cowboys Newsletter

He found a more direct football metaphor in a letter about another troublesome business venture, an oil exploration syndicate.

> Mr. Robert W. Berry
> President
> Exploration Drilling Company
> 1909 First National Building
> Tulsa 3, Oklahoma
>
> Dear Bob:
>
> Next year we are planning to merge the Syndicate with the Dallas Cowboys, since both are sporting ventures and are yielding approximately the same return on investment. This, of course, assumes that the Commissioner will approve the merger by not classing the Syndicate as a gambling institution. Personally, I think this would be the correct interpretation since, to me, the word "gamble" connotes some possibility of winning, which would certainly be an implausible connotation in our case . . .

He sent Ramon Jarrell a photocopy of a page torn from a scientific journal, in which the learned author expressed in a footnote a sociological theory on the sexual symbolisms of the oil business:

> . . . but one American sociologist has taken such an analysis beyond its usual grounds by extrapolating the fact that Clint Murchison, [Sr.] an early Texas oil millionaire, had one of the bedrooms in his house equipped with eight beds "so a group of us boys can talk oil all night." This led the good professor to conclude that oil was the most sexual of economic pursuits. "There is," he wrote, "the business of drilling, drilling, drilling, a sort of economic Don Juanism in which the Earth itself represents the desired women but in which only a minority of affairs are satisfactory. The striking of oil becomes a graphic analogue of the orgasm, notably in the case of a gusher. The symbolism of the derricks and the well-shafts hardly needs comment, nor does the rhythmic rocking of the pumping machinery. Then, just in case we doubt the truth of his interpretation, along comes Murchison to give the whole game away. Of all places, it is the bedroom in which these nightlong orgies of talk take place, substituting the oil business for the bedroom's proper business."

Clint added a somewhat wistful footnote to the footnote:

> Ramon:
>
> The only thing wrong with this footnote is that my Dad could never keep his eyes open past the 10 o'clock news.

Paul Trousdale, his periodic partner on several ventures, had become disenchanted with the prospects for a Hawaiian development. Clint agreed, and then some:

> February 1, 1968
>
> Mr. Paul W. Trousdale
> Los Angeles, California
>
> Dear Paul:
>
> I agree in general with your comments concerning the Centex-Trousdale joint venture in Hawaii; there simply isn't enough business in the area at this time to justify the necessary overhead of the operation . . . I agree that because of the overhead situation it would be best to sell Kaopa to another builder.
>
> . . . There is, however, one thing which bothers me. In your list of equipment owned by the joint venture there was an even number of all items such as trucks and table saws, which could presumably be divided if we were unable to sell them to a third party. However, you listed only one fork saw; thus, one of us must accept a saw and the other a fork. I suggest we flip a coin.

For most of his career he found himself necessarily cast among legions of lawyers, some of whom he actually liked. He may have given a glimpse of his shaky respect for the profession in a letter to an attorney who was on his side at the time:

> May 10, 1984
>
> Mr. Orrin W. Johnson
> Johnson & Davis
> 402 East Van Buren
> Harlingen, Texas 78550
>
> Dear Orrin:
>
> I agree in general that we should proceed with the Forni litigation, but so that we will know what we are talking about, we should try to get an estimate of attorney fees from this point on to completion.

> I would suggest a settlement except that I am reminded of the comment of an English barrister who had a similar case involving the interpretation of certain obscure covenants in a will. Unbeknownst to him, the heirs got together and made a settlement, at which point the barrister said, "What a beautiful estate to be wasted on the heirs."

Shortly before the opening of Clint's pet Dallas Cowboy restaurant in New York, he heard from Kyle Rote, a former Dallas high-schooler and SMU standout who had gone on to star for the New York Giants. Rote was publishing a New York newsletter and had asked Clint if he could reprint a column Clint had written for the Cowboy newspaper.

In return, Rote would see that the opening of the restaurant would not go unreported in the New York media.

> August 4, 1971
>
> Mr. Kyle Rote
> New York Insider's Newsletter, Inc.
> 235 East 45 Street
> New York, New York 10017
>
> Dear Kyle:
>
> We hope the Dallas Cowboy is opening on September 18. Naturally, I am more than happy to accept a spread on the restaurant in your Newsletter in lieu of my usual reprint fee ($50 to the Dallas Boys' Club).
>
> Pesci is going on the payroll. Best chili and barbecue in town.
>
> I will keep you advised.
>
> Sincerely,
>
> CLINT

But as it happened, the restaurant was to suffer from opening night jitters that lasted several weeks. According to a transplanted Texan who had written to Clint to complain, it also suffered from bland chili, timid barbecue, and irascible help. Clint replied:

> November 29, 1971
>
> Mr. Joe M. Turner
> CIBA Pharmaceutical Company
> Summit, New Jersey
>
> Dear Mr. Turner:
>
> If you ever tried to teach an Italian in New York how to cook Texas style food, you would find that it was a much more difficult task than

Classic Clint

manufacturing pharmaceuticals, and with a hell of a lot smaller markup.

However, I think that all of our problems attendant to the opening of the restaurant are now solved and the food is excellent. There are one or two changes and additions that will be made in the next four to six weeks; by Christmas, we will have the best chili and barbecue that you can buy anywhere, including Athens.

Our host, Peter Pesci, is actually a delightful individual, but I understand he did get a little uptight, what with the confusion attendant to opening. He's calmed down now; I understand that he has even gotten to like the chili.

Very truly yours,

CLINT MURCHISON JR.

On occasion, to the initial dismay of those around him, Clint would choose the most awkward moment to go farthest into left field. The result was usually what he'd intended, a disarming *non sequitur*.

There was an episode involving a Houston banker, whose name some of Clint's associates had misspelled in earlier correspondence. Clint seized the day:

April 6, 1973

Mr. Frank E. McGonagill, Jr.
Senior Vice President
Bank of the Southwest
Houston, Texas 77001

Dear Frank:

I noted that in the letters to you from Messrs. Barrett and Hewett that your name was spelled with two "n's" and one "l," while on the letterhead of your reply the spelling was with one "n" and two "l's." Since Barrett and Hewett seldom make mistakes of this type, it occurred to me that your letterhead might be printed incorrectly.

You might ask your secretary to check this out.

Sincerely,

CLINT

Maybe there was just something about bankers and their names:

> October 10, 1978
>
> Mr. John C. Archibald
> Senior Vice President
> Corporate Banking Department
> The Chase Manhattan Bank, N.A.
> 1 Chase Manhattan Plaza
> New York, New York 10015
>
> Dear John:
>
> I was correct in the statement that the gentleman from whom we bought the Georgetown estate was a Standard Oil heir, and I have further determined why I was unable to remember his name, which is a rather weird one: John D. Archbold. All that money and he doesn't even know how to spell his own name.

By the beginning of the 1980s marine salvage and undersea probing technology had reached the point where expeditions were discovering the sunken *Titanic*, thinking of raising the *Bismarck*, bringing up Spanish galleons and their treasures from the Caribbean and from Gulf and Atlantic waters off Florida. Paul Trousdale and Clint had exchanged data on an opportunity to finance an expedition hoping to discover the hulk of the *Pinta*, one of the three ships in Columbus' voyage.

> October 29, 1980
>
> Mr. Paul Trousdale
> Los Angeles, California
>
> Dear Paul:
>
> Enclosed is all the dope I could come up with on the *Pinta* expedition. It appears that the monetary recovery is negligible as is the possibility of proving that the wreck is actually the *Pinta* (even though it may prove to be of the same vintage).
>
> I am an authority on this because Norman Scott and I worked many wrecks together. He worked; I got wrecked.

Classic Clint

Later the same year a worried woman in Brackenridge, Pa., wrote a personal letter addressed to Clint at his office in Dallas. Brackenridge in 1980 was a town of 4,297, about 20 miles northeast of Pittsburgh off Highway 28. She enclosed a T-shirt bearing the message *Pull for Steel*, along with a clipping from a western Pennsylvania newspaper reporting that the far-flung Murchison Interests of Dallas, Texas, were on the verge of acquiring Alleghany Ludlum Industries, Inc., a steel plant and the area's main employer. She wrote the letter cold-turkey, in a firm, feminine longhand:

> Dec. 2, 1980
>
> Dear Mr. Murchison:
>
> Let me introduce myself. my name is Vera DiPerna— owner of a small "newsstand" called 'Town News' here in Brackenridge.
>
> We are next door across the street from Alleghany Ludlum Steel and most of the mill men come through our store everyday.
>
> Enclosed is an article which was in one of our neighboring newspapers.
>
> It will tell you a little of how we feel here and our concern.
>
> I would like you to tell me—are we going to work and make the steel we all love and need? Will this change help with jobs, work we—I—need?
>
> I also hope this letter reaches you and that *you* will read it.
>
> My men here are waiting and are interested in whether or not you will answer my letter.
>
> Some say Vera, forget it, but Vera is not going to forget it. I feel you will contact me and if possible we can meet and talk.
>
> I am one of the little people (per se) however without the little people—what!!
>
> Wear in good health my little gift of our 'Pull for Steel' jersey. Hoping to hear from you.
>
> With regards,
>
> Vera DiPerna

When Mrs. DiPerna opened the largish return envelope from Clint a day or two after New Year's Day of 1981, she found that his letter of reply was nestled in a Dallas Cowboys T-shirt.

Almost Strictly Business

December 30, 1980

Mrs. Vera DiPerna
Brackenridge, Pennsylvania

Dear Mrs. DiPerna:

As you probably know, my proposed purchase of Alleghany Ludlum Industries, Inc., was not consummated; therefore, a statement of my proposed objectives may be moot. I have no reason to believe, however, that the new owners hold any different objectives from mine: To continue the operation of the company as the viable entity that it now is. Had I not considered the company well-run and well-manned, I would not have made my offer. I consider that a continuation of management and operations as they now exist to be in the best interest of all.

And I think I know as well as anyone that that plant on the river is of little value without the people in it.

I appreciate the T-shirt; I'll wear yours if you'll wear mine.

A man—in fact, a Murchison—sent Clint an envelope packet that included a cover letter and four pages, typed, single-spaced, containing detailed descriptions of several dozen shotguns, including 20 gauge, 28 gauge, 410 gauge, 16 gauge, and 12 gauge. The guns ranged in price from $39,900 for an "AHE 20 Acme Steel Full & Full Straight Stock with Skeleton Butt, 15-inch pull, Burl wood, factory hinged front trigger, beautiful floral engraving on receiver" to only $450 for a "12 Gauge Underlever Straight Stock Splinter Forearm, Steel Butt Plate." Clint may or may not have noticed the letter was dated on what used to be called Armistice Day.

       Fred S. Murchison
       Pearsall, Texas

Nov. 11, 1981

Clint W. Murchison
1st National Bk. Building
Dallas, Texas 75202

Dear Clint:

I felt since we are related and very few of my family is left that I might drop you a line with this list and let you know I have not disgraced the name as of yet and am always looking for good cheerleaders. If my wife saw this last statement I'm afraid I would have to admit it never crosses my mind. In all honesty I always asked if I am related to you and I must admit I am quite proud of the name. I had a wonderful grandfather by the name of S.L. (Sid) Murchison from Crockett, Tx. My father Fred Cook Murchison died when I was two. I am now 42. I have one living uncle, a Dr. Robert Atmar of San Antonio and an aunt, Mrs. Laura "Sugar" Atmar of Fla., as I said not too many left in my family. I have ranched for the last twenty years and bought and sold ranches. I have now sold out and moved closer into town, the list I have sent you is a collection I have put together over the years. I do not know if you are interested in firearms but in making a list of names to send this list to I felt it might be a good time to get acquainted. I know there are quite a few Murchisons in Dallas but I have never lived near or met any other Murchisons and I have always felt I might be the only one!

Good luck with the Cowboys!

Sincerely,

FRED S. MURCHISON

CLINT MURCHISON, JR.
Dallas, Texas

January 7, 1982

Mr. Fred S. Murchison
Pearsall, Texas

Dear Fred:

Although I am not a gun collector, I appreciate your thinking of me in sending the itemization of your collection. I agree that there are few Murchisons around; however, in 1961 the Cowboys managed to sign Ola Lee Murchison, who pronounced the "ch" as in "Charley" rather than as in "Christmas," as I do. I guess he changed this because he later told me that my sons always referred to him as "Cousin Ola." Not only was "Cousin Ola" one of the few previously unknown Murchisons I have met, but he was the only black one.

Sincerely,

CLINT

Collector's-item shotguns weren't the only high-ticket mail offers he declined.

> June 23, 1978
>
> Mr. Scott Shanklin
> Autohaus
> 14185 Dallas Parkway
> Dallas, Texas
>
> Dear Mr. Shanklin:
>
> I appreciate your offer of the 6.9 Mercedes, but I am surprised at your price. I had heard that Autohaus was a "real go-getter," but I think I should tell you that Van Winkle has priced the same car to me for $32,300.
>
> You are not only not in the ball park, but out of the whole damn county.
>
> Sincerely,
>
> cc: Mr. James Stephenson
>
> Van Winkle Motor Company
> 4023 Oak Lawn Avenue
> Dallas, Texas

His son Robert says Clint bought three Mercedes at one time a year later, having decided that he liked luxury cars after all. "He decided to buy the three because it was around that time federal emission standards had been imposed on imported cars, and he wasn't sure how the converters were going to affect their performance and reliability.

The Mercedes Hat-Trick was a dramatic turnaround from the previous car habits for which he had been perversely famous: one of the world's wealthiest men driving to work in nondescript and sometimes shabby-looking blue-collar cars.

Previously, he had just been indifferent about cars. "Dad didn't care about prestige or looks as long as it got him from Point A to Point B," Robert said. "I remember he drove a couple of Buick Skylarks and a Pontiac LeMans. Usually they were cars my mother had driven for a couple of years, and then Dad would take them over. He'd drive those cars until they were five, six years old."

Classic Clint

In Robert's view, the definitive clunker story occurred the day Clint was rushing to a press conference at Texas Stadium, when the shameful car he was driving just gave out while he was driving on the freeway through the Trinity River-bottoms industrial district.

"He coasted off the freeway onto the parking lot of some warehouse. He went inside and asked the secretary if he could use the phone.

"She looked at this guy standing there, and then looked out the window at what he'd been driving, and kind of shuddered but told him to go ahead and use the phone.

"I don't know if she could hear what he was saying on the phone, but I think she changed her impression of him after about 15 minutes, when a helicopter landed on the parking lot to take him the rest of the way."

It wasn't generally known in Dallas that the guy next to you stuck in expressway traffic in the nondescript car might well be Clint Murchison—which could have been the point. Steve Schneider had some thoughts about it, though, expressed in another guerrilla-warfare letter to their mutual friend, Buick dealer Finley Ewing, with copies to several who'd ever expressed misgivings about being seen publicly in Clint's clunkers:

> **Dear Finley:**
>
> On Saturday evening last, I was at the Chateaubriand Restaurant with The King in *his* Buick. After din-din, and plenty of sauce, we went back to the parking lot for his BUICK, and it was nowhere to be found. Along with the parking attendant, our furtive King earnestly searched the lot, but to no avail.
>
> Having gone home by cab, we awaited the call from the police, for surely the BUICK was stolen. Instead, the parking attendant called and said that the car had been found right on the lot—when all the other cars had left, there it was! In quizzing the boy about this, his only explanation was that they had noticed it earlier but everybody had dismissed it because they thought it was just a great big mud ball. He later noticed the wheels sticking out and investigated closer. The boy also pointed out that The King himself, with Scotch cup clutched in his hand, had passed by it three times and didn't see it. Even the Red Baron (Schneider) missed it, which is about as tough a test as I know of!

Almost Strictly Business

This is a testimonial to the fact that Orand Buick sells the most inconspicuous car in town—now doesn't that make you feel better?

**cc: Henry Lindlsey III
Bedford S. Wynne
Theodore H. Strauss
Jack C. Vaughn
The King**

*Steve — Thanks to the oil deals you have put me in, I can live in style.
Clint*

Sportsman-Philanthropist CLINT MURCHISON, JR. -- the little man with the big heart -- heads for the SUPER BOWL in his private plane!!

Clint's Red Baron Period

Steve Schneider's Christmas cards had an aviation theme, so he thought Clint should have an airplane pose too. When Clint saw the results, he sent it back to Schneider with the inscription.

Chapter Eight
Not-So-Strange Bedfellows

> *"I just want you to know how much I appreciate what you did to put me over. I shall never forget it."*
> —U.S. Senator-elect Lyndon Johnson to Clint Murchison, Sr., 1948

> *"All I can say to you is ta do cluibh peil ag ineset go h-an maith. Buac aill maith tu!!"*
> —U.S. Senator Edward Kennedy to Clint Murchison, Jr., 1972

Clint Murchison, Jr., rarely expressed himself publicly on politics and politicians, but his attitude toward them may have been what one would expect from a multimillionaire, Petroleum Club Democrat whose almost painful personal shyness prevented him from speaking to people on elevators. Not much of a back-slapper was Clint.

He didn't have anything against influence, however. For years he was represented in Washington, D.C. by good friends, kindred spirits, and skillful lobbyists like Tom Webb and Irv Davidson. His father's pen pals, over the years, had ranged from Franklin Roosevelt to Dwight Eisenhower and LBJ.

The torch was accordingly passed to the son, whose own personal contact with the new generation of state and federal power of the nation was less mentorish and more playful.

Clint's files point out how, one way or another, the celebrities of historical eras always seem to end up knowing each other. Edgar Allan Poe knew Robert E. Lee from West Point. Likewise, Ulysses Grant knew Jefferson Davis. Al Jolson knew Albert Einstein. Ernest Hemingway knew Marlene Dietrich, Muhammad Ali met Saddam Hussein.

In the 1962 Texas gubernatorial primary, John D. Connally led the seven-man field with 431,498 votes. His closest foe was Don Yarborough, with 317,986. Because Price Daniel and other candidates together polled more than a half million votes, a second primary was necessary. In those days a victory in the Democratic primary was deemed tantamount (a word fallen into disuse since Texas became a legitimate two-party state) to election in the general balloting in November.

Connally, despite his comfortable margin in the first primary, barely squeaked past Yarborough in the second primary, 565,174 to 538,924.

In Connally's victory mail came the droll congratulations of Clint Murchison, Jr.:

Dear John:

What the heck, the first time around Lyndon won by only 49 votes.

Sincerely, Clint

It was not only impertinent, but arcanely accurate. Lyndon's notorious 1948 "stuffed-ballot-box" victory in Duval County over Coke Stevenson was famous for its 87 votes—but that was after a recount of his original margin of 49.

Not-So-Strange Bedfellows

When Clint's longtime friend and minority Cowboy stockholder, Bedford Wynne, was named by President John F. Kennedy to chair a fundraising dinner, Clint responded playfully:

> January 2, 1963
>
> The President
> The White House
> Washington, D.C.
>
> My dear Sir:
>
> I was naturally pleased at the selection of my football partner, Bedford Wynne, to serve as chairman of the Second Anniversary Inaugural Salute Dinner; however, let's hope he does a better job selling tickets for you than he does for the Dallas Cowboys.
>
> Respectfully,
>
> Clint Murchison Jr.

New Mexico senator Clinton P. Anderson and Clint's father had a long relationship over the senator's years involved in oil and gas legislation. In 1965 Anderson had suffered a circulatory ailment.

> July 15, 1965
>
> My dear Senator:
>
> It never concerns me when some friend goes numb in the brain since I know so many people in that condition already, but I did become worried when Bob told me you were numb in the leg. I am certainly glad the problem cleared up promptly.
>
> Sincerely,

Sometimes Clint liked to make life a scene from *Harvey*, in which the main character, played by James Stewart in the film, asks "What did you have in mind?" to anyone who says "May I help you?"

Dallas district state senator Jim Wade knew Clint not only as a constituent but as an occasional tippling buddy. When Wade's office included Clint on the mailing list of one of those let-me-know-if-I-can-ever-help-you form letters, Clint replied promptly:

Classic Clint

> January 20, 1967
> Honorable Jim Wade
> Texas State Senate
> Austin, Texas
>
> Dear Jim:
>
> Thank you for your letter of January 17 and your offer therein of assistance. You can, of course, assist me in many ways.
>
> What is your telephone number?

A campaign letter from Lt. Gov. Ben Barnes got the same treatment:

> September 4, 1970
> The Honorable Ben Barnes
> State Capitol
> Austin, Texas
>
> Dear Ben:
>
> I know that you appreciate my friendship and support, and I want to say that I certainly appreciate your offer of assistance from either you or your office.
>
> What do you have in mind?
>
> Sincerely,

Clint was able to mix the p.r. gesture with football interests when the governor of Florida wrote in 1968 to ask his support for holding future Super Bowls in his state. Super Bowls I and II had been played in California.

> May 10, 1968
> The Honorable Claude R. Kirk Jr.
> Governor of the State of Florida
> Tallahassee, Florida
>
> Dear Governor Kirk:
>
> As an owner of the Dallas Cowboys, I am certainly pleased by your interest in the Annual World Championship Game which, as you pointed out, was a tremendous success when held last year in Miami. My personal position is that the game, being national in scope and interest, should be alternated between Miami and Los Angeles, and I will be lobbying for this concept at the league meeting next week. It happens that the game probably cannot be held in Miami next year because of the Playoff Bowl; this is, however, probably a nonrecurring problem. In any event, I fully expect that the game will be played in

Miami in January, 1970, as I am equally expectant that the Dallas Cowboys will be a participant at that time.

Sincerely,

CLINT MURCHISON JR.

Clint was off on both counts; in the Super Bowl of 1970, Kansas City defeated Minnesota, 16-6, at Tulane Stadium in New Orleans. But Miami had landed the 1969 Super Bowl, when Joe Namath's Jets upset the Baltimore Colts, 16-7.

Congratulations on the reelection of Louisiana Sen. Russell Long in 1968:

August 20, 1968

The Honorable Russell Long
United States Senate
Washington, D.C.

Dear Russell:

You may recall in our last conversation in Washington I said I would be disappointed if you didn't receive 90% of the vote. Naturally, I'm a little disappointed, but then I guess 87% is close enough.

In 1969, as Congress was considering versions of tax reform, Clint was rankled by a *Time* magazine story listing what it thought were privileged tax advantages enjoyed by landlords. Clint didn't bother with letters to the editor. He sent a marked copy of the offending passage in a letter to the top.

April 11, 1969

Mr. James Linen, President
TIME, Inc.
TIME and LIFE Building
New York, N.Y.

Dear Jim:

TIME, April 4, 1969:

Real estate owners enjoy a triple tax break. Like other borrowers, they can deduct the interest paid on their loans. They may also deduct all the operating costs of a building from rental income. Finally, they may

Classic Clint

opt for "double depreciation"—they can deduct for the deterioration of their property at twice the rate at which the law presumes it is.

With the clipping of the article, Clint wrote:

And how about that loophole permitted publishers, whereby they are allowed to deduct as a business expense the salaries paid their editors?

The extraordinary point about this particular flam, apparently a hand-out from the PR staff of the Treasury Department, is that it was carried by both news services and printed in most newspapers and several magazines without editorial comment. Even by a magazine whose tremendous success is in part based on its adroit mixture of reportorial and editorial observation.

Sincerely,

CLINT MURCHISON JR.

During the Senate Watergate hearings, Clint's name had been brought up in connection with the money trail of political contributions involving Howard Hughes and President Nixon's mysterious friend Bebe Rebozo. Clint was anxious to set the record straight about political contacts he *didn't* have.

May 7, 1974

PERSONAL

Mr. Sam Dash
Senate Watergate Committee
United States Senate
Washington, D.C.

RE: Inquiry to me by Mr. Lee Sheehie
     concerning Hughes-Rebozo political contribution.

Dear Mr. Dash:

I have been advised by Mr. Sheehie that the Senate Watergate Committee is desirous of obtaining any information which I might have concerning the investigation referred to above. I wish to make the following comments:

1. I have never met Mr. Rebozo. Several years ago, he was seated next to me at a board meeting of the Boys' Clubs of America at which I was in attendance, but we did not speak.

2. I do not know Mr. Howard Hughes. From what I have read, there is some question in my mind whether anyone speaks to Howard Hughes.

3. I do know Mr. Robert A. Maheu. I believe I have seen him once since the matter originally surfaced in the newspapers; this was at a large party and our conversation was limited to a greeting.

4. I do know Mr. Richard Danner, and I have seen him once or twice since the aforementioned newspaper stories, but my conversations with Mr. Danner were entirely social in nature; the matter involved did not arise even in a frivolous way.

5. From any source other than the news media, I have no knowledge whatsoever concerning the purported political contribution from Howard Hughes to the Nixon Presidential campaign via Mr. Rebozo or otherwise.

I would be happy to attest to this statement before a United States Attorney here, or before you on my next visit to Washington, which I expect will be in June.

I have, as you know, previously provided you with a statement as to my own political contributions in recent presidential races.

I appreciate your consideration in accepting this letter from me in lieu of a personal appearance at this time in Washington.

Very truly yours,

CLINT MURCHISON, JR.

In the arts of influence, it's not only who you know, but knowing what to ask for. Clint left no doubts as to what would please him in a later memo to Louisiana Sen. Long. Congress once again was mulling the tightening of tax laws on capital gains and interest deductions. (He signed the letter in red ink.)

October 17, 1969

The Honorable Russell Long
United States Senate
Washington, D.C.

Dear Russell:

Memo for October 24:

I certainly hope that you fight a determined battle to retain the alternative tax on long-term capital gains and also to eliminate the proposed restrictions on the deductibility of interest which are

Classic Clint

included in the House-passed rules on Limit on Deductibility of Interest and Allocation of Deductions.

Sincerely,

p.s. I haven't run out of blue ink; that red is my blood.

There had been an appeal to a fancier Washington address in 1966, when the proposed football leagues merger seemed stalled in Congress' hopper.

September 27, 1966

Dear Lyndon:

Although Congressman Celler has publicly and privately encouraged a merger of the National Football League and American Football League, he seems reluctant to report out Hale Boggs' bill to legalize the merger.

The bill, a companion to S. 3816 passed unanimously yesterday by voice vote of the Senate, is in the national interest, as evidenced by the fact that it has no opposition; but dear to my heart is the fact that it is in the National (Football League) interest.

I know a call from Pennsylvania Avenue wouldn't hurt and it might help Dallas win the championship, which would be another first for Texas. I would surely appreciate it.

Sincerely,

CLINT

By 1970 environmental issues had begun to creep into the news. Nevada Sen. Howard Cannon was involved in some problems Nevada farmers and their cattle were having with a growing incidence of limestone dust. Awkwardly enough, some of this limestone dust was being kicked up by one of Clint's companies, Centex Corporation.

March 3, 1970

The Honorable Howard Cannon
United States Senate
Washington, D.C.

Dear Howard:

Re: Limestone dust problem
Fernley, Nevada

> The biggest cow I ever saw was raised on a diet of limestone dust; of course, her teats broke off the day she calved.
>
> Sincerely,
>
> Clint

The outspoken Dr. John Kenneth Galbraith, Harvard economist, onetime Ambassador to India, and professional intellectual, spent the seventies being an irritant to various Republicans and conservative doctrines on everything from Vietnam policy to Keynesian economics. It's unknown whether what he said to rankle Clint occurred on one of the networks' Sunday "issues" shows or otherwise in some article or speech. Nevertheless, Clint dropped him a line on Sept. 9, 1970:

> Dr. John Kenneth Galbraith
> Cambridge, Massachusetts
>
> Dear Dr. Galbraith:
>
> I agree with you that the Democratic Party should be run by intellectuals like you and me instead of by Texas fat cats and party hacks like George Meany.
>
> After all, it was people like us who gave the world Red China, the Korean War, the Berlin Wall, and Fidel Castro. These are all now established institutions, and we should be in there taking credit for them.

In the Dallas city elections in the spring of 1971, the mayor's office went, in a stunning upset, to a former television sports anchorman, Wes Wise, who had run an independent and skimpily financed campaign calling for the ouster of the long-entrenched Citizens Charter Association slate. Although Clint's nemesis from the stadium cold war, J. Erik Jonsson, did not run for reelection, Clint still enjoyed the slap to the CCA. He wrote to the newly elected mayor:

> April 21, 1971
>
> Dear Wes:
>
> What I really like to see is an elected official without any obligations to the fat cats. Or to the skinny ones, either, for that matter.
>
> Congratulations!

Christmas 1971 — New Year's 1972 were happy holidays for Dallas and Texas football fans. Coach Darrell Royal's University of Texas Longhorns would be in Dallas to meet Penn State in the Cotton Bowl

Classic Clint

Classic on New Year's Day. On the next day, the Cowboys hosted the San Francisco 49ers in the National Conference championship game. Clint had run into Royal at one of the many Dallas functions going on in advance of the bowl game and wrote him on Dec. 20:

> Darrell:
>
> The other night you mentioned to me that the reason you had not been to Texas Stadium was that you had not been invited. IF the Cowboys beat Minnesota on Christmas Day, then the NFC championship game will be played at Texas Stadium on January 2. I understand that you will be in town that weekend, and I hope that you will be my guest for this game, if played.
>
> President and Mrs. Johnson will also be my guests. Not being shy like you, he invited himself.

The Cowboys did beat the Vikings, setting the stage for the championship meeting with the 49ers. Clint's son Robert was among the party group of 28 in Clint's "double-wide" Circle Suite for the game. Over the years, Clint's guests in the suite ranged from Willie Nelson to Clint Eastwood, Jerry Jeff Walker, Norman Lear, Burt Reynolds, and Henry Kissinger. President Johnson had been out of office for four years. He had driven up from the Hill Country for the game with Lady Bird.

Robert Murchison remembers the game had a frustrating start for the favored Cowboys, who were unable to score in the first half. Neither could the 49ers. It was 0-0 at halftime. But in the second half the Cowboys began to establish their dominance while the defense held San Francisco at, er, bay. Just as the rally was getting underway and the Cowboys were on their way to a 14-3 victory, Clint leaned across to President Johnson and said, "Here come the Duval County results." As Robert remembers it, LBJ laughed harder than anyone. Two days after the game, Clint sent a note to President Johnson:

> January 4, 1972
>
> Mr. President:
>
> Best line of the day:
>
> "President Nixon called the Cowboys' locker room and President Johnson answered the phone."
>
> Clint

Once enamored of a pet gag, Clint let neither the problems of linguistics nor the passage of time defeat him. Two weeks after St. Patrick's Day of 1971, he sent a letter to an Irish-American celebrity:

> March 31, 1971
>
> The Honorable Edward M. Kennedy
> United States Senate
> Washington, D.C.
>
> A Chara Dhilis,
>
> Bhios i Boston La le Phadraic agus ta bronmor orm nac raibh tu 'san cathair cun onoir do bhronnad ar do naomh naisiunta. Naire ort!!!!
>
> Is mise, le meas mor,
>
> CLINT

The letter was in Gaelic, the ancient and official language of Ireland. Where and how Clint found someone to translate for him, his friends can't guess and don't even want to know. Time passed—about a year and a half, with no word back. This may have involved one of history's longest shrugs, but meanwhile Clint had run into Sen. Kennedy at a Redskin game in Washington and remembered that he had never replied to his Gaelic letter. Back in Dallas, he wrote again:

> October 30, 1972
>
> The Honorable Edward M. Kennedy
> United States Senate
> Washington, D.C.
>
> Dear Ted:
>
> I have always been impressed by your personal attention to detail, such as in your recent note to me after the Cowboys-Redskins game, with one exception. Last year, when I happened to be in Boston on St. Patrick's Day, and when I attempted to contact you, I learned that you were elsewhere. This political error I attempted to call to your attention in a letter written in Gaelic. A year later, having never received a reply, I mentioned the oversight to Senator (John) Tunney, who promised to call it to your attention.
>
> My question is, politics being what it is, particularly in an election year, would I have gotten more attention if I had written it in Hebrew?
>
> Sincerely,
>
> CLINT

Classic Clint

To this, Kennedy replied:

> United States Senate
> WASHINGTON, D.C. 20510
>
> A Cara Clint:
>
> I do have your letter, but it has taken all this time to get it translated.
>
> All I can say to you is ta do cluibh peil ag ineset go h-an maith.
>
> Buac aill maith tu!!
>
> Best,
>
> TED

We are beholden to Deirdre Boyle, of the Irish Embassy in Washington, for this critique of the Murchison and Kennedy Gaelic Papers:

"Mr. Murchison's stuff is OK, not the best Gaelic, you know, but it's all right. It says 'I was in Boston for St. Patrick's Day and was disappointed that you were not there, in the city, to honor the sorrow of your patron saint. Shame on you!' The last line is 'I am yours truly.'

"Senator Kennedy's says—I don't understand this, but what it says is, 'Your football boys are scoring good goals.' It ends 'Good chap, or good fellow.'"

The Cowboys were playing Miami in the Super Bowl. A few weeks before, President Nixon had sent a suggested play for the Washington Redskins to use in a playoff game. The Redskin coach, George Allen, had used it—losing yardage on the Nixonian end-around reverse. On January 8, 1972, Clint and Tom Landry got another presidential message, a telegram, on the eve of their Super Bowl appearance.

> WESTERN UNION
>
> AUSTIN, TEXAS
> JANUARY 8, 1972
> TOM LANDRY
> DALLAS COWBOYS
> 6116 NORTH CENTRAL EXPRESSWAY
> DALLAS, TEXAS
>
> MY PRAYERS AND MY PRESENCE WILL BE WITH YOU IN NEW ORLEANS ALTHOUGH I HAVE NO PLANS TO SEND IN ANY PLAYS.
>
> LYNDON B. JOHNSON
>
> CC: MR. CLINT MURCHISON JR.

Not-So-Strange Bedfellows

1977: Another year, another administration, another Congress toying with the idea of tax reforms. President Jimmy Carter had plunged a swizzle stick into the heart of American Business with his notorious threat to bring in more tax revenue by denying American Business its age-old right to the tax-deductible three-martini lunch. Clint wrote again to Louisiana Sen. Long:

> Re: Administration Proposals
> for tax reform legislation
>
> Dear Russell:
>
> A friend of mine asked Bob Strauss to tell Jimmy Carter on the next occasion they spoke that if the Lord hadn't intended businessmen to have three-martini lunches, He wouldn't have put all those olive trees in the Holy Land.
>
> I am passing this information along solely in the interest of good legislation.

He didn't go in for needlepoint inspiration and homily, but occasionally he came across a quotation that impressed him and sent them out to cronies on his mailing list. Sometimes they were relevant to a current event, a personal situation, or both. To the perennial second-guessing and Monday-morning quarterbacking going on by critics of the Cowboys and their management, he liked a quote from Theodore Roosevelt. It had come from Steve Schneider, the Pen Pal from Hell, during the midst of Clint's spotlighted problems with the city fathers on the stadium dispute:

> It is not the critic who counts, not the man who points out how the strong man stumbles or where the doer of deeds could have done them better. The credit belongs to the man who is actually in the arena; whose face is marred by dust and sweat and blood; who strives valiantly, who errs and comes up short again and again, who knows the great enthusiasms, the great devotions and spends himself in a worthy cause; who at the best knows in the end the triumphs of high achievement; and who at the worst, if he fails, at least fails while daring greatly; so that his place shall never be with those cold and trivial souls who know neither defeat nor victory.

(Schneider had added an inspiring note when he had sent it in 1964, the last of the Cowboys' losing years.)

Classic Clint

> "And after five years, I think it can honestly be said, you sure got a crappy team."

More in line with his droll outlook, and even his irreverent one, was the earlier letter he wrote to President Lyndon Johnson.

> March 29, 1967
>
> The President
> The White House
> Washington, D.C.
>
> Dear Mr. President:
>
> I understand that you have been requested to ask that the Department of the Interior change the name of Byrd Mountain in Antarctica to Harold Byrd* Mountain. While you are at it, I hope that you will also request that Interior change the name of Royal Gorge in Colorado to Darrell Royal Gorge, and I also hope that you will ask Secretary Rusk to begin negotiations with Kenya to get them to change the name of Murchison Falls to Clint Murchison, Jr. Falls. Coach Royal and I would appreciate your prompt attention to these matters.
>
> p.s. I have always wondered, is Harold Byrd any relation to Lady Bird?

* Harold Byrd, an earthy Dallas oilman, was a distant relative of Adm. Richard Byrd

---

He had also learned that one of LBJ's cabinet members collected spoonerisms, Sam Goldwynisms, and other slips of the tongue:

> The Honorable Willard Works
> Secretary of Labor
> Washington, D.C.
>
> Dear Mr. Secretary:
>
> Add to your collection of "Monumental Metaphors" this little gem from the late Senator Joe McCarthy: "That's the most unheard of thing I ever heard of."
>
> Yours very truly,
>
> CLINT MURCHISON JR.

Hubert Humphrey, the populist Minnesota senator and vice president under Lyndon Johnson, was known neither for his eloquence nor for having Clint Murchison, Jr., as an admirer. But upon Humphrey's death in 1978, Clint sent out a sort of sampler collection of some of Humphrey's capsule philosophies. Among the recipients was *Dallas Times Herald* editorial columnist Felix R. McKnight. Clint added a note with the sampler to McKnight:

> **Felix:**
> **Several of these quotations are, I believe, worthy of further dissemination. If you missed them I think you will enjoy them.**

The source of the collection is uncertain, but Clint may have liked the appreciation of Humphrey's remarks: "They were rarely memorable, but they were invariably heartfelt. They expressed rather than camouflaged the real man . . ."

On speaking his mind "I've seen all these people that hem and haw. They never quite get around to saying where they are or who they are or what they are, what they want, where they've been, or where they're going. You have to make some judgments; you just can't keep waiting for more evidence."

On 'The Politics of Joy' "Happiness is contagious, just exactly like being miserable. People have to believe that they can do better. They've got to know that there's somebody that wants to help and work with them, somebody that hasn't tossed in the towel."

On helping others "Compassion is not weakness, and concern for the unfortunate is not socialism."

On ruthlessness "I know a lot of people tell me I'm not tough enough. Listen, there are enough tough people in the world."

On showing emotions "A fellow that doesn't have any tears doesn't have any heart."

On being snubbed by President Johnson (who thought he had leaked a story to the press) "I'm the living example that a man can be in the deep freeze for at least two weeks and still live. But then he'd give you that quick thaw. A wink with one of those eyes was just like two cymbals coming together in a clash. He'd forgiven me in one flick of an eyelid."

On foreign policy "We can't be the world's policeman, but we can be the world's idealist."

Classic Clint

On adversity "Some people look upon any setback as the end. They're always looking for the benediction rather than the invocation. Most of us have enough problems so that any day we could fold up and say, 'I've had it.' But you can't quit. That isn't the way our country was built."

On love "The greatest gift that has come to me is the affection of so many—far more important than people feeling sorry for me. In fact, feeling sorry for someone is simply to give him a little pain reliever. Love is a healing force."

He may have been in a more sardonic mood the day he sent out this note to several buddies, seeming to enjoy the recent discomfiture of Sen. George McGovern. McGovern had respectfully called on Lyndon Johnson at the latter's Pedernales Ranch during McGovern's bid for the presidential nomination and had been dismissed without even getting a tour of the ranch.

Notable Quotes

President Johnson, as he downed his last bite of apple pie during his luncheon with Senator McGovern:

"Come back again, George, when I have a little more time to show you the ranch."

Clint sent it out with no further comment.

A 1979 letter accompanied a Dallas Cowboys warmup jacket:

The Honorable Brendan T. Byrne
Governor of New Jersey

Dear Governor Byrne:

I was surprised to learn from Ramon Jarrell that you are sporting a Pittsburgh Steeler jacket. Certainly you will agree that a man of your stature should only wear the best, which is herewith enclosed.

I appreciate the assistance which you and your office are giving Ramon.

Sincerely,

CLINT MURCHISON JR.

Not-So-Strange Bedfellows

In the same year, Clint wrote Price Daniel, who was about to be honored at a dinner commemorating his 40th anniversary in public service as U.S. Senator, lieutenant governor and governor.

> My dear Governor:
>
> I want you to know that I consider it an honor to serve as a member of the Sponsors Committee for your Appreciation Dinner. You have made a singular contribution to our state and to our country during your illustrious career.
>
> But forty years? For a man of your youth, you must have started at age eleven.
>
> Sincerely,
>
> CLINT

June 1980: At the conventions later in the summer, the Democrats would renominate Jimmy Carter to run against Ronald Reagan, who at nearly 70 was getting on up there. Clint read this memo from his secretary Ruth Woodard:

> Gov Pat Brown's office called. The Gov is being honored on his 75th birthday on June 17 in L.A. They want to include your name on honorary list of friends.

Clint hastily scribbled an OK on that memo and then sent the former California governor, who with his son Gov. Jerry Brown had given the state a rare father-son gubernatorial parlay, a note:

> Honorable Edmund G. Brown
> Beverly Hills, California
>
> Dear Pat:
>
> Belated congratulations on your 75th. Now that you are mandatory retirement age, I suggest that we nominate you for president on August 11. This will not only give you something to do, but it may straighten out the current disarray in the Party.
>
> Sincerely,
>
> CLINT

Classic Clint

In 1980 Clint was an investor in an Oklahoma City radio station managed by Ken Dowe, who had known Clint during his Dallas radio career as Granny Emma, a falsetto-voiced reactionary biddy. For the Oklahoma station's election night coverage, Clint and Dowe had managed to recruit none other than veteran House Speaker Carl Albert, recently retired, to come into the studio and do election commentary.

> November 10, 1980
> The Honorable Carl Albert
> McAlester, Oklahoma
> Dear Carl:
>
> I appreciate your doing the color for Ken Dowe on election night. He said he got a number of calls about it—including one from a competitor who was listening to our election coverage instead of his own.
>
> You apparently have quite a following in Oklahoma. Did you ever consider entering politics?

Ken Dowe recalled later: "I had spent a lot of time that year working with the Republican Party in Oklahoma. Mr. Albert, of course, had been a major Democrat. Clint and I often joked about my Republicanism and Clint's corresponding involvement with the Texas Democrats. There was a big Republican sweep in 1980, and the day after the election I called Clint to rub it in. For several minutes I waxed eloquent, I thought, about the great rise of the GOP and the fall of the Democrats.

"'So, Clint, you'll have to admit,' I said, 'our side won and yours lost.'
There was a long pause.
'Not so,' Clint said.
'Why not?' I asked him.
Clint said: 'Not so . . . because I'm on ALL sides.' And so he was."

Clint's onetime next-door neighbor Annette Strauss became Dallas' first woman mayor in 1987. One of Clint's mischievous contributions to her political career was a bizarre plan for the solution to one of the city's lingering traffic problems, Central Expressway traffic. As it happened, Clint and Annette had had a kind of automotive relationship from the first, as her husband Ted Strauss recalls.

In the 1950s the Strausses and the Murchisons were youthful couples with growing families, neighbors on Wateka Avenue in an upscale wooded neighborhood of North Dallas called Greenway Park.

"Annette, at the time, had an embarrassing inability to remember to put the car into 'park' when she pulled into our driveway," Ted Strauss recalls. "One day it crept backward down our driveway, slowly gathering momentum until it crashed into Clint's beautiful brick wall. Clint's three sons, little guys in khaki, came over to the house and told her what she'd done. When I called Clint that evening to assure him I'd take responsibility, he was polite, quiet, and noncommittal. While I kept waiting to hear from him about a repair bill, the brick wall was just left that way, at an angle dangerous to life and limb, for at least several months.

"Then I came home one afternoon and as I drove into my garage, the fence seemed to have been 'cleaned out.' I assumed repair work was underway. I was wrong. When I got inside Annette told me the same three little boys had come to ring our doorbell and in doleful tones had said, 'Well, you did it *again*!'

There was more than one impromptu Demolition Derby in that Murchison driveway on Wateka. Clint III says, "Dad had a kind of strange habit when he drove home. He'd roar into the driveway at pretty high speed, drive right into the garage, and then hit the brakes and squeal to a halt just in front of the rear wall, trying to scare us, I guess. Most of the time he made it. But a couple of times, maybe when he was coming home from one of the clubs, he didn't stop in time. The back of that garage wall had some dangling sheetrock and dented paneling."

Clint's suggestion for the future Mayor Strauss's traffic platform should be viewed in the framework of the decades of Dallas' civic agonizing over what to do about Central: add a monorail, add a conventional elevated train, widen it, fill it with buses, go around it, plow it under, or forget about it in a tempting episode of mass mega-amnesia. But Clint had a different option.

Classic Clint

Dear Annette:

I have been attempting to come up with a platform for you which would assure your election and I think I have finally found it. Of course, the most obvious platform would concern DART (*note: Dallas Area Rapid Transit*) but that involves the railroad and there will be too much of that in this election anyway.

What I finally concluded is original, innovative, daring, striking, and a great crowd pleaser. It is something so simple that no one else has thought about it: CENTRAL EXPRESSWAY UNDERGROUND! Tunnel the new roadway beneath the existing one! No unsightly structures through residential neighborhoods resulting from raised structures! No condemnation of valuable commercial land resulting from a widening of the Expressway!

Think of the catchy election slogans:

"Home Alive in '95!"

"In from the Sticks in '96!"

"A Bit of Heaven in '97!"

The existing roadway would be broken up and sodded with grass; this ecological improvement would not only get the (environmentalist) vote, but by providing a place for a jogging trail would capture the hearts of Kenneth Cooper's Aerobics minions also.

I suggest we get together next week and brainstorm this approach. The more I think about it, the more excited I get. Gov. Mark White, watch out!

Sincerely,

CLINT

Ted Strauss later said that Clint considered the gag had backfired on him; he was almost crestfallen to learn that when she read the letter, Annette Strauss had thought he was serious. Eventually, a citizens' expressway solution committee actually considered Clint's plan among the options.

Chapter Nine
Inspirations and Other Outrages

> *"I can remember so well his standing in the doorway of my office with a very solemn look (but always with a twinkle in his eye) and dictating a letter to someone which turned out to be a joke . . . They always turned out well and they made the recipient's day . . ."*
> —Ruth Woodard, his secretary for 13 years

There was some kind of joke in nearly every letter, note, memo, reminder, broadside, manifesto, brief, deposition, *aide-memoire*, or caption that he ever wrote. But as Picasso might shift his media from ink sketches to sculpture, Clint frequently moved into the heavier duty, industrial strength category of gags, the practical joke that required time, thought, verisimilitude, equipment, props, and collaborators.

These capers were nearly always ignited by an event, a gaffe, somebody's misstep or weakness, no matter how trivial or even near-tragic the episode might have seemed. Near-tragic, in fact, was pretty fair game.

Classic Clint

In early June of 1963 Clint took a large group of about a dozen friends on a bird-hunting excursion to Clint, Sr.'s 75,000-acre spread, Hacienda Acuña, in the Mexican state of Tamaulipas.

During one of the shoots, one of the teenage Mexican boys working as a retriever was grazed by a couple of pellets from insuranceman Jack Jones' shotgun. The boy hadn't been badly hurt, but he had bled. And the more the story got recounted and embellished that night after dinner and the next day, the worse the boy had been wounded and the more Jack Jones had had to drink.

Clint thought of more embellishments on the flight back to Dallas. Back in his office, he sent a letter to ranch manager Roy Reed.

> June 10, 1963
>
> Dear Roy:
>
> I wish you would have the enclosed letter written down there and mailed from Gonzales to:
>
> > Jack W. Jones
> > Corrigan-Jordan Insurance Agency
> > 211 North Ervay
> > Dallas, Texas
>
> The letter should ostensibly be from the boy he put the buckshot into. So have it written on cheap stationery and in poor, but legible, handwriting. It should also be written in Spanish, so make the best translation you can.
>
> p.s. To heighten the effect, drop a couple of drops of blood on Jack's copy. This need not be human blood, however.

The transit of the letter to the Acuña ranch, its translation, and remailing from the interior of Mexico took two weeks. The handwriting in the Spanish, blood-dappled version was in a rounded, tortuous script that met Clint's specifications.

Inspirations and Other Outrages

> Estimado Señor Jones —
>
> Quiero disculparme de Usted por la inconvenencia que le cause a Usted por correr enfente de su escopeta la semana ante pasada. Ojalá que mi acción sin pensar no le molesto en ninguna manera. Francamente, yo no pensé que Usted iba a tirar como Usted tenia una botella de cerveza en su mano (para tirar) derecha, pero yo debería por mas agusado para llegar a una conclusión tan ridiculo. Yo nunca uso mi cerebro. Ya me siente bien y los doctores dicen que me dejan salir del hospital en un mes. La herida no me molestia mucho, pero a veces la sangre me ensucia la ropa algo
>
> Su segura servidor
> Cinca Martinez

The letter in Spanish to Jack Jones from Cinca Martinez. It looked more authentic with the bloodstains.

Classic Clint

It took Jones, the letter's victim, most of a day to get it translated.

> **Estimado Senor Jones (Dear Mr. Jones):**
>
> I wish to relieve you of the blame for the inconvenience which I may have caused you for running in front of your gun week before last. Oh, how I wish that my thoughtless action did not bother you in any way. Frankly, I did not think that you were going to shoot, as you were holding a bottle of beer in your right hand (your shooting arm) but I should have been smarter than to reach such a ridiculous conclusion. I never use my head. Now I am feeling well and the doctors say that they are going to let me leave the hospital in a month. The wound does not bother me much, but at times the blood soils my clothing a little.
>
> Sincerely yours,
>
> Cinca Martinez

Jones went immediately to Dudley Ramsden at Neiman-Marcus, where there was a tailor of Mexican descent in the alterations room. "As he began reading the note aloud," Jones says, "his face turned dark. Then he took me over to a corner where he could translate it in private. I was panicked. The kid was in the hospital! I didn't get an inkling it might be a gag until I finally started thinking about the name at the bottom of the letter—Cinca Martinez. Five martinis."

Matthew, Mark, Luke & Clint

In the spring of 1968 Clint flew to Spanish Cay with a group of Cowboys front-office staffers and virtually the whole Dallas-Fort Worth pro-football sportswriting media for a week of deep-sea fishing and evening revelries. It was a week of restful retreat, Coca-Conga seminars, and the give-and-take that Clint enjoyed so much with sportswriters. Cowboy staffers along included Tex Schramm, Al Ward, Curt Mosher, and Tom Hardin. The writers were Andy Anderson of the *Fort Worth Press* and Frank Luksa of the *Star-Telegram*; Walter Robertson, then sports editor of the *Dallas News*, and Bob St. John, the Cowboy beat writer; and *Dallas Times Herald's* Blackie Sherrod and Cowboy beat writer Steve Perkins.

At the end of the trip the writers, stumped on what to give the man who had everything, in fact found something he didn't have; at Sherrod's creative instigation, they sent him a gift-wrapped six-pack of Gideon Bibles, one for each guest bungalow on the island.

It was a coup that Clint felt compelled to counter. But how? Jim Stroman, Clint's office aide in those days, remembers how the project proceeded:

"Clint called Rev. Tom Shipp at the Lovers Lane Methodist Church and he asked if he could send him any quotations in the Bible that had to do with scribes. Then he told me to go to a book store and pick up 12 cheap Bibles. Have you ever tried to find *cheap* Bibles? There aren't any. I finally bought some from a Salvation Army chapel. It occurred to me later I should have called Joe Cavagnaro at the Statler Hilton Hotel, which had them in all their rooms, but I didn't think of it in time.

"After Clint got the Bibles, he spent most of a morning going through the relevant passages of each one of them, using a red marking pencil to underline the quotations that Rev. Shipp had sent him.

"Then he told me to just tear out the pages of the quotations he had marked in each set, so he wouldn't have to send each sportswriter the whole Bible.

"I said, 'Tear up the Bible? Are you sure? Is there any other way we can . . .'

"He reached over, picked up a Bible, and ripped out a page. 'Like this,' he said."

The quotations were:

Job 13:26 *For thou writest bitter things against me, and makest me to possess the iniquities of my youth.*

Jer. 8:8 *. . . the pen of the scribes is in vain.*

Matt. 5:20 *For I say unto you, That except your righteousness shall exceed the righteousness of the scribes and the Pharisees, ye shall in no case enter into the kingdom of heaven.*

Matt. 7:29 *For he taught them as one having authority, and not as the scribes.*

Luke 20:46 *Beware of the scribes, which desire to walk in long robes, and love greetings in the markets, and the highest seats in the synagogues, and the chief rooms at feasts.*

He mailed the packets to each of the guests, starting with Blackie Sherrod.

When Trivia Turns Crucial

In a column written after Clint's death, Sherrod found himself drawn to memories of the capers.

> It was a loss that more people weren't exposed to the Murchison humor, which sat up there at the very top. Not the broad basic tricks his Fun Loving Rover Boys pulled. The time he had a goat tied to the stair railing to my apartment. (Card: "You got my goat with what you wrote, so am delivering same.") He also slyly alerted TV cameramen so that they showed up immediately and their lights so frightened the poor goat that he chose the mathematical center of the parlor rug as a bathroom.
>
> There were delightful subtleties. Example: There were his frequent notes. Certainly I don't imply to have been in the close Murchison circle. I was on the remote fringe, but he had a copious fringe.
>
> He wrote frequent nominations for "Whatever Happened To . . ." targets, only they would be intriguingly obscure. I remember one as "George R. Elliott" that I never could make and, in some disgust, he identified the private who spotted radar blips of Japanese planes approaching Pearl Harbor, and whose report was ignored by superiors.
>
> When he played trivia, he didn't fool with statistics and such: name two quarterbacks who played in Yankee Stadium with the initials Y.A.T. . . .
>
> . . . On a boat in the Caribbean, Clint ignored actions of comrades in the stern and on the flying bridge. He stretched on a bunk in the cabin and read a book. Sparkling day, trolling smooth seas, fish of astounding varieties practically leaping in the boat. His pals chided him so unmercifully finally he put aside his book without a word, took over a fighting chair, almost immediately got a strike. In an amazingly

short time, he boated a 65-pound grouper, easily the biggest catch of the day, arose, socked the rod back in the slot and with magnificent deadpan, slowly looked everyone in the face. Still silent, he turned and went back to his bunk and book. I don't think he would have traded that scene for a Superbowl. I remember him as a man of great humor . . .

In his "Clint's Corner" column in the Dallas Cowboys Insiders Newsletter of January 15, 1971, the issue before the Cowboys' first Super Bowl appearance against Baltimore, Clint showed his fondness for trivia, and for Blackie Sherrod.

Name Two Quarterbacks
With the Initials Y.A.T.
Who Played in Yankee Stadium

Do you remember when, in the movies, Jack Oakie used to run 92 yards for the winning touchdown? If you do, you're my age or older, and you'd better call right now about your annual physical. This was about the time W. C. Fields gave a flinty glance at Baby Leroy and remarked that "children should be patted on the head until dead," and when Mae West asserted that "I started out as pure as the driven snow, but then I drifted a little."

All this may not seem important to you, but you sure have to know about this period, among other things, if you want to be any good at playing Trivia. Trivia is not simply a compendium of trivial information (Where is the highest sand dune in the world?*); to qualify as true trivia, an event must at one time have been extraordinary, and now but dimly remembered; a person must have been of transcendental fame, and now buried in oblivion.

I once asked Blackie Sherrod, who is either pretty good at the game or exploits an unflagging research staff, to name the individual who had played for the New York Rangers (hockey), the Brooklyn Dodgers (baseball), and the New York Knickerbockers (basketball). I won't keep you waiting; the answer is Gladys Gooding, the organist. THAT is trivia.

One of the greatest experts in this field is a pal of mine from New York City, Spencer Martin. Last year, just as the World Cup soccer matches drew to a close in Mexico, I happened to be in New York, conversing with several men, when we were interrupted by a knock at the door. Expecting Spencer, I opened the door and without introduction asked, "Spenny, we've been wondering, who is the most highly paid team athlete in the world?" I could tell by the glint in his eye that I had him: "Pele," he announced triumphantly. "That, Spenny," I replied condescendingly, "is his nickname. What's his NAME?" Spencer worked on it for 10 minutes, but never came out with Edson Arantes do Nascimento . . .

This particular confrontation ended in a victory for me worth savoring, for Spencer usually comes out ahead. Once, for instance, I popped this one on him: "Name the referee who permitted Dartmouth a fifth down against Cornell in 1940." In the closing seconds of the game, Dartmouth had scored the winning touchdown on the redundant down and the result was chaos, if not throughout the world, at least throughout the Ivy League, an organization, I might add, which has been revitalized by our own Calvin Hill.

I happened to know the referee's name because his son and I had attended high school together, and I supposed that this would give me an edge. Spencer, however, was undaunted. "Freisell," he shouted (Spenny shouts), "and what was the name of the captain of the Cornell team?" That glint in his eye again. I had a sinking feeling as I realized that THIS time I was done in. The astonishing answer was "Brud" Holland, who only two months before had been named as the United States Ambassador to Sweden. Football players turn up in the strangest places.

But my favorite rejoinder came from the old pro, Blackie (the one with the indefatigable research staff). As you know, he begins his Sunday column with the expression, "Scattershooting while wondering whatever happened to 'X'. Generally, 'X' is the name of an individual who qualifies as a candidate for trivia. And so one day I sent Blackie a two-page note.

Page One:

Blackie, while you're scattershooting, why don't you wonder whatever happened to someone important, such as

1. Dave Barry
2. Fred Noonan
3. Benny Lom
4. Joe Forner
5. Sal Durante
6. Anna Sage

Page Two:
1. The referee who gave the long count in the Dempsey-Tunney fight, September 22, 1927.
2. Amelia Earhart's navigator. Did the Japs get him, too?

Inspirations and Other Outrages

3. The University of California player who tackled his teammate, Roy Riegels, from behind when Riegels made his famous "wrong-way" run in the Rose Bowl.
4. The Irish-American who was beaten in the 1908 Olympic Marathon when the British officials carried the flagging Italian, Pietro Dorandi, across the finish line.
5. The spectator who caught Roger Maris' 61st home run.
6. The gal who fingered Dillinger.

About three weeks later (after, I'm told, numerous exultations to, and even verbal lashings of, his desperately overwrought research staff), Blackie replied, again in a two-page note.

Page One:

"And poor old Sgt. Joe Lockhart,

Page Two:

". . . Who quite fruitlessly spotted the Jap fleet on radar." Four years later, on the anniversary of Pearl Harbor Day, I found in my newspaper a tip which would have negated this reply: the Sergeant spelled his name not Lockhart, but Lockhard.

But I was too late; an expert on Trivia must be swift and decisive.

I was done in again.

*Southwest Africa; 10 will get you five you had it in North Africa, but that's trivial.

It was typically devilish of Clint not to have answered in his column the tantalizing question posed in the headline: Name two quarterbacks with the initials Y.A.T. who played in Yankee Stadium. Most fans knew immediately that one of them was Y.A. Tittle, the veteran New York Giants and San Francisco 49ers quarterback. The other was Army's postwar All-American quarterback, whom sports fans knew as Arnold Tucker. His full name was Young Arnold Tucker.

Clint and Blackie had other trivia challenges. Once Clint headed a note on another topic with the provocative query,

"Scattershooting while wondering whatever happened to Max Yasgur . . ."

Classic Clint

Yasgur was the upstate New York farmer on whose property the Woodstock festival had been held.

Another long-running trivia problem involved the mystery of what the I. stood for in the middle name of Dr. S. I. Hayakawa, who had gained some fame as an educator, semanticist, and onetime California political candidate.

Clint had challenged Blackie, and several weeks later the answer came back from Blackie:

> Dear Sir:
> His middle name is Ichiye.
> It's taken a while.

Clint replied:

> May 7, 1976:
> Blackie:
> I learned of Ichiye long ago—but it wasn't easy. After weeks of discussion with such astute fact-finders as Spencer Martin, Bob Cochran and yourself, a cutie (who happened to learn of my befuddlement) gave me a call and said, "It's Ichiye." I asked in amazement how she could possibly have information unavailable to all of my learned friends; "I looked it up in Who's Who," was her prompt rejoinder. What will these girls think of next?

On Fish & Other Exotics

Those "fish of astounding varieties" that had so impressed Sherrod had had a similar effect on Ed Sabol of NFL Films, when he had visited Spanish Cay. He learned that Clint had taken movies of the undersea glories in his SCUBA diving, and they discussed NFL Films' producing a feature on the tropical fish of Spanish Cay, editing Clint's own undersea home movies. The film, "Abaco Reef," was produced, with the sepulchral voice-over of John Facenda, the Philadelphia TV anchor who narrated NFL Films for years. The credits read: "Starring ... The Murchisons—and Other Fish."

In one letter, Sabol had asked if Clint knew the names of the species of fish that were to be shown.

June 23, 1969
Mr. Edwin Sabol
President
NFL Films
250 North 13 Street
Philadelphia, Pennsylvania

Dear Ed:

I don't know the names of the fish either. When I edit these films, I refer to them as "little blue jobbies," "red jobbies with white spots," etc. However, for your personal information, I am enclosing two books which picture a great number of the fish I photographed. The list attached to each book indicates where these may be found. I would appreciate your returning the books after you have finished with them. In any event, after the film has been put together, I think it will be necessary to borrow an ichthyologist from the University of Pennsylvania in order that no mistakes are made in the commentary.

As to the length of the film, I am inclined to think 1600 feet might be a little too long. Maybe we should plan on taking, say, 1200 feet of the most interesting shots and doing a first-class production on them . . . I could assist you in the editing . . .

As to plot: you mentioned that the shots had a great deal of similarity. I might point out that so do nudie movies, and they do all right.

How To Succeed at Spanish Cay

The idyllic private island, 160 miles east of Miami, had a 5,000-foot paved airstrip and landscaping designed by the longtime king of the business, Joe O. Lambert. There was a large main building and six guest bungalows, connected by a covered walkway. Clint had designed the island house, too, as he had 6200 Forest Lane. Its look was a tropical version of the Dallas home: one-story, low-slung, sprawling, with screened-in rooms and open terraces, and lanais. It was not air-conditioned; ocean breezes cooled it. Clint loved going there and treated it as a personal fiefdom, a fact fully appreciated by Steve Schneider in his advice to Ted Strauss, who was about to make his first trip to Spanish Cay:

> Organized improvisation is what he wants—demands! You know what the sun is to the planets. Around HIM, boy, around Little Caesar! Hand him the world and his comment will be, "What else have you got?" He likes Al Jolson . . . but not in the morning. Lyrical poems—Byron,

Keats, that sort of stuff—are good for the morning. A little pantomime with his sliced oranges will do for variety. For Jolson, he particularly likes "Toot Toot Tootsie, Goodbye" . . . reminds him of Jane. And when you do "I Only Have Eyes for You," be sure and look at *him*. Save the juggling and acrobatic stuff for the beach. On this I suggest subtlety—make it clear that you know he can do it better than you.

Always laugh at his jokes; of course, this will keep you laughing every time he opens his mouth 'cause you never know whether he's joking or not (he's not joking about the Cowboys). Sometimes he will sit for long periods of time staring at the ocean and then break into a grin and give a slight chuckle. Don't worry about this, he's just recalling to mind some good friend who went broke or some cousin who died unexpectedly.

Everyone is impressed with his champagne fountain. I'll let you in on a little secret—he borrowed the glasses from John Dabney and John Dabney doesn't know it. In fact, the British are still trying to figure out the note he gave them for the island, secured by preferred stock in Daisy Air Rifle, registered in Allan Kirby's name, with a stock power attached from Bobby Baker . . . Lots of luck . . . and tell Annette not to get upset when he calls her "Hey, You." At least he does recognize that she is there.

Fools rush in,

STEPHEN W. SCHNEIDER

Quick—What Rhymes with Duck?

He enjoyed tweaking *Time* magazine's policies, officials, and eccentricities. It was 1968. LBJ had dropped out. There had been riots by the public and the police, and beatings at the Democratic National Convention in Chicago. The three presidential tickets were Nixon-Agnew, Humphrey-Muskie, and Wallace-LeMay.

October 9, 1968

Mr. James R. Shepley
Publisher
Time Magazine
Time-Life Building
New York, N.Y.

Dear Jim:

I took your candidate-watcher test in the October 4 issue and am happy to say that I scored 100%. Now, here's one for you:

What was the favorite word of *Time* editors in 1960-61? In 1966?

What is their favorite today?

What happened to *Time's* Poet Laureate?

Score yourself an expert *Time* reader if you identified the favorite word in 1960 as "acerbic," and in 1966 as "dialogue"; the favorite word today is apparently "angst" (rhymes with Pangst). The Poet Laureate is, of course, the fellow who filled in all of the parenthetical "rhymes withs"; since he hasn't been heard from recently, we may assume that he retired in a huff after President Eisenhower gave Bandaranaike an unfair poetical advantage by his ambassadorial appointment of Maxwell Gluck (which even a Ceylonese can rhyme with "duck") . . ."

Gagnum Opus

The Dudley Ramsden Rolls Royce Interment Caper, perhaps Clint's logistical masterpiece, came into the Hall of Fame in 1977. Clint's secretary Ruth Woodard recalls its beginnings:

"Mr. Murchison saw the story in the newspaper about a man who had been buried in his car. He immediately thought of Dudley Ramsden, who was famous in his circle for being so proud of his own cars. We went to work."

The article had appeared in an Ann Landers column:

> Dear Ann Landers: I wonder how many of your readers wonder what happened to some of the people whose letters have appeared in your column. I, for one, am consumed with curiosity about the man who wanted to be buried (after his death, of course) sitting up, behind the wheel of his beloved Packard.
>
> Please, Ann, fill me in on this. It's been years since I read that letter, and I've been wondering about it ever since. Can you give me an update?
>
> —An Elephant in Petaluma
>
> Dear Pet: Elephant, indeed! That letter appeared at least 15 years ago and I remember it well. Only it wasn't a Packard. It was a 1939 Dodge.

Classic Clint

> The man wrote to ask if it was legal, and I told him it depends on the charter of the cemetery. I advised that he enlist the help of a funeral director to find a cemetery that would permit such a burial because he would probably need to buy two lots.
>
> I don't know if the man is still living. I suspect he is, because if he had been buried in his 1939 Dodge, it surely would have made the papers.

In mulling his global contacts for the right props to give this dawning depredation the right stuff, he remembered that he himself was the partner in a joint venture with Paul Trousdale in a Hawaiian enterprise known as Valley of the Temples. It was a cemetery. The cemetery already had a handsome color brochure, of course. Clint got Trousdale to ship him some of the letterhead stationery from Valley of the Temples.

The letterhead itself carried the proper exotic ambience, notably the address: 47-200 Kahekili Highway, Kaneohe, Hawaii 96744. Clint recruited an artist for some special illustration work that would accompany the offer Dudley Ramsden was about to receive.

He received it in mid-July, 1977:

> **VALLEY OF THE TEMPLES**
> **AN ENDOWMENT CARE MEMORIAL PARK**
>
> July 12, 1977
>
> Mr. Dudley Ramsden
> 8206 Inwood Road
> Dallas, Texas 75209
>
> Dear Mr. Ramsden:
>
> Since we have observed the increased popularity in this country of the desire of certain distinguished people to be interred in their automobiles, this institution, Valley of the Temples, has elected to feature this very specialized type of Memorial Estate Development.
>
> Please be assured that the offer of these services is not being made to the general public but only to those people of suitable distinction and who possess the quality of automobile (the Vehicle of Interment) befitting this particular approach to the selection of a suitable final resting place.

Inspirations and Other Outrages

I am enclosing a brochure of Valley of the Temples together with a photograph of the area we have elected to reserve for Automobile Interment; I believe you will find the latter breathtaking in every respect. I am also enclosing a cross section of a typical interment which emphasizes the lasting qualities of the care which we provide.

Yours very truly,

JOHN J. POWERS, JR.

47-200 KAHEKILI HIGHWAY / KANEOHE, HAWAII 96744
TELEPHONE: 239-8811

The signature of John J. Powers was remarkably similar to the handwriting of Ruth Woodard.

The cross-section diagram pictured a man leaning at a 45-degree angle in the front seat of a Rolls Royce sedan.

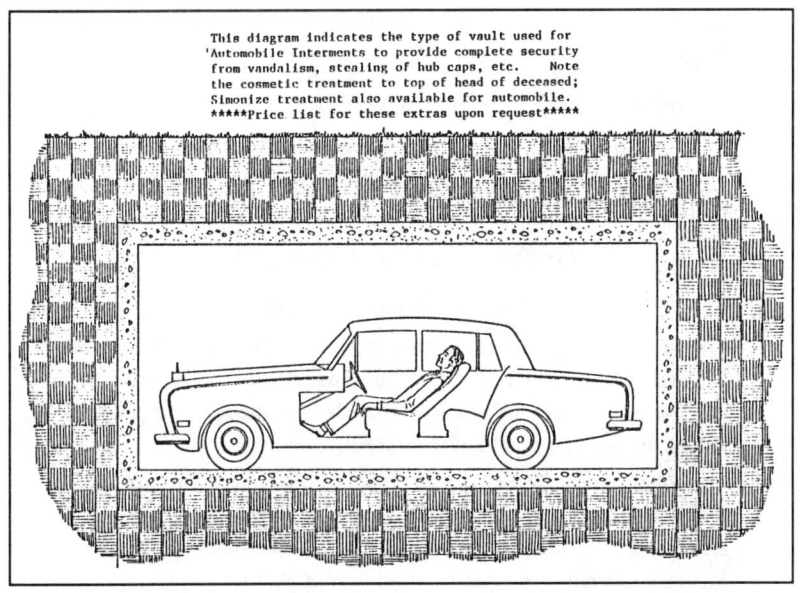

This graphic was part of the elaborate car-burial brochure offered to his friend Dudley Ramsden.

Clint was so proud of the final look of the package that he asked Jack Jones, the victim of the Shot-Mexican-Youngster caper, to help him by assembling the packets and sending them to a privileged mailing

Classic Clint

list of the Clued-In. It was such a good gag that Clint wanted the knowledge of it restricted to a select circle—just Jack Vaughn, Carroll L. Webb, Jr., Robert Wigley, Toddie Lee Wynne, Jr., Basil Georges, Guy (Murph) Foote, Max Thomas, William G. Webb, Ben R. Briggs, Guy Carter, Grant Fitts, Jack Garrett, Jr., George S. Hiland, William F. Neale, Jr., William B. Oliver, Tex Schramm, Charles Seay, Roy H. Bettis, Tom Buell, Sanders Campbell, Leo Corrigan, Jr., William Dinwiddie, Finley Ewing, Jr., Jones, Tom Laros, Herman Lay, Harold Lilley, Kenneth Moore, George Nicoud, Jr., Peter O'Donnell, Jr., Niel W. Platter, John Rauscher, Jr., Steve Schneider, Robert H. Stewart, John Taylor, and Paul Thayer.

Clint had added a note to the original Ann Landers clipping that had inspired it:

Friends:

The Burier lives! Only it wasn't a 1939 Dodge, either—it was a 1974 Rolls Royce. I thought you might like an update.

Ruth Woodard recalled: "When it finally dawned on Dudley that it was a joke, he thought it was hilarious, too."

There was a final chapter to the caper seven years later, when Clint sent to the same mailing list an actual headline and Associated Press story from the *Dallas Times Herald* of March 2, 1984:

Man Buried Cadillac-style

CHICAGO—A man who was buried in a coffin built to look like his beloved Cadillac Seville, drawing 5,000 people to the funeral home, was "very car-conscious" and had requested the special arrangements before his death, a funeral director said.

The coffin bearing Willie M. Stokes, Jr., who was buried Wednesday, had flashing head and tail lights, a steering wheel, a chrome grille and the Cadillac insignia. It also carried the word "WIMP," the name Stokes displayed on his personalized license plates.

"We took the casket to a body-and-fender factory in Indianapolis to get the authentic Cadillac grille and trunk design," said Spencer Leak, vice president of A.R. Leak Funeral Home.

Stokes, 26, was shot to death Friday by three men in the parking lot of the South Side motel where he lived, police said.

Inspirations and Other Outrages

Evidence of Fowl Play

The stunt that brought Clint Murchison his first, and most, national notoriety as a caperist, the one that may have launched him into major-league mischief as a hobby, the one that caused the most hard feelings on one side and the biggest guffaws on the other, the one he personally was most unexpansive about, was the one that didn't quite happen. It was the Chicken Deal.

It happened at the old D.C. Stadium in Washington during the Christmas season of 1961, the Cowboys' second season in the NFL. It also happened because it was the Christmas season.

It made *Life* magazine, which was writing in 1966 about "the good old days" of the Cowboys' early years. "Clint discovered," wrote John R. McDermott in the magazine's issue of Dec. 16, 1966, "that the Redskin management, which took pride in its halftime shows, had planned a Christmas motif for the Redskins-Cowboys intermission: Santa Claus would appear on a sled drawn by a team of Alaskan huskies. The night before the game Murchison and his pals seeded the entire field with cracked corn and somehow cached 200 chickens, flown in from Texas, under the stadium. According to Clint's gleeful concept, chickens would attack chicken feed and dogs would attack chickens as the band played "Jingle Bells." The plot was foiled at the last minute by alert stadium guards."

Modern historians agree that *Life* correctly described the scenario, but neglected two relevant points: (1) The lingering tension between Redskins owner George Preston Marshall and Clint over the 1959 kidnapping of the Redskins' Fight Song; and (2) Clint's crony and Centex partner Bob Thompson wasn't given nearly enough credit for his input into the scheme.

Washington Daily News sports columnist Morrie Siegel was able to fill out some details of the plot in the edition of the Monday following the game:

> It started out as small talk among a group of Texans who winged up to see the final hassle of the season. By midafternon Saturday the Texas contingent had employed the services of a local connection who made arrangements for the clambake. This included purchasing 10 coops of chickens to be secreted, the best way possible, into the stadium.

Classic Clint

It also included a lick of intramural sabotage. Somebody on the stadium crew, our operatives report, had been gotten to and had spread the field from goal post to goal post with chicken feed. The timing was to have coincided with the arrival on the field of Santa Claus.

Shortly before blastoff, general manager (Dick) McCann got wind of the plot. McCann tried a diplomatic approach. The Texas delegation couldn't be convinced that there might be some in the stadium, notably George Marshall, who likes his chicken only one way—in the pot at Duke Zeibert's—who might not think it funny.

That's when McCann called in the gendarmes, who arrested the chickens while they were cooped up in the dugout awaiting their release. It was fortunate the plot was killed. Santa arrived in a sled pulled by nine thoroughbred Alaskan Huskies. Though outnumbered by the chickens 200-9, the dogs had to be made the favorites . . .

There was an internal document from the general manager, McCann, intended for owner Marshall. Even for a poultry topic, it is a model of the investigative procedural report:

MEMORANDUM ON CHICKEN INCIDENT AT COWBOYS GAME ON DEC. 17

The crates of chickens (4 or 5) were brought to the Stadium in a truck that followed the Cowboys' players' bus.

The crates were carried in by two boys who were wearing Field Tags that had been issued to the Cowboys' publicity director.

The two boys said to the gateman that the chickens were to be used at the half.

While arrangements were being made to remove the chickens, Bob Thompson emerged from the runway off the Cowboys' dressing room and asked (Irv) Davidson, "What's with the chickens?" Davidson complained that "These so-and-so's—this McCann—won't let us use them." Thompson tried to protest, but then desisted.

Jim Silman, TV producer, said that the presence of the chickens was known to Davey O'Brien and Tom Harmon (network broadcasters).

The plan was to release the chickens just at halftime.

I am enclosing a copy of Morrie Siegel's column from Monday's *Washington Daily News*.

RICHARD P. McCANN

General Manager

Inspirations and Other Outrages

In the nation's capital the great Chicken Probe continued. On December 19, the NFL's new commissioner Pete Rozelle was sent a packet from George Preston Marshall.

> December 19, 1961
>
> Dear Pete:
>
> The enclosed tickets were picked up in the hands of two bellhops from the Sheraton Carlton Hotel. These two boys were hired to handle this chicken deal and somehow got these passes through the Dallas team.
>
> Enclosed you will find copy of Siegel's article yesterday. Siegel had information on Saturday this was going to be done.
>
> The visiting box, as you know, is next to mine, and I must say I have never seen more booze passed around than I saw personally in this box.
>
> Thompson is a very wild and desperate man. What he would do, there is nothing I would put past him in connection with this sort of thing. Saturday night at their party at which there must have been 300 people at the Sheraton Carlton he fired a gun several times. A few weeks ago he thought I was at Duke's and he came into the restaurant with a horse.
>
> I am one who likes fun as well as anyone else, but where it involves the National Football League this kind of thing is out of line.
>
> McCann did a great job of breaking it up and he has had two threatening anonymous calls as of yesterday.
>
> I am afraid that serious repercussions could develop in the future. Both Bedford and Clint should realize how important this is. I don't know of anyone that can stop it but you. Thank God it was blocked here.
>
> Best,
>
> GEORGE PRESTON MARSHALL
>
> 3 Encl:
>
> 1. 2 Field passes—Game 12/17
> 2. Report from R. P. McCann
> 3. Morris Siegel's Column

Classic Clint

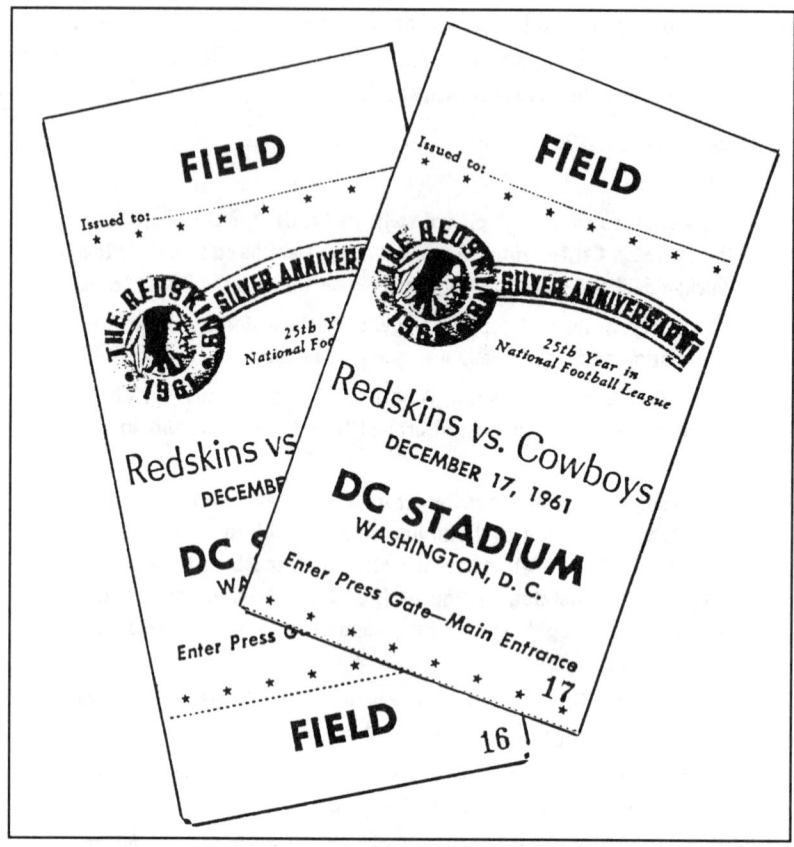

Redskin security guards seized these field passes carried by Clint's co-conspirators in the Chicken caper. Well, conspirators might be too strong a word. They were hotel bellhops hired to carry the crates of chickens inside the stadium. —photocopy courtesy of Pete Rozelle

The next day, Dec. 20, there was another packet addressed to Rozelle.

Dear Pete:

. . . I am sending you a picture which we were quite fortunately able to get of the removal of the chickens, and the arrow points to Mr. Thompson, of the Dallas Cowboys, watching the operation.

I am glad to send you this, in case Dallas states this man had nothing to do with it.

Best,

GEORGE PRESTON MARSHALL

Inspirations and Other Outrages

The situation presented an interesting problem to Rozelle, who was still new to the job and must have known that millions of Americans were wondering just what it is an NFL Commissioner *does*. Apparently he did nothing for a while on the "chicken deal," because *Life* magazine's article from five years later picked up the thread of the story:

"But for the next several weeks—though he changed his private number four times—Marshall heard clucking noises at the other end nearly every time he picked up the phone. He finally wrote an outraged letter to the league commissioner asking that Murchison be ordered to cease and desist, and this seemed to squelch Marshall's well-heeled tormentor. But Clint was only biding his time. When the Cowboys came to Washington the following fall, he hired a man dressed as a huge chicken to cavort on the field just before game time. It was a well-thought-out gesture, but poorly executed. 'Damn fool came running out right in the middle of *The Star-Spangled Banner*,' mutters a Cowboy official in disgust."

Eight years after the Chicken incident, there was an exchange of letters between Clint and George Preston Marshall's successor as owner of the Washington Redskins, Edward Bennett Williams, who had hired Vince Lombardi as the new head coach and general manager of the team.

>February 19, 1969
>
>Mr. Edward Bennett Williams
>1000 Hill Building
>839 17th Street, N.W.
>Washington, D.C.
>
>Dear Ed:
>
>What I want to know is, in the future will you or Vince be in charge of the arrangements for your halftime shows?
>
>Sincerely,
>CLINT

Classic Clint

**Edward Bennett Williams
1000 Hill Building
Washington 6, D.C.**

February 21, 1969

Dear Clint:

V I N C E.

But part of his contract is that he will follow the previous administration's policy on chickens.

Sincerely,

ED

With Green Bay Packer legend Vince Lombardi at an NFL meeting in Miami, 1964. —photo courtesy of Dallas Cowboys Newsletter

Chapter Ten
Letters from the Stomach

"If we let the Yankees get away claiming the invention of the hamburger, they'll be going after chili next."

He operated in worldly circles that might consider the term Texas cuisine an oxymoron, but Clint's favorite food was the sovereign menu of Texas—the chuck wagon trinity of burgers, barbecue, and chili. He launched some historical detective work and believed he had found the origin not only of the hamburger, but of french fries. He started several food businesses, all relating to his favorites. Exasperated by "trying to teach New York Italians how to cook chili," he finally began exporting his own version from his "Cowboy Kitchen" commissary in Dallas to his own restaurant in midtown Manhattan, which he considered a cultural wasteland when it came to chili, Tex-Mex, and barbecue cooking. On a night out during an NFL owners' meeting in North Miami Beach, he discovered a modest, 90-seat spot that served baby-back ribs along with unique onion rings packed in compressed loaves. With Clint's financial backing and marketing resources, the Tony Roma's chain would grow to more than 140 units by 1991.

For a man who could be so picky on points ranging from his own impeccable wardrobe and precise crewcut to the clinical ambience of Texas Stadium, he loved to eat in some strange places, his sons say.

The sons' puzzlement over the dad's idea of a good burger was probably generational. The great burgers Clint remembered from his youth were served up off spattering griddles onto warm, butter-scorched buns with chopped fresh trimmings and tomatoes that hadn't come from Sinaloa. By the eighties, burgers had become something else, with arugula and radicchio garnish.

"He enjoyed eating at joints," says Burk Murchison. "He called them hamburger stands and barbecue places; I called 'em joints. There was a quote he used either from Pop (Clint Sr.) or my grandfather on my mother's side: 'You can't eat atmosphere.' Dad was of the same school."

For a long time Clint's favorite joint was the little barbecue stand in the basement arcade of the Statler Hilton. Called the Saddle and Spur, it was wedged between a beauty salon, a drug store, and a shoe-repair shop. It was a one-man operation; Dudley Neal leased the space from the hotel, serving hickory smoked beef brisket, sliced or chopped, and piled on the undersized buns common to Texas barbecue spots. Customers sat on wooden chairs designed like school desks and were expected to deposit their own wrappers, drink cans, and milk cartons in the trash can on the way out. "Dad wanted to back Neal in a whole chain, but he said he was too busy running the one he had," Burk said.

"For a while his favorite burger spot was a drive-in complete with carhops that served oldtimey burgers, fries, and shakes. Once he told me he had really enjoyed going there until the day he saw a cockroach chasing the carhop around the parking lot and back inside.

"Later, his favorite was Club Schmitz, a place he'd stumbled across on the way to Love Field once. Dad was a real stickler when it came to the way he liked his burgers, and he really liked theirs. They were fairly inedible, from my standpoint. He liked his patties thin and flat. He kind of liked 'em greasy, so he was really in luck at Club Schmitz."

Says Robert Murchison: "I've seen him eat some real sliders."

Clint's days at the remarkable Club Schmitz, in his fading days with his favorite friends, are described in a later chapter. Clint would speak of it affectionately as the only place he'd seen where the flies fought to get *out* instead of in. High praise in the ground rules of his perverse humor.

Letters from the Stomach

"Hamburgers were his favorite thing for fixing at home," Burk says. "Away from home, he'd usually have them with mustard, lettuce, tomatoes, and pickles. But the only way he'd have them at home was with a glob of Miracle Whip, to which he'd add sweet-pickle relish. He put the same stuff on his barbecue sandwiches at home. Two of his favorite snacks were catsup on crackers, and white bread-and-catsup sandwiches." Anyone born after World War II finds it hard to understand, much less appreciate, the tolerance for a catsup sandwich. But during the war years, catsup was one of the few foods not on the wartime rationing list. Clint wasn't the only American who developed a fondness for the catsup sandwich.

Clint had firm opinions about the ways other people served food:

On Astrodome hot dogs (a letter to Houston Oiler owner Bud Adams, August 27, 1971, after attending the Cowboys-Oilers pre-season game).

> Bud,
> Last night I had a hot dog at the Astrodome. Some comments:
> 1. It was difficult for me to determine the quality of the bun because it was cold, below room temperature. A possible explanation for this was that
> 2. The frankfurter had apparently been recently removed from the refrigerator, warmed perhaps in the process of passing through the vendor's hands. My impression was that the meat, if heated, would not have been of satisfactory quality.
> 3. The mustard was probably all right, since it is difficult to louse up mustard. But, again, its exact taste was camouflaged by
> 4. The relish, which was a bland, neither sweet nor sour, variety which I have found occasionally in second-rate New York delicatessens.
>
> It appeared that this entire exercise constituted an effort to hold down sales of the product. The opinion of those with me, all of whom seemed capable of paying the $7 admission fee to the stadium, was that a more satisfactory procedure for limiting sales would have been to increase the price of the product by, say, 10 cents and serve a hot, tasty wiener, rather than that gooey, inedible mess.
> CLINT.

Classic Clint

Upon the defeat of his Dallas Cowboy Restaurant chili team at the Terlingua World Championship Cookoff, a letter of protest to Dallas columnist and Terlingua cookoff cofounder Frank X. Tolbert:

> November 8, 1971
>
> Mr. Frank Tolbert
> The Dallas Morning News
> Dallas, Texas
>
> Dear Frank:
>
> I was considering filing a protest of the judges' decision at the Terlingua cookoff, since it is quite obvious to me and all of the Dallas Cowboy Restaurant personnel that the judges were under the influence of something other than chili peppers. However, I have just learned that C. V. Wood, the so-called Super Bowl chili champion, was using a highly illegal green chili. Therefore, I conclude that George Wright, representing the State of New York and the Dallas Cowboy Restaurant therein, won by default.
>
> We are now prepared to defend our championship against any and all comers, even if necessary from atop the London Bridge, from whence, I might add, Mr. Wood should jump, green chili and all.
>
> cc: C.V. Wood, Chili Faker

(Ed. Note: C.V. Wood, a Californian who later wrested a version of the chili cookoff away for a California site, was the promoter who bought, dismantled, and shipped the London Bridge, block by block, to a resort site at Lake Havasu City, Arizona.)

In September 1984, Clint noticed an article in the *Dallas News* about the origin and success of the Dallas-based Wyatt's Cafeteria chain. At the time there were 118 of the cafeterias in nine states, serving 45 million meals a year. The article had concluded:

> The chain was started in 1945 with a cafeteria on Abrams Road in the Lakewood area of Dallas.

Clint felt compelled to write the Wyatt's executive who had been quoted throughout the article.

Letters from the Stomach

September 6, 1984
Mr. H. Lynn Packer
Wyatt Cafeterias Inc.
10726 Plano Road
Dallas, TX 75238

Dear Mr. Packer:

The first official Wyatt's Cafeteria may have been opened in Lakewood in 1945, but I expect Earle (Wyatt, the founder) got the idea for it in 1932 when he put a hot plate at the end of the butcher's counter in the store on Preston Road, a hamburger stand ("Eadie's Famous") south of Lovers Lane. He (or the butcher) served full meals, but I generally opted for the barbecue sandwich and a bottle of milk.

Clint would have been about nine at the time. His recollection is of interest to anyone who knows that present part of the Dallas area, Preston Road near Lovers Lane, as one of its toniest commercial sections.

Clint had kept a permanent residence in New York City for years, and in 1969 he finally got tired of despairing over the availability in the Big Apple of chili, barbecue, and Texas burgers. The restaurant was on East 49th Street and featured one of Manhattan's traditional restaurant punctuations, a curbside awning. The awning was emblazoned with the Dallas Cowboy helmet and logo.

Once, Lamar Hunt passed on to Clint an irate letter from some customer at The Dallas Cowboy, who may have suffered scorched tastebuds from his bowl of Cowboy chili. He was not the first to confuse the two rich Dallasites who both had NFL football teams.

October 17, 1972
Lamar,
Didn't I tell you? Whenever someone comes into my New York restaurant and complains, I have instructed the maitre d' to tell him that you are the owner.
This way, I avoid a lot of crank letters.
CLINT.

Classic Clint

The Dallas Cowboy Restaurant got so much publicity that it came to the attention of the NFL copyright guardians. Clint one day received a document that had been forwarded to his office by Tex Schramm at the Cowboys office:

UNANIMOUS RESOLUTION OF EXECUTIVE COMMITTEE OF NFL PROPERTIES

Whereas there is a restaurant on East 49th Street in New York, New York, which is owned by Clint Murchison, Jr., and which has been heretofore operated publicly under the name "The Dallas Cowboy"

And whereas said restaurant has been publicly operated by using and employing the Dallas Cowboy club name and football helmet as part of the publicity and/or advertising of the restaurant

And whereas this committee has been entrusted with the obligation of establishing and implementing policies and guidelines established by the Board of Directors of NFL Properties in respect to the use of club helmets, logos, emblem colors and designs in connection with any commercial products and services

And whereas this committee has been instructed that no NFL club owner may use any club name, emblem, helmet, logo or colors in connection with any commercial product or service without the consent of the Board of Directors of NFLP

Now therefore it is hereby resolved that

The restaurant at 49th Street, New York, New York, operated under the name "The Dallas Cowboy" must discontinue immediately the use of the expression "Dallas Cowboy" as the restaurant name and in any advertising or promotion thereof; further no further use can be made therein of the helmet of the Dallas Cowboys in association with the name of any advertising and promotion thereof; nothing herein contained shall prevent the use of the single name "Dallas" or the single word "Cowboys" in the advertising or promotion thereof, but no use can be made of the two words Dallas or Cowboys jointly or in any combination.

The resolution was signed by the clubowner-members of the committee, Lou Spadia of the 49ers, Dan Rooney of the Steelers, and Bill Sullivan of the Patriots.

Clint replied with a classic three-way one-liner:

> July 12, 1973
>
> Mr. Lou Spadia
> Mr. Dan Rooney
> Mr. Bill Sullivan
>
> Gentlemen:
>
> Gee, fellows, it's only a game!
>
> Sincerely,
>
> CLINT

He renamed it The Cowboy. Without the helmet.

He had the native Texan's allegiance to chili, or at least to the *idea* of chili and its cook-off culture of culinary anarchy, but his closest friends agree that Clint's favorite lunch was a barbecue beef sandwich and a carton of milk (after they stopped putting milk in little bottles, as it had been in 1932). And after a lifetime of barbecue sandwiches, a man gets to know his way around a bottle of Tabasco Sauce. In 1984 he was noticing something different about his Tabasco, whose premium version is made only by the McIlhenny Company. He took his concern straight to the top.

> May 10, 1984
>
> Mr. Walter S. McIlhenny
> McIlhenny Company
> Avery Island, Louisiana 70513
>
> Dear Walter:
>
> This letter is written to make a suggestion which I hope will be helpful.
>
> I noticed for the last several months it has been very difficult to start the flow of Tabasco from a standard size bottle. Like a bottle of catsup, it is very difficult to get a drop of sauce until the neck is empty. Perhaps the bottle should only be filled to that point; this would make the first drop easier to obtain and save you some Tabasco, too.

Clint's son Robert was away at Yale in 1974. That year he sent Clint an article from *The New York Times* reporting the imminent closing of a New Haven landmark, a hamburger hangout called Louis Lunch.

The *Times* article characterized the spot as "The birthplace of the American hamburger . . . in 1900." The site was in danger of being razed to make way for a medical complex, the story said.

> January 29. 1974
>
> Dear Robert,
>
> I recall years ago my Dad telling me of a conversation he had had with his father concerning sandwiches.
>
> It seems that before Dad was born (in 1895) his father regularly ate a wonderful sandwich prepared by an old man named Dave who served from behind the counter at Stirman's Drugstore in Athens. The sandwich consisted of a flat patty of ground round served between two thick slices of monkey bread, each browned on the outside (the first bun?). For flavor, he added a mixture of ground mustard seeds in mayonnaise, and sliced cucumber pickles. As a side order, you could get fried potatoes with thick tomato sauce all over them, a concoction invented by a fellow from Paris, Texas.
>
> The sandwiches were so good that the local Chamber of Commerce got together a kitty and sent Dave to the St. Louis World's Fair in 1904 to advertise their city. A fancy dan reporter from the old New York *Tribune* interviewed Dave (who'd probably never heard of France), who in answer to a query replied that the potatoes came "from Paris." About two weeks later, the *Tribune* reported that hamburgers had been invented at the St. Louis Fair, and that they were best served with "French fried potatoes."
>
> Louis Lunch is a fraud, and the quicker they build that medical complex, the better.
>
> Love,
>
> Dad
>
> cc: Mr. Ray Kroc, President
>   McDonald's Corporation

Clint passed a copy of his letter to Robert on to Frank X. Tolbert, the Dallas columnist:

> Frank:
> It may be somewhat fanciful, but let's face it; if we let the Yankees get away claiming the invention of hamburgers, they'll be going after chili next.
> C.

Tolbert was the cofounder of the Terlingua chili cookoff and the crusading patron of the Farkleberry, an arboreal object that grew on a tree indigenous to parts of East Texas. He promoted a drink called the Farkletini, a martini with a Farkleberry instead of an olive. Tolbert traveled the state in search of engaging bits of lore exactly like the hamburger legend.

Tolbert was delighted when he read on in the *New York Times* story, which in its meticulous drive for journalistic fairness and accuracy had contacted McDonald's for its view of the hamburger's origin.

The *Times* had written, "A serious challenge to the title is a theory supported by the McDonald's Corporation, the giant nationwide hamburger chain. Historians at McDonald's Hamburger University have researched the problem and claim the inventor was an unknown food vendor at the St. Louis Fair of 1904."

To an investigative folklorist like Tolbert, that paragraph must have been the hamburger-origin-quest version of a smoking gun.

Now Tolbert took over the story: "In Athens last week, I talked with a number of Clint Murchison, Sr.'s friends, including Bill Perryman. Bill was the only one who had heard Clint Sr. tell of the first hamburgers being composed at the Athens drug store in the late 1880s or early 1890s. And so far I've had no luck trying to find out the full name of Mysterious Dave the inventor . . ."

Tolbert spent the ensuing weeks researching the mystery of Dave, eventually coming up with some oldtimers in the area who remembered him as Fletcher Davis, aka Old Dave, aka Uncle Fletch.

Clint was doing research, too, and learned that in his spare time from inventing the hamburger, Fletcher Davis also worked as a road striper: a man who painted center stripes on roads before there were

Classic Clint

machines that did it. "He single-handedly painted the center stripe on the road from Athens to Murchison," Clint wrote Tolbert. "Were these the first road stripes in the world?"

Clint wrote Tolbert again:

> September 1, 1976
>
> Dear Frank:
>
> In going through some old family records, I came across a souvenir brochure of the 1904 St. Louis World's Fair, a photograph from which I am enclosing. There was a very faint arrow (which I have overlined) on the photograph pointing to what was described on the reverse side of the page as indicating the location of Old Dave's (Uncle Fletch's) original hamburger stand.
>
> I am forwarding a copy of this to Ray Kroc, chairman of McDonald's, so that the archives of the College of Hamburgers will be up to date; I think that with this and with the contents of your last hamburger column, the authentic recognition of the creator of this great invention should be firmly established and that the controversy, if there really was one, can be laid finally to rest.

A long search of the archives yielded this view of the St. Louis World's Fair of 1904, with Clint's hand-printed legend of where Uncle Fletch Davis' hamburger concession stood on the midway. —photo courtesy of Frank X. Tolbert Family

In March of 1984 the first Fletch Davis Memorial World Hamburger Cookoff was held in Athens, where a historical plaque on the town square honoring Fletcher Davis had been unveiled by a group headed by Clint. Athens, the ancestral Murchison hometown, was happy to host the cookoff, even though it was already the home of the Black-Eyed Pea Jamboree and the Old Fiddlers' Reunion event.

The winner of that first cookoff was a truck driver who said he'd eaten so many bad hamburgers on the road, he knew what a good one should taste like. His recipe called for bacon grease folded into the meat pattie.

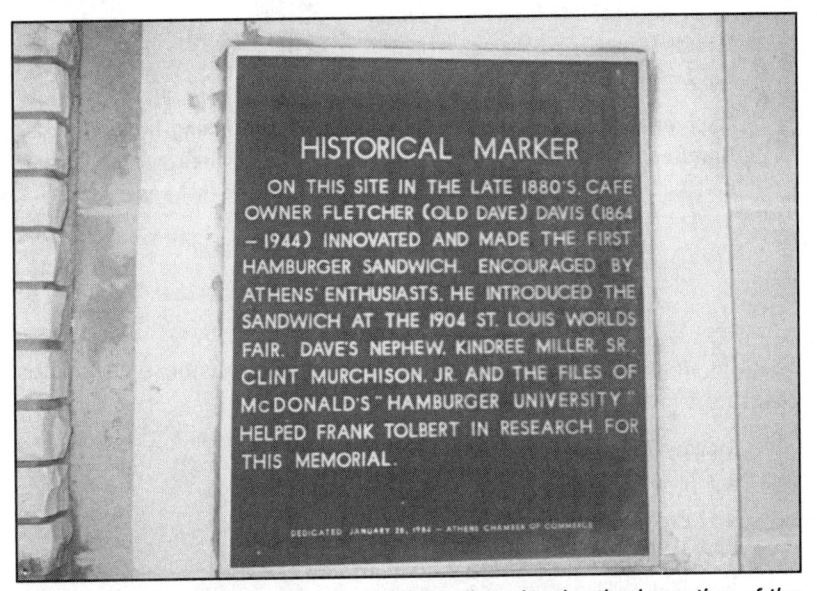

The plaque commemorating what Clint believed to be the invention of the hamburger is on the town square in Athens, Texas.

New Haven, Connecticut, did not go gentle into obscurity as the non-home of the hamburger. It still insists that Louis' Lunch was first. It has a historical plaque in honor of the first hamburger, too—at 261 Crown Street, some blocks from the site of the original luncheonette, torn down to make room for the medical complex.

Classic Clint

One of the reasons Clint avoided the social circuit of dinner parties was the sure knowledge that he would be encountering something like *Coquilles St. Jacques* instead of the beloved burgers, chili, or barbecue. Once he was confronted with the peril of being served this kind of frou-frou cuisine in his own home. A friend had queried him whether he would be interested in hiring a European-trained chef, who was currently in Dallas, at liberty and available.

> **November 12, 1963**
>
> Mr. S. J. Hay
> Chairman of the Board
> Great National Life Insurance Company
> Dallas, Texas
>
> Dear S. J.:
>
> I appreciate your sending me the information concerning the chef. However, I am going to turn it down since the children and I eat nothing but hamburgers. Please do not reveal to Jane that I have not availed myself of this opportunity.

For the man who had everything, friends and business associates resorted to food and drink novelties.

> **January 15, 1963**
>
> Mr. H. W. B. White
> 212 Esplanade Building
> International Market Place
> Honolulu, Hawaii
>
> Dear Hod:
>
> Thank you for the electric pepper shaker. I am certainly glad that you recognize that I have been working much too hard this past year, and that every little energy-saving aid helps.

His friend Phil Schepps was a Dallas liquor distributor. Upon the introduction of a new brand of Scotch whisky called 100 Pipers, Schepps sent a trial bottle to Clint.

September 13, 1965

Dear Phil:

I have finished the bottle of Scotch which you were kind enough to send, and as soon as my head clears I will give you a complete report on it. I do remember that the first couple of jiggers was great.

He appreciated the homemade stuff the most, even when it came at a traumatic time, like Kathleen Bradshaw's gift on his 53rd birthday:

September 20, 1976

Dear Kathleen:

Thank you for the bread and butter pickles, and the bread to go with them; I was particularly surprised, since I don't have birthdays any more.

But the best homemade stuff of all was his own peach ice cream creation, which he enjoyed at all times of the year, having filled the freezer with the peaches from each summer's crop. He disclosed the recipe in letters he sent to his grandchildren in 1982. The letters were accompanied by ice cream machines.

September 20, 1982

I have been worried about you boys not getting enough peach ice cream, so I hope that this machine and this recipe will remedy the situation.

PEACH ICE CREAM

1 can Eagle Brand milk
1 to 2 cups sugar (to taste)   Try first recipe with 1 cup of sugar.
                Also, peaches' sweetness will make a difference
8 eggs beaten
2 tsp. vanilla
2 cups whole milk
1 quart peaches, peeled and pureed in blender
1 pint Half and Half
1/2 pint whipping cream

Classic Clint

> (1) Mix condensed milk, 8 eggs, sugar, milk and beat. Put on low fire and cook until custard coats the spoon. Add vanilla. Let mixture cool.
>
> (2) Mix pureed peaches and the Half and Half together
>
> (3) Add two above mixtures together. Add whipping cream.
>
> (4) Freeze in ice cream freezer for about 20 minutes
>
> (5) HAVE AT IT!
>
> p.s. After freezing, the ice cream can be kept in the refrigerator freezer, but before serving, whip it in a Waring Blender until soft; it actually tastes better about two days later rather than when just frozen.

(Later, as his illness advanced and sugar was eliminated from his diet, he claimed that he had a sucrose version that was indistinguishable from the original. But, regrettably or not, no Lite version of Clint's Peach Ice Cream recipe exists.)

"When he got it in his mind he wanted some barbecue, there wasn't much that could stop him from going to get it," Bob Foley said. "This seemed to happen quite a lot right after we'd had a couple of pops in a bar after work. He'd get to thinking about barbecue, and we'd drive out to this kind of cruddy-looking barbecue joint in East Dallas.

"This particular day, I had traded with (Dallas criminal lawyer) Frank Wright for an old Volkswagen he'd taken in from some burglar or something for his fee. I had left my car at home, and I was going to take this one over and give it to my kid so I wouldn't have to drive him to high school every day.

"When Clint said 'Barbecue,' I said, 'Clint, I don't have any car today to drive out there.' And he didn't have a car that day. I said, 'All I've got is that old Volkswagen out there at the curb with a damn manual gear shift. And I've never driven one of those little things.'

"He said, 'Oh, we can handle that!.'

"So we go out there to the curb, and of course it's also in the middle of a gigantic thunder and lightning storm and the sky's real dark. He's sittin' in that little car, peerin' around and saying, 'Now, when I say clutch, you push that thing in, and I'll handle the gears.' Off we jumped. We went all the way out to that place in a driving rainstorm, driving the car that way, just to get him some barbecue."

Neither snow nor Scotch nor Volkswagen clutches kept Clint from visiting Jack Walton's Barbecue, a favorite joint. —photo courtesy of John Sears

"I think Dad's alltime favorite barbecue place was the old original Jack Walton's on Haskell," Burk Murchison says. "At one time, back in the forties and fifties, it had been part of a thriving chain. One by one they'd closed, and this remaining one, the original, had been bought by a Greek couple, Nick and Dena Papanikolaou. Dad just loved it. When he became ill, one of the ways his friends would be with him would be to take him out to lunch, and it was nearly always either Walton's or Club Schmitz. With Walton's in the early eighties, he even went so far as to try to buy it and relocate it out to one of the hot restaurant districts in far north Dallas, around Beltline and Midway. He'd also wanted to involve Dudley Neal in it, the man who had operated the other barbecue place he liked, the Saddle and Spur at the Statler Hilton. He was thrilled about starting up another barbecue place, but because of his failing health and the financial situation, they never did it.

"At that time I was trying to help him out on it, do some coordination and whatever he needed. He'd always insisted that Walton's barbecue tasted notably different, superior, and his theory as to why it was great was because of the custom wood they were using to smoke the briskets. He said the wood gave the meat a unique taste. I went over to check it out one day, walked back through the kitchen with an eye for this magical wood pile. They weren't smoking anything at the time, but over in the corner of the room they had a burnt-out grate over a fire that was made from what looked like pieces of broken up shipping pallets. It looked like scrap wood. And this was the cooking secret that made it so great? I didn't really have the heart to tell Dad that the secret was definately not the wood."

Another part of the Murchison food business that did become a reality was Tolbert's Chili Parlor, as a result of Clint's fondness for the Texas chili culture and his friendship with its chief guru, Frank Tolbert. In 1984 Clint's sons Burk and Robert reached an agreement with Tolbert to build and operate an intended chain of the chili parlors that had begun as a carefully dilapidated joint on Main Street near the Dallas County Courthouse.

Chapter Eleven
Miscellaneous Mischief

Dear Don:
Help!
Sincerely,
CLINT MURCHISON, JR.

With Reference to References

Given his pervasive presence in the business and financial world, his clout as owner of the Cowboys and more than 200 companies, his many board and advisory memberships, and his willingness to help a friend, a reference from Clint Murchison, Jr., was a golden credential.

His letters of reference, like his letters on any other subject, had that irrepressible urge to joke. As his boyhood friend Kenneth Swanson perceived, Clint was like his father in that he rarely troubled to check the background of a potential associate. He may not have taken the idea of references that seriously.

> Dear Fred:
> ... It happens that a young man (blond and rather tall) applied for a job with one of our companies and has given your name as a reference. He indicates that he expects the latter to be quite favorable, since he is, in fact, your illegimate son. In order to save you time, just check one of the blanks below and ask your secretary to return this note.
> _____ Chip off the old block.
> _____ Bad seed.

Classic Clint

Mr. Ward Skinner
Dallas, Texas

Dear Ward:

In the Marine Corps I was always taught that it wasn't necessary to have any character to join the Army. However, I am happy to be used as a reference for you in that regard.

Mr. Berry R. Cox
Dallas, Texas

Dear Berry:

I am happy to be a reference for you. Fortunately, I am skilled at avoiding the truth.

Clint was a director of Pepperdine University, a college near Los Angeles with limited enrollment and highly sought-after admissions. An employee of Clint's Tecon Realty Corporation in Hawaii had a son who was anxious to attend Pepperdine, and who happened to have had his picture made with Tom Landry on one of Landry's trips to Hawaii for the Pro Bowl. The father had enclosed the photo in his letter to Clint's office.

February 29, 1980
Mr. C. Doug Plank
Malibu, California

Dear Mr. Plank:

I want to strongly recommend as a candidate for admission to Pepperdine this Fall, Raymond Heitzman, who is the son of an employee of mine in Honolulu. I think you will find him to be a qualified academician and an exemplary citizen. The enclosed photograph of Raymond and Tom Landry was taken about two months ago. Landry is the one with no hair.

Hard-Cell Promotion

It was a common event for his office to receive requests for Cowboys T-shirts, jerseys, decals, cups, caps, and pictures. Some of the requests were less common than others:

> Oct. 13, 1982
>
> Clint W. Murchison, Jr.
> Dallas Cowboys
> 6116 N. Central Expressway
> Dallas, TX 75206
>
> Dear Mr. Murchison:
>
> I'm writing to you in regards to one of our favorite subjects, 'The Dallas Cowboys.' Being from Dallas, I was hoping to attend the games this season; however, due to the football strike and the fact that I'm doing many years in the Arizona State Prison, I probably will not attend for a while.
>
> I would like to ask you one favor. The biggest part of our day is spent watching sports my favorite is football. Since I can't attend, I was hoping you would send me one official Dallas Football Jersey in ex large. I realize that your not in business to give things away, but if you would make this one exception and send one jersey and any info on the team I would be very greatful.
>
> Thank you,
>
> RON STACEY
>
> Arizona State Prison
> Florence, Arizona
>
> PS I promise not to tell the fellows here where I received it. Thanks.

Clint sent the jersey and a note to the fan:

> Dear Mr. Stacey:
>
> When you get this on, don't run out of there.

He also sent a copy of the prisoner's letter to Tex Schramm with an observation:

> Tex:
>
> It's too bad the strike is keeping this fan from seeing the games.

Classic Clint

Clint surrounded by his four eldest grandchildren George, Burk, David, and C. W. (from l. to r.). —photo courtesy of Jerry Hughes

Clint's Theory of Relativity

A letter from the same year, 1982, freezes a moment of the Clint the public never knew, the affectionately newsy grandfather writing with intelligence and respect to a homesick camper. The letter was to C. W. Murchison IV, then 8, who was away at the Cimarroncita Ranch Camp for Boys in Ute Park, New Mexico:

> June 28, 1982
>
> Dear C. W.:
>
> Seeing all those kids in the water on Saturday at Burkito's birthday party made me think of you and that cold mountain water in New Mexico. The first time I swam in a mountain stream was in New Mexico in 1932 when I was eight years old (note the similarities). I remember it was real cold but we had a lot of fun. We would stay in the water as long as we could and then get out and lie down on a rock in the sun and bake like a lizard.

Another thing we used to do was find a lot of arrow heads which I suppose you are doing now. If you can, bring me back one and I will put it in my collection, which includes one found in an excavation in downtown Dallas.

I don't know whether George (C. W.'s younger brother) had developed his fancy basketball dribble before you left, but he is really hot; he can dribble the ball under his leg and behind his back. However, I expect that he is not tall enough to play for the Mavericks.

Don't have so much fun out there that you won't want to come home, because we all miss you. I will see you soon.

With love,

Frigid mountain streams were one thing, but it can get really uncomfortable, and expensive, when chilly weather comes to those Manhattan apartments.

September 18, 1968

Mr. Don Bokmaier
Building Superintendent
445 Park Avenue
New York, New York

Dear Mr. Bokmaier:

Since it is getting near steam time again, I think we had better straighten out the meter problem with respect to the twenty-second floor. The attached bill copy represents the unpaid balance of the charges since Dec. 20, 1967. You will note that on last March 18, I paid $1,000 on the account. You will note also that the charges for the previous year occupancy averaged approximately $1,000 per year. I will be in the apartment on September 27.

Very truly yours,
CLINT MURCHISON, JR.

Six weeks passed.

> October 30, 1968
>
> Mr. Don Bokmaier
> Building Superintendent
> 445 Park Avenue
> New York, New York   Re: Consolidated Edison
>
> Dear Don:
>
> Help!
>
> Sincerely,
>
> CLINT MURCHISON, JR.

> May 21, 1976
>
> Mr. Bruce Jacobi
> Cortland Corporation
> 711 Fifth Avenue
> New York, New York
>
> Dear Bruce:
>
> ... Enclosed are the Con-Ed bills for the past five years. Note that by applying the Sulzberger-Rolfe figure of $253.67 to the April, 1976 Con-Ed Bill of $2,489.57, my total utility cost for the month of April is in excess of $2,700, as compared to approximately $400 for the month of April, 1971.
>
> I know Con-Ed wants to complete that new generating plant on the Hudson, but I think it is unfair for them to insist that I shoulder its total cost.
>
> Sincerely,
>
> CLINT

By 1981 the financial world had been riveted first by the efforts of the Dallas Hunt Brothers, Bunker and Herbert, to corner the silver market, and then stunned by the subsequent collapse.

Clint had discovered a faded page from his grandfather T. F. Murchison's ledger diary of the First National Bank of Athens, Texas, dated Nov. 13, 1894. In a shaky Spencerian script it read:

Miscellaneous Mischief

> *An impartial historian ten years from now will say that the Silver Craze wrecked this country commercially and financially in 1893 and wrecked the Democratic Party in 1894. —T. F. Murchison.*

Clint sent it on to Bunker Hunt on January 22, 1981.

> Dear Bunker:
>
> This note was written by my grandfather the year before my father was born. Apparently things haven't changed much since then.
>
> C.

By early January of 1976 the Cowboys were on the way to the first of two Super Bowl meetings with the Pittsburgh Steelers. A Murchison friend in Kuwait, banker Ali Al-Bader, had promised to send Clint and Anne a package containing some sure-fire Kuwaiti good luck totems, called *sajat* and *daff*. Clint's secretary Ruth Woodard remembers them as being a collection of small tambourine-like objects.

On January 12, a discombobulated Ali Bader had written:

> Dear Clint:
>
> My secretary did it again, she sent the letter without the parcel. Now, this is the "Sajat" and the "Daff" that will carry Anne to the Superbowl!

By the time the packet arrived from Kuwait, the Steelers had beaten the Cowboys on Jan. 18, 21-17.

> January 27, 1976
>
> Mr. A.R. Al-Bader
> Kuwait Real Estate Bank
> P.O. Box 22822
> Kuwait
>
> Dear Ali:
>
> I am sorry the sajat and daff did not reach us in time for the Super Bowl. As a matter of fact, I am sorry about the sajat and daff period. I find it very difficult to rest with those damn things clanging all around the bedroom. Anne is determined to be completely prepared for our next party.
>
> I hope to see you soon in Kuwait.

Classic Clint

By early 1982 more of Clint's mail, and even his wisecracks, showed a preoccupation with health. He knew his was failing. He remembered a Maine banker's story of going swimming in the chilly waters off New England.

> March 26, 1982
>
> Mr. Paul G. Bailey
> Executive Vice President
> Midlantic National Bank
> Edison, New Jersey 08818
>
> Dear Paul:
>
> A friend of mine, Chandler Lindsley, is the granddaughter of Franklin Roosevelt. I asked her where her grandfather was swimming the afternoon of the day on which he was stricken with polio. She said he had swum in the Bay of Fundy (there being no pool at Campobello). She further confirmed the summertime temperature of the water as being, as you said, 50 or 55 degrees. What other wild habits do you people from Maine have for recreation?

Quiche Alert!

Aware of Clint's grim new interest in evolutionary research, and his fondness for bizarre mail, his friend Dr. Ken Altschuler of the University of Texas Health Science Center at Dallas sent him a copy of a painfully learned treatise in a technical journal, with the note:

> I thought you'd be interested in the attached. I've asterisked the most important lines, which you must memorize for later discussion. Of course, I understand it fully (?) . . .

The material was from somebody's monograph on Evolutionary Gradualism:

> At the levels of microevolution and speciation, the extreme saltationist claim that new species arise all at once, fully formed, by a fortunate macromutation would be anti-Darwinian, but no serious thinker now advances such a view . . . Legitimate claims range from the saltational origin of key features by developmental shifts of dissociable segments of ontogeny to the origin of reproductive isolation (speciation) by major and rapidly incorporated genetic changes that precede the acquisition of adaptive, phenotypic differences. Are such styles of evolution anti-Darwininan? What can one say except "yes and no" . . . Indeed, Eldredge and I originally

proposed punctuated equilibrium as the expected geological consequence of Mayr's Theory of Peripatetic Speciation . . .

April 17, 1982
Dear Ken:
I see that the author of the article from *Science* collaborated with Eldredge in proposing a "punctuated equilibrium as the expected geological consequence of Mayr's theory of peripatetic speciation."
No wonder that he answers key questions with "yes and no." I know Eldredge; he is a well-known quiche eater.

To make jokes about evolution and equilibrium was a stunning testament to his inner steeliness, and, at that point, perhaps to his optimism and indomitable confidence. It was the year of the onset of the illness that he referred to first as "The wobblies." It was a problem of equlibrium and of slurred speech. He had a joke for it, of course: he said it had started only after he had *stopped* drinking.

Much later, the sportswriters would identify it as ALS, amyotropic lateral sclerosis, suitably ironic for the sports page because it was better known as Lou Gehrig's Disease. Cosmically ironic, maybe, but incorrect. Clint would learn from neurologists that he had olivopontine cerebellar atrophy, even rarer, but just as relentless and with a special meanness.

Chapter Twelve
Public Wobblies, Private Strength

". . . He has very little of his motor functions remaining, but the twinkle is still in his eye."
—Anne Murchison

August 7, 1978
Henry W. Dodge Jr., M.D.
Los Angeles, California
Dear Bill:
I appreciate your advice on the micro-neurosurgery. I was probably looking for an excuse to delay the surgery for another year anyway.
Sincerely,
CLINT

Clint had consulted Dr. Dodge, an ear specialist, for some disturbing problems he had begun to have, involving popping noises and episodes of losing his balance. Periodic falls in the shower were the first symptoms. Then there was difficulty in walking. His secretary Ruth Woodard said he had complained of the sudden noises, describing them as, "It's like firecrackers going off in my head."

He had stopped drinking in 1976. Now, when he'd join friends for lunch at the Petroleum Club, others in the room would see him lurching to or from the table and think he was drunk. On a Cowboys road trip in 1982, he fell in a hotel bathroom and cracked two ribs.

He no longer drove; one night when Bob Foley had picked him up at the airport to drive him home, he turned to the stockbroker and said, "D-d-did you n-n-notice this didn't s-s-start getting bad until I *quit* drinking?"

"I would watch him walking down the hall of the office for the restroom," Ruth said. "He'd be touching the wall with his fingertips to keep his balance."

In 1983 Clint summoned Tex Schramm to his home to tell him that because of his health, he was going to sell the Cowboys. Schramm told author Jane Wolfe that Clint had begun by explaining that his neurological problems stemmed from a flaw in the vestigial part of his brain that controlled gait and equilibrium.

From early animals, that part had retained its role in humans even as the rest of the brain grew in size through evolution. It probably accounted for Clint's curiosity about the scientific articles on evolution he had asked Dr. Altschuler to send him.

His friends cherish the stories they witnessed of the steel of his spirit and his courage in laughing at the wobblies and the slurring of the speech in its early stages. But he was even braver than that.

He had been in his suite at Baylor Hospital in Dallas when George Owen came to visit him.

"It's bad," he told Owen.

"I asked him how bad," Owen recalled. "He said they'd told him it was eventually going to be terminal, and that he only had a few years. I said, '*How* few years?' And he just shrugged and said, 'Seven, four, five, ten; who knows.'"

The general belief after the Dallas tests was that Clint had a sclerosis ailment similar to Lou Gehrig's Disease, but the ultimate diagnosis came from Dr. Jerome Posner of Sloan-Kettering Institute in New York: olivopontine cerebellar atrophy, perhaps even rarer and meaner than the other. His mental faculties would remain undiminished; he would just be unable to say, or even write, what he was thinking.

Public Wobblies, Private Strength

His son Burk remembers, "By the time Elise and I were married, in 1982, Dad was using a cane." Even before that obvious sign of something amiss, word had leaked to the sports media. Blackie Sherrod wrote of hearing about it by accident from a sportswriting colleague who was trying to promote financial backing for a film.

"I called a contact in the NFL office to get Clint Murchison's number, and I told him what I wanted," the writer told Sherrod, "and the fellow said Murchison wouldn't be interested, that he was very sick."

"It was my first inkling," Sherrod wrote. "Shortly later, after a Cowboy road game, I noticed—perhaps *looking* for some sign—that Clint was a bit unsteady as we walked through the stands to the locker room. His speech was just the tiny bit slurred. It was almost as if he were intoxicated. A week after, at a Cowboys press luncheon, I got Tex Schramm aside and asked, without preamble, if Clint were sick. Tex didn't sidestep.

"Yes, he is. I don't know much about it because he will not talk about it . . ."

His intimates still believe that had it been almost any other ailment, one that didn't prevent him from communicating, Clint could have untangled the cascading problems of creditors' panic and bankruptcy actions that followed first the fact of his illness, and then the news of it.

There were many who contemplated at the time the brutal meanness of Clint's last days. I was one of them, as a columnist for the *Dallas Times Herald*:

". . . It was galling, it was stunning, to be the former owner of the Dallas Cowboys and the Tony Roma chain and the Palm Springs Racquet Club and 97 other corporations and to hear that in Idaho and Maine they were circulating chain letters that had your name mentioned where the Philippine generals and the Indonesian presidents used to be—the apochryphal celebrities who had foolishly broken the chain and had had bad things happen to them later . . ."

There was nothing apochryphal about Clint's fix.

Paul Trousdale remembered a particular chain letter (it mentioned a Philippine "General Tagak" who had been blighted because he broke the chain).

Classic Clint

"Dick Reynolds sent Clint the chain letter with a dollar inside. The instructions were to keep the dollar and send the letter to 10 friends, and he'd eventually get $64,280 back. Clint put the dollar in his pocket and tore up the letter. About a week later, Reynolds called and asked, 'Did you send the letter on?' Clint said no, it was a silly idea. So Reynolds sent another chain letter to Clint. Once again, Clint tore up the letter and pocketed the dollar. That night, at 3 o'clock in the morning, there was a knock at Reynolds' door in Austin. When he opened the door, a delivery boy stood there with a baby pig. There was a chain letter with the pig. 'Send a pig with this letter to 10 friends, and if no one breaks the chain you'll soon be receiving 64,280 little pigs.'"

Even terminally ill, he was still as clever as ever, but now nobody could know. The zingers, the gem-cut ad libs, were still in there rolling around in his head, but they couldn't get out. "That was a part of the tragedy that a lot of people didn't understand," a California friend said. "They saw him in the wheelchair, unable to move or talk, and they thought he'd lost touch. But he hadn't. He heard, he understood. You could see the effort in his eyes when he wanted to tell you something. He was still the same guy inside and couldn't let you know."

As he received and replied to mail from concerned people around the world, his endurance and his continuing courtesies during the illness were beyond stoicism.

He had to decline an invitation from Mrs. Wofford Cain to attend the dedication of the Cain Civic Center in the town of Athens:

> September 6, 1983
>
> Dear Effie:
>
> Sorry I won't be able to go to the dedication; in the photograph the building looks magnificent. It reminds me of a question Burk asked me one night after returning from his second-grade geography class. "Daddy," he asked, "was Athens, Greece named after Athens, Texas?"

To a suggestion that he seek help from a Swiss clinic:

May 21, 1984

Mr. Sash Spencer
Holding Services Corporation
685 Fifth Avenue
New York, NY 10022

Dear Sash:

Before my dad died, he tried living cell therapy in Switzerland; we had to shear him twice a month.

September 16, 1983

Mr. Nathan Berkowitz
Denver, Colorado

Dear Nat:

Thank you for your letter. It is true that I am ill—but that's not so bad considering the alternatives.

December 8, 1983

Mr. Nat Shore
Miami, Florida

Dear Nat:

Thank you for your suggestion regarding the Mayo Clinic. I have been trying to work up a trip to Rochester, and am presently waiting for the snow to melt.

February 22, 1985

Mr. Gordon McLendon
Lake Dallas, Texas

Dear Gordon:

Thank you for the letter; come by and shoot the breeze anytime. I am pretty easy to talk to now since I can't talk back.

Bob Asher, who had played college football at Vanderbilt and had been a tackle on that 1970 Dallas Cowboy team of bootstrap destiny, wrote from Chicago. Life after football had found him as a stockbroker:

> Dear Mr. Murchison:
>
> I recently read an article in the Wall Street Journal concerning your recent difficulties. As one of your former players, I only wished to drop you a line of support.
>
> Since Dallas I have known difficulties in my life, but never one due to my relationship with you or the Dallas Cowboys. The people I had met, and the moments I had enjoyed through your good will in the community were among the very best a person could ever know. I read where your health was failing and wonder how our Lord could ever allow you to suffer knowing your devotion to him. I have a small glimpse of what it is like being slightly handicapped physically (and financially), and can offer you one experience I've had. After I have worked through a tribulating experience, I always seem to enjoy a greater ability to feel the sensitivity and love of those around me, particularly family and friends. The greatest man who ever lived taught that this feeling was a much greater gift than any financial reward and I know he's right.
>
> Mr. Murchison, with your entourage of friends and admirers I guarantee you your best moments lie ahead of you. I only hope this letter finds its way to you as I am certainly one of your admirers and wish you a quick recovery and the very best in life for many years to come.
>
> Sincerely,
>
> ROBERT D. ASHER

Max Sherman had become Dean of the Lyndon B. Johnson School of Public Affairs at the University of Texas in Austin.

> Dear Clint:
>
> A few years ago when I was a candidate for Attorney General of Texas you supported me. I appreciated your encouragement and the fact that even after things did not go as we had hoped, you were still willing to give me advice and counsel. I appreciated not only the financial support, but also the words of encouragement and the fact that you were available to visit with me personally.

> As I read the various stories concerning your affairs and your health, I want to express our thanks for all that you have done for so many and, in most instances, without a great deal of fanfare. Please know that Gene Alice and I have remembered you in our prayers.

Dr. Jerome Posner, the neural specialist in New York, had affirmed that Clint's medical condition would not allow him to testify in the blizzard of civil lawsuits involving his financial troubles.

> January 23, 1984
> Dr. Jerome Posner
> New York, New York
>
> Dear Jerry:
>
> I appreciate your affidavits concerning my inability to testify in lawsuits. Mums the word.

For what it said about interrupted futures, his note to Kenneth E. Field of the Bramalea Corporation, the man who had first fielded the famous "Picky Picky Picky" letter, was most poignant of all. Field had written Clint and mentioned the imminent completion of the InterFirst Tower:

> June 6, 1984
>
> Dear Ken:
>
> Thank you for the nice note. I never told you, but if my health had not failed I planned to be on the 70th floor; however, you will have to do without me.

By that summer of 1984, Clint's interests in the Cowboys and Texas Stadium had been acquired by Bum Bright's investment group. The days of Circle Suites were over:

> July 20, 1984
> Mr. Holt Bettis
> Dallas, Texas
>
> Dear Holt:
>
> I, too, went to the Michael Jackson concert Sunday night; I had to borrow a box.

Classic Clint

He heard from Louisiana Senator Russell Long, who had been told a note was better than a phone call for communicating with Clint.

> **Dear Russell:**
>
> Thank you for your kind note. My difficulty, caused by a neurological problem, is the reason that I am unable to talk. Some look upon this as an asset—but at least it eliminates me from the burgeoning field of senatorial candidates.
>
> **Give my best to Carolyn.**

A year later, Clint had sent Sen. Long a campaign contribution, though a much more modest one than in other times. Long had returned it.

> **August 27, 1985**
>
> **Dear Russell:**
>
> If you don't quit returning campaign contributions, people will think you retired because you are getting senile.

John Schoellkopf, the Dallas investor who had served on the Boys Club boards with Clint, wrote him the same year:

> **Dear Clint:**
>
> D Magazine came snooping by last week to see if I could enlighten them on the real Clint. I was forced to confess that after a dozen years with you at the Boys Club, I was not too sure I knew anything about you except that the Boys Club was about the best darn charity in town and Clint, Jr. was mainly responsible.
>
> I know these are tough times for you and I'm a little ashamed that I haven't communicated anything friendly in a while. Not that you and I were bosom buddies, but I always appreciated your friendship, and, to D Magazine's misfortune, I got only good to say about you . . .
>
> You once told me that your Dad could have made a lot more money if he had not spent so much time helping younger men that he liked. I always thought your courtesy to me was in the same vein.
>
> Best of luck, Clint, and if you ever want some company, give me a call.
>
> **JOHN L. SCHOELLKOPF**

Public Wobblies, Private Strength

Maybe he was helpless, but he remained relentlessly wry. Going through one of the biggest personal bankruptcies in history, Clint replied to Bill Seiden, who had sent him a leather memo case:

Thank you for the only notes I'm not afraid to sign.

Losing a fortune, and staying ill. Either one of these conditions is enough to make for a pretty rainy parade, and Clint had them both. But a whole new sub-legend of stories would rise from his indomitable impishness.

His son Burk recalls a family gathering on a Christmas Eve; "It underlined a side of Dad in which he used his humor to needle people. Dad was already pretty ill by now. He was having trouble communicating, so Anne had to do the interpreting. He'd mumble a few words, and then Anne would announce what he'd said."

His daughter, Coke Anne Saunders, and her husband, Richard, were visiting the family from New York. "Coke Anne was very, very pregnant with their first child, and she was sensitive about it," Burk said. "Dad said he'd heard about a man whose wife had just had a baby. As he's walking up to the maternity room window to see the baby, the doctor taps him on the shoulder and says, 'I'm sorry to tell you that instead of a baby, your wife has just given birth to a very large ear.'

'An ear?'

'Yes, but there's good news and bad news,' the doctor said.

"The father asked, 'What's the good news?' as he turned to tap on the window the way new fathers do, hoping to get the attention of their newborns.

"The doctor said, 'Well, it's alive and healthy.'
Then the father asked, 'What's the bad news?'
'It's deaf.'"

Burk recalled, "Dad was just grinning and glowing while Anne translated for him. Coke Anne was mostly just pretty miffed. She couldn't believe how hard the rest of us were laughing. Richard thought it was funny, too."

Clint could laugh at his own discomfiture, even when it was caused by a child's ironic misspelling. In July of 1986 he sent a note and a clipping of a cartoon panel to his grandson Burkito:

Dear Burk:
I guess it's really summer because I just got a watermelon.
The guy in the strip reminds me of you.
Love,
Granddad.
p.s. Note how I spelled 'Granddead.'

Young Burk had misspelled it the latter way in a "Dear Granddead" letter home from camp.

"Even in the darkest days," says his son Burk, "he kept that unfailing sense of humor. He had several people taking care of him, helping him in and out of the wheelchair, doing things for him, helping him eat, and so on. Jim Busby was usually one of them.

"One night Dad had trouble sleeping and was in bed, awake, listening to the radio near dawn. Jim was sitting with him. Dad was listening to one of those swap-and-shop shows on the radio. The host got a call from a rural-sounding lady who said she had some bricks for sale.

"'The host said, 'Bricks, huh? Could you tell us what kind of bricks they are?'
She said, 'Thayuh RED!'

"Dad just came apart at the seams. Jim said tears came to his eyes. He couldn't stop laughing for four or five minutes."

Ken Dowe, the disc jockey whom Clint had backed in the radio business, recalls:

"After he became confined to the wheelchair, I was living in California most of the time, but when I was in Dallas I liked to stop by for a visit. I tried to have several jokes on hand, which he'd usually enjoy. He snickered, and his eyes gleamed, though he couldn't say much. When he did try to talk, it was difficult to understand him. But I could, if I listened carefully. On one visit, I gave him some bad news. Our

Public Wobblies, Private Strength

mutual friend Snuff Garrett (whom Clint also had backed in a music publishing venture) had suffered a stroke. Clint already knew it."

"Yessssssss," he said, He . . . and . . . I . . . . are . . . going . . . . to . . . t-t-take . . . sssssssspeech lessssons togggeeeether!"

"No joke, Clint. It's terrible about Snuff," Dowe said.

"No! N-n-not t-t-terrrrible! C-c-can't use his l-l-left arm. T-t-that's GOOD!"

"Aw, Clint, why's it good?"

"He k-k-keeeps his monnneeey in his l-l-leeft pocket!"

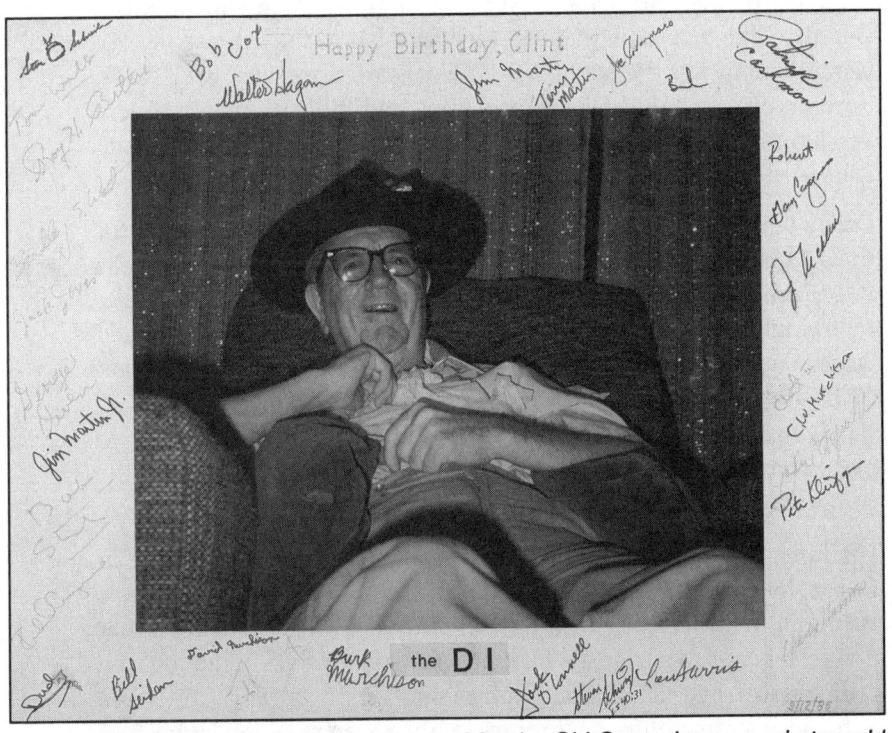

Friends and family signed the card for the Old Campaigner on what would be his last birthday — September 12, 1986.

Louis Farris, Jr., has a story of those days, too. "It was the summer of 1986, and we were driving to the barber shop in Preston Center after another one of those delightful Club Schmitz lunches he loved so much, the greasy burger with not much meat, mustard and french fries with catsup, and a glass of milk. Clint was telling a story that drifted from a strong beginning to a faint mumble that had us holding our breath, so we could hear every tortured syllable. Finally he had finished, and nobody knew what he'd said. Then I asked him, 'Clint, do you ever get tired of people asking you what you said?'

"He got that little smile, looked at me and said, 'What did you say?'" Farris treasures another story, from the days just before Clint was confined to the wheelchair. "We'd had lunch at the Royal Oaks Country Club in a room that was on a level below the parking lot. We were climbing up the stairs when Clint started to sway backwards. Several of us grabbed to brace him, and Billy Kilmer, the old Washington quarterback, reached him first. 'Don't worry, Clint,' Kilmer said, 'you know I never fumble.'"

Clint's dialogues with Steve Schneider were usually sardonic ones for the 30 years they had been close. The ultimate of what Schneider calls the "Reality Crack" may have come on the day in 1986 at the wake following Mitch Lewis's memorial. Lewis, an immensely talented writer, advertising consultant, and radio executive for Gordon McLendon, had also handled projects for Clint. They had been from Saudi Arabia to Stockholm together and had had a drink or two everywhere in between; Mitch's phrase "The Clangs" had been the codeword for hangover from the Rover Boys days.

His funeral had been in Santa Fe. There was a memorial service in Dallas, followed by a wake at the bar of the Melrose Hotel. Clint was sitting in his wheelchair at the hotel entrance when he noticed that Schneider was laboriously making his way up the ramp on the crutches he had used since contracting polio as a young man. Schneider strained his way to the top, then stopped, looked down at Clint, and panted in mock smugness, "Well, Clint, we finally got rid of Ol' Mitch."

Public Wobblies, Private Strength

At Christmastime, 1986, Anne wrote their holiday newsletter:

> Dear Friends and Loved Ones:
>
> Today or tomorrow Clint and I are moving into our new house, and we are so excited. It will be wonderful to be settled and into our new home. Even Clint is optimistic and enthusiastic, which is quite a surprise to all. Who would have ever thought that he would be glad to leave 6200? . . .
>
> Clint is quite frail. He has very little of his motor functions remaining, but the twinkle is still in his eye. We have shared many giggles and laughs together (thank goodness for humor in this world) and, I might add, a few tears (thank goodness for the tears as well) . . . Our legal problems look like there is an end in sight. There are a few more hurdles ahead of us but the turmoil is beginning to settle down. We have a lovely new home and enough money to meet our needs. We are grateful to the Lord for every day that we live . . .

The holiday message was dated December 22, 1986. Clint had 98 days.

Clint married Anne on May 3, 1976. She stood by him during the tough years. —photo courtesy of Jerry Hughes

Chapter Thirteen
'The Other Side Of Silence'

". . . Grandad's walking? He's talking?"
—*Bradley West*

The memorial service for Clint Murchison, Jr., was at Shady Grove Church in Grand Prairie, on April 2, 1987. Grand Prairie, aptly named, is one of the oldest towns of the vast midcities flatness that ties together Dallas and Fort Worth. Here begins the "big-sky" country that separates the two skylines, and for that matter the two Texases, East and West. There are years when spring blooms early and balmily in the area, but this wasn't one of those years. On this second of April, there was a thinness to the blue sky, a hint of a chill behind the lemony sun, and a high, still herringbone roof of clouds.

Grand Prairie sits in a relatively low-lying part of the Trinity River bottomlands west of Dallas. The city is a contradiction, part rows of blue-collar strip businesses, muffler shops, used car lots, and the air of severe fundamentalism, and part high-rise office complexes to the north, lining Interstate 30, where there is a multimillion-dollar amusement park sprawl—Six Flags over Texas, hotels, restaurants, water parks, Wax Museum, and, farther west, Arlington Stadium.

From one of those high-rises in Grand Prairie, on the day of Clint's funeral, one could look north to the higher ground of old "Turkey Knob" in Irving and see Xanadu, Texas Stadium, its bulbous brightness shimmering in the hazy distance.

Classic Clint

There were 1,600 in the church, and another contradiction: one group "Brother Clint's" fellow church members from his few years of membership in the church, the other group his coteries from before, many of them incredulous at the fundamentalist tone and trappings of Shady Grove, with its colorful airiness and its giant TV screen looming from the pulpit/stage.

The service began with the words of Shady Grove's pastor, Rev. Olen Griffing, Clint's minister during his born-again decade of the eighties.

"We come here today to this building, to honor Clint Murchison, Jr. . . . He was a person who lived his faith. And we come here to honor him and honor his life. And this service is in answer to his desires. I want all of you to know that Brother Clint left specific instructions as to this kind of celebration. He said, 'I want this to be a celebration of my homegoing . . .'"

Ralph Sanford, a Murchison friend who also had embraced religion, was next.

"Clint W. Murchison, Jr., was born Sept. 12, 1923, in Wichita Falls, Texas. Our brother Clint went home to be with Jesus March the 30th, 1987. Clint is survived by his wife, Anne, and children, Clint III and his sons C. W. and George; Burk and his sons Burk and David and his daughter Christine Elise; daughter Coke Anne Saunders and her daughter Courtney Cain Murchison Saunders; son Robert F. Murchison and their mother, Jane Haber; stepson Frank Heavner and stepdaughter Wendy West and her sons Bradley and Bryan and her daughter Loren West.

"Brother Clint graduated from Duke University and also Massachusetts Institute of Technology. In honorary societies he was a member of Chi Beta Chi and also Phi Beta Kappa. Military service: second lieutenant, United States Marine Corps Reserve. Civic activities: member, board of trustees, Pepperdine University, M.I.T., St. Mark's School of Texas, Marine Military Academy, past member, board of trustees, Lawrenceville School. Among Clint's many honorary and humanitarian and distinguished service awards are those from the Boys Clubs of America and the Boys Club of Dallas; the Herbert Hoover Humanitarian Award, Bronze Keystone 15- and 20-year awards, dedication of Oak Cliff Boys Club as the Clint Murchison, Jr., Building, and the Man and Boy Award. Also

'The Other Side Of Silence'

Murchison Science Building, Pepperdine University; Distinguished Civilian Service Award from the United States Air Force. Also Texas Business Hall of Fame, and lastly, founder of the Dallas Cowboys. May we pray:

"Father, we bless you today. Father, we thank you that we as people had the opportunity to share just a portion of brother Clint's life. Many here were with him for many years, and some, just a few years. But father as we gather together I pray that would magnify your name, because Lord, I know, in fact, Lord, in a humorous way, I can almost see Clint standing in the portals of heaven with that grin on his face, saying 'Go for it!'. . ."

There was discomfort and a nervous shuffling among the "B.C." faction of Clint's friend in the audience. Some were torn between their respect for the occasion, their unfamiliarity with the ambiance of fundamentalism, and the suspicion whether this ceremony could have been Clint's final and biggest joke of all.

The next speaker was Tom Landry.

". . . You know, my first encounter with Clint Murchison was in 1960, when Tex and I flew down from New York to have a press conference about the Cowboys. The day before I was in a championship game in New York against Baltimore, and unfortunately they beat us. But as I stepped off the plane I saw Clint for the first time. And those of you who know Clint, the first impression is not always the best one. He has that slight build and that burr haircut, and he's got those horn-rimmed glasses on, and he really didn't make much of an impact. He didn't look like much of a football player, that's for sure. Clint and I are about the same age. Clint's just one year older than me; his birthday is one day after mine. And I was always grateful for that, because he threw great parties. I could usually have my party and then come to his party, too. We had a lot of fun in those days.

"But he had a great impact on my life. He probably had the greatest impact of anybody that I know. Because you know the story very well. When I came to Dallas to coach the Cowboys in 1960, football wasn't really my career, I didn't feel, but I thought I would come on down and try my hand at it, because I had spent a lot of years in football. And I knew that I wouldn't survive, because nobody survives with an expansion club. You get fired in about the third year after you try to

Classic Clint

coach one of 'em. And then camp came around in 1964, when I guess everybody wanted a new coach, and Clint's answer to that was, he gave me a 10-year contract. And so that was a great impact in my life, because to me as a Christian—and I was only a Christian for one year before I came to Dallas in 1960—this was God's way of saying to me 'This is where you should be, in coaching.' You know the story from then on. In '65 we were a .500 team, in 1966 we started 20 years of winning football. That's a record that's hard to match in professional football, because we're in a tough business, football. But it was Clint. A lot of people were wondering why we were successful. I got my praise, Tex got his praise, Gil (Brandt) got his, the organization . . . but it was Clint Murchison that brought us together. It was his roots.

"Stability is the only way that you can have a long-running successful organization in pro football, and he gave us the stability that we wanted. And the amazing thing about Clint was that he was an optimist. He didn't ever believe that things were not gonna be worked out the way he wanted them. He loved the Cowboys. And every time we got into a valley, you could count on one thing. A letter would show up. It might not have but one word in it, it may not have but one sentence. But it always lifted your spirits and got you back on the right track. So this is important in the Cowboy history.

"But I think in his contributions to the Cowboys and their winning seasons, he made even a greater contribution, to Dallas, Texas . . . The sixties were tough times for Dallas. With the assassination of John Kennedy, we were known worldwide as the City of Hate. Nobody had a good image of us. Our pride was down as a city. But because of the Cowboys, and because of our winning tradition as we started to win, we changed that.

"People focused their attention on football, and on our winning. And we became America's Team, which was hard to live down, but it was kind of true. And it changed the vision that people have for us in Dallas.

"I guess the thing that I'm the sorriest for, right now, as Clint has gone away from us, is that he wasn't recognized by the city of Dallas for the great contribution he made to the welfare of our city. But I sure know that we owe him a great debt of gratitude. You know that Clint is a Christian, as you heard today, and he became a Christian a lot later than I did. But he became a Christian, I think, through Anne and through her contribution to him, and there isn't any question to me that this is the strength that pulled him through these last few years. You never did see Clint when his eyes didn't kind of sparkle and he smiled at you even when he couldn't talk. Yet even the other day, when Tex and I went into the hospital, you could see that little smile trying to come out again.

"These are great times for me to think about, and it makes me a little bit emotional when I think about them. But we're celebrating today because he is a child of God. And I want to close with this: I'd like to share a story with you—I asked Anne if I could share it, because it had a big impact on me. When Alicia and I went over there to see her Tuesday night, she was telling us this story because Clint had passed away the night before, and she was trying to know how to tell the grandchildren that he wasn't going to be with them anymore. She brought Bradley out, 5 years old, sat him down, and she tried to say as gently as she could that Grandpa had gone to be with Jesus. Bradley looked at her a little bit there, and all of a sudden his face started to light up, his eyes got big, he smiled and said, 'You mean that Grandpa is well? He's talking? He's walking?'

"That's a great story. I'm kind of emotional when I think about it. But I'm sure that Anne assured him that that was true, that he was with Jesus, that he was talking, that he was walking, in heaven today..."

The next eulogist was Jack O'Connell, president of one of the few Murchison companies that had survived the bankruptcy reorganizations.

"I stand here today for myself, to be sure, but as a messenger for hundreds and hundreds of people around the world whose lives have been touched by Clint W. Murchison, Jr. Each of us cherishes, in some special way, that touch he gave our lives. Some of us had a business relationship with him; he gave full faith and credit, full support in an undying way forever, to any project in which he was interested.

"Some of us are the duly elected leaders of our cities, our states, and our nation. He supported the government of this country very very strongly. Some of us are parents of children whose education he provided, hospital bills he paid for; some of us are with the Boys Clubs of America, the Marine Military Academy, all levels of life, all

Classic Clint

levels of society: he just quietly did what it took to get the job done, very privately. It was a pleasure to have been part of his life. I know, going way back, of a 17-year-old stable boy who came with a property that Clint, Sr., bought and made his homestead. Clint, Jr., took care of that man, right up to the very end, to Sparkman-Hillcrest (funeral home) where Clint himself rests today.

"That was his style. His legacy is his family, everything that revolves around his family, his children, his grandchildren. And thousands and thousands of people all over the world whose lives are better off for his having spent his four quarters here on earth. There was no overtime in his life. I would be proud to finish the four quarters of my life with his record."

Next was attorney Marshall Simmons, the lawyer, the veteran of all of those depositions and the "Deviled-Egg War" with Clint. He began abashedly:

"I wish I could have gone first. It is a great honor to me to be asked to stand up here and talk about Clint. I had the privilege of being one of his lawyers for 20 years. Clint was a blessing in my life, in my professional life and my personal life. Like has been said, he changed my life in every way for the better. A lot of lawyers say the practice of law would be great if it weren't for clients. They didn't have the good fortune to represent Clint. In all of his businesses and his relationships I think he was just like he was with Tex Schramm; he gave you the reins and he let you run with them. He didn't want to hear from me any more than was absolutely necessary.

"He spoiled me forever as a standard for clients; it was great fun representing Clint. He's a trial lawyer's dream. For one thing, every lawyer who ever had to take his deposition was scared to death. They were in awe. They would come in, ask his name and address, then thank him very much and go home. Every time a lawyer takes a deposition—I'm sure most of you know this—they serve a subpoena to bring all of your files. Well, Clint and I would go to the deposition and he didn't bring anything. The lawyer would say 'Didn't you get that subpoena?' and I'd say yes. 'Well, did you bring everything?' I'd say yes. He'd say 'Well where is it?' and I'd say 'Ask Clint.'

"Then they'd say 'Well Mr. Murchison, did you bring your files?' And he'd say, 'I don't have any files.'

'The Other Side Of Silence'

'Don't you write letters?'
'Occasionally.'
'Don't you keep copies?'
'No.'
'Don't you get letters?'
'Yes.'
'What do you do with them?'
'I read them.'
'*Then* what do you do with them?'
He said, 'I throw 'em away.' If you've ever been in Clint's office and looked behind his desk, you know exactly what I'm talking about.

"The private Clint Murchison, Jr., that I had the good fortune to get to know was a very warm and generous person. As those who know him well would say he was generous to a fault. If everybody whom Clint has helped financially would come back in here today and put it up here on this stage, we'd be back in the top 10.

"I have been in awe of Clint's ability to deal with this adversity in these last years. I don't know how he did it. I know I could not have done it that well, and I understand the Lord has played a major part in that, but I saw Clint, and he never, never complained, he never acted pitiful, he never felt sorry for himself. Oh, God, what an inspiration, to me and to anyone who was with him in these days. One week ago today, Jack O'Connell and I stood at Clint's bed in the hospital and reminisced and told stories, and Clint *laughed*. He lay there in that bed and laughed as best he could.

"His sense of humor was just wonderful. I miss that now. I could stand here now and—you know, the trial lawyer's got four minutes, we bill by the hour!—but I think if Clint had been able to say something to me in his last days and if he knew that I was gonna have the opportunity to stand up here, I'd probably ask him if I could tell this one story, and I know he would say yes.

"About five years ago we were in a lawsuit and Clint's deposition was being taken by an outstanding Dallas lawyer named Stanley Neely, a friend of mine and a friend of Clint's. He had great respect for Clint, and admiration. He'd been taking this deposition for a couple of days and he got toward the end, and just kind of for fun he handed Clint an annual statement from Tecon Corporation which had

Classic Clint

been published many years before. And he said, 'Now Clint, I want you to look at the last page of that report. Well, not the *last* page because that's where the accountants do all that business, but the last thing in there and he says, 'Now look at that picture.' And there was a picture there of Clint when he was about 40, I guess. And Stan says, 'Clint, who is that?'

"Clint actually took off his glasses to look. He peered for a moment, then he looked up and said, 'Gable?'"

The next eulogist, Harv Oostdyk, came from a part of Clint's life that had begun after the good times, high living, private jets, and boardrooms. Oostdyk's common denominator with Clint was his new spiritually oriented life, and a new set of worldly concerns.

Oostdyk said, "One time I was in Clint's office, talking with him, and he showed me a letter that had come from a foreign country. The envelope said

> Clint Murchison
> Texas
> U.S.A.

"Now, you and I, if they just get one number of the ZIP Code wrong...

"Yes, Clint was famous. To describe Clint, I would use *silence*. I only got to know him in 1981. But Clint was dominated by silence. It was the sort of way he was, and then a terrible disease ravaged his body, and he was reduced to silence.

"I got to penetrate that silence. I had lots of long, long talks with Clint. I found out what was at least partially behind his silence. I did it on one theme, the theme of the poor. If you wanted to describe the ghetto, the ghetto is what lies on the other side of silence.

"Most people in North Dallas, they don't know very much about that silence. George Eliot wrote these words: 'If we had a keen vision and feeling of all ordinary human life, it would be like hearing the grass grow and the squirrel's heart beat, and we should die of that roar, which lies on the other side of silence.' I shared that silence with Clint: the way poor people hurt, the way they feel hopelessness, the incredible resources that our society makes available to the poor; and how we have no capacity to take that resource and to give it to the poor in a coordinated way. It would only take a few powerful people in America who could begin to use their influence to see that the resources our society has provided could truly reach the poor . . . I honestly believe that if Clint could have stayed healthy, Clint could have been the man who from his pinnacle of strength and personality and conceptual ability, could have led a new day for the poor.

"But Clint deteriorated in his health, and Clint is now dead. But a foundation that he helped create was able to put together something called the Murchison Forum. ". . . His son Burk Murchison has accepted the challenge to take that mantle and to finish that task . . . perhaps one day across America a man who had few words will be reponsible for millions of words being spoken to the hearts and needs of the poor . . ."

Pastor Griffing said, "Burk Murchison has written a statement in honor of his father and has asked that I read it on behalf of his brothers Clint and Robert and his sister, Coke Anne, and their respective families, and also on behalf of his and Elise's sons Burk and David and their daughter Elise.

"In recent years, as Dad's physical wellbeing deteriorated and his so-called financial empire came apart at the seams, I felt that the expression of his many attributes as a person and a father were being lost to those around him. On the one hand, his illness cost him his finely honed skills as a communicator. Other than a word here or a phrase there, his interaction was often limited to a nod, a smile, or a sparkle in his eyes. The accompanying tragedy of his financial crisis exacerbated this loss. The normalcy and closeness of his family and his business relationships were undermined and often replaced by bitterness, heartbreak, and resentment.

"I did not want these memories, those of his final tragic years, to be those that predominated, and in consequence I sought out something that might serve as a reflection of Dad in earlier, happier times. There was much to draw from, but I finally was able to make the selection of such an example. It is an article that he wrote for the Dallas Cowboys Newsletter in the Fall of 1970. It is one of a series of articles that he wrote for the Newsletter that season, and it now serves as the prologue of *Clint's Corner*, a compendium of that same series.

Classic Clint

"The Fall of 1970 was a good time for Dad. The Texans had long since moved to Kansas City, his struggles were over with the mayor and City Hall concerning the issues of replacing the Cotton Bowl, and the Cowboys were soon to move to Texas Stadium. But most importantly, despite Dandy Don's premature retirement, the Cowboys were doing something that was very dear to Dad's heart: they were winning." In my mind, this article exemplifies qualities in Dad that I hope will remain with us always: his love of life, his brilliant, quirky sense of humor, his sensitivity, his staggering intelligence, and his keen sense of articulation.

"It reads as follows:"

> As you will shortly see, I am no journalist. I am not unhappy about this. Their long hours and low pay are only partially offset by the interesting work. For instance, I would love, in order to meet a deadline, to be able to reach Lamar Hunt, Gale Sayers, or Erik Jonsson by telephone at 10 o'clock in the evening—or, in one of those instances, at almost any time within a month. But not at the expense of having to stay in the office past midnight.
>
> However, the publisher of this newsletter volunteered to make a contribution to the Boys Club of Dallas to compensate me for my efforts. And since I am a great believer in the Boys Club, I agreed. If you don't like what you read, send money to the club, 3004 N. Westmoreland. And when your donations equal that of the publisher, which isn't much, I'll quit.
>
> In this column, I'm not going to discuss the direct administration, as such, of the Cowboys. I'll leave that to those who know a lot more about it than I. But there are related matters which will perhaps be of interest in both a current and a historical sense. For example, some of you may wish to know, what was the real reason for the Cowboys' moving to Irving? How did Schramm acquire the nickname Tex? Why do grown men act like kids over football? (I'll answer that now: they don't; in football, kids act like grown men.) Do the Cowboys make money? (I don't mean Bob Lilly or Bob Hayes, I mean ME). Follow the bouncing ball through this season, and we will explore these and other subjects.
>
> One more thing, about format: if you have any unresolved problems in the area of general management, as opposed to scouting, coaching or playing, let me know and I'll try to answer. But please don't send in any complaints such as the one I received in November, 1963, a few days before Green Bay met Chicago in a game which would decide

'The Other Side Of Silence'

> the winner of a very close Western Conference championship race (the Cowboys were 3-7 at this point). A woman from Fort Worth wrote, 'I am the spokesman for a group of girls in Fort Worth who are the most ardent boosters of the Cowboys in this area. From 1960 until today, we have suffered through thick and thin, and have put up with every indignity in the support of our team. But when you black out Chicago-Green Bay and force us to watch the Cowboys-Philadelphia game on television, you are going too far.'
>
> Don't send this type of complaint to me. Send it to Don Meredith, American Broadcasting Company, 7 W. 66th St., New York, N.Y. He's used to it. I'm sensitive.

The pastor said, "We received one more word, from Tom Webb, a friend of Clint's in Washington." He read it:

"I was fortunate to know Clint both professionally and socially for almost 35 years. He was the finest, kindest, most unselfish and talented individual I have ever known. I was extremely lucky to have known the three greatest individuals in the world: namely, my father, J. Edgar Hoover, and Clint. He has taken a big piece of me by his passing. He was truly number one . . ."

For some that day at Shady Grove, Tom Webb's tribute and his mention of J. Edgar Hoover brought a flicker of a smile, the memory of one of Clint's best gags floating back from across the decades of portent and change, history and horseplay. In 1960 Hoover, the only Director the FBI ever had and a friend of the Murchisons from his fondness for their Del Mar racetrack, flew to Dallas for a weekend of revelry with Clint and Bob Thompson, at whose home he was quietly staying. When Hoover had entered the empty house, he found the greeting gift the boys had left him: a jackass hitched to the staircase.

Roger Staubach's thoughts that morning during the eulogies may have been of shaving. "I had a ritual on game days that included my not shaving until after the game," the Cowboys' quarterback wrote to Burk Murchison after the funeral.

"Part of this ritual was for Clint to come up to me in the locker room while I was shaving. If we had won the game, he would come in with a bright smile and a humorous comment. If I'd had three touchdown passes, he would say, with a smile, 'Sorry you had such a bad day.'

Classic Clint

"If it had been a bad day, interceptions and a loss, he knew that I would take it hard. Yet, he could still cheer me up for a few minutes with a joke or a funny comment.

"There are times even now, when I am shaving, that I flash back on the memories of Clint in the Dallas Cowboys locker room, and I am glad that I had the opportunity to know him."

Clint's widow Anne later would write:

"Clint's character held up well in the face of such great (financial) humiliation, but as if that were not enough, he endured a cruel and unusual physical affliction which ultimately robbed him of any dignity he had left. He had almost no voluntary movements in his body. He could not lift an arm nor move a leg. At the very end, he had great difficulty swallowing foods and was ultimately put on a feeding tube. He could not cause a sound to come forth from his mouth, nor form intelligible words. It is even grimmer than I tell you here . . .

"Clint once said to me that if he could have just one function of his body back . . . it would be his speech. Our family has chuckled often about the fact that this man who never said much when he could talk only now desired to do just that . . . I never entered a room where he was that he did not smile broadly, nor that his eyes did not twinkle . . .

"Our pastor used an interesting scripture at the graveside family service. He quoted, . . . *the voice of Abel still speaks*. His point was this—Clint Murchison's life will continue to speak to all of us for years to come . . ."

Indeed it does, as do his previous deeds and devilry from long before. Each year on his birthday, September 12, Clint's sons and friends have gathered in the back room of a Tony Roma's in Dallas to hash over tales already told, and to trade new ones freshly remembered.

Oddly, the image that returns to many of them in these remembrances is that of Club Schmitz, his fond and unlikely social headquarters during his last days. There is a constancy to the affectionate puzzlement in their head-shaking anecdotes: "I never knew what he saw in that place, but lemme tell you what happened to us there once . . ."

"The place had different ways of surprising you," says Clint III. "One Saturday, when my sons C. W. and George were about 10 and 6, we went there with Dad, and a couple of fellows who looked like steamfitters were up drinking beer and playing at the shuffleboard table. My kids went up and watched them play for a while, and then these guys stood back and let the boys play, showed 'em how to slide the pucks and keep score. I thought it was a nice thing to do, so I sent 'em over a couple of beers. Just as a kind of thank-you. But a few minutes later, they sent me over a couple of beers. Reciprocating, you know. Keeping things even."

Clint's favorite line about Club Schmitz was, "It's the only place I know where the flies fight to get OUT instead of in," but his delivery of the line always suggested affection rather than distaste. "During his last years, whenever you'd ask where he wanted to be taken for lunch, it was always either Club Schmitz or Walton's barbecue, but usually Club Schmitz," says Burk Murchison.

Club Schmitz, "the neighborhood spot without a neighborhood," was Clint's favorite hangout in his last years. —photo courtesy of John Sears

Classic Clint

For Clint III and his sons George (l.) and C. W. (r.), a call on grandad often ended in a journey to Club Schmitz.

As Clint himself could be an ambivalent contrast of the earthy and the urbane, so Club Schmitz may be a sort of institutional version of this contradiction; part funky and part trendy, a gathering spot for power brokers and housepainters, "a neighborhood bar without a neighborhood," as its co-owner Bob Schmitz calls it. 'D' Magazine of Dallas, customarily elitist in its view of the merits of bars and restaurants, called Club Schmitz "as simpatico an eat-and-drink depot as you could ask to see . . ." Not the least of Club Schmitz's distinctions is that it's a beer joint with an unlisted phone.

Since Clint's last years were also a time of dramatic change and disappearing landmarks in Dallas, he probably appreciated Club Schmitz for its continuity, too. It opened in 1946 and first found favor as an oasis for commuters between Dallas and Irving; depending on the direction one was traveling, it was either the first or last wet spot. It has remained under the same family's ownership for nearly half a century. Beer is the only drink served over the bar, and highchairs are available for customers who want to bring their kids. "Hot Chili, Cold Bud" says a sign over the bar. With these kinds of amenities, plus the house specialty hamburger with the spattering-grill taste Clint would remember from his youth, it would be a place a bankrupt millionaire could enjoy.

One of his last outings before his death was to Club Schmitz with Joe Cavagnaro, the Texas Stadium manager. "This one day, I called him, and no one else had showed up at his house. So it would be just Clint and me. With the condition he was in, I was worried sick about how I was going to get him up the steps to the place so he could get his burger and fries. But we got out there, and there was a bunch of truck drivers and bearded guys and everything; he was more used to that crowd than I was. And when we pulled up I got more help than I needed, and I never saw people show so much respect to anybody as they did to Clint when I rolled him inside there. Some of them moved the tables so we could get him through the doorway, and while we were there they came over and patted him on the back and hugged him, said it was good to see him getting out.

"Later, when we were leaving, we got out to the parking lot and these two big burly guys came over to the car. I thought our luck had run out, we were about to get mugged or something. But Clint rolled the window down and these guys just reached in the car, patted him on the shoulder and said, "Mr. Murchison, we're praying for you."

His closeness with his family and friends, and holding court at Club Schmitz were the main pleasures of his final days. "What set Clint Murchison, Jr., apart was that he enjoyed the hell out of his money," Gary Cartwright wrote in a valedictory titled "Too Rich To Worry, Too Bright To Care."

He had enjoyed the money on his own terms, using the wealth while keeping the attendant fame and fanciness at arm's length. He had been rich enough to own a box at Ascot, but hadn't really cared about the trappings of the royal milieu, just as he had preferred his own home-burgers to a live-in gourmet chef. He had owned America's Team and a private tropical paradise and had been the shy focus of five Super Bowls. At the end he had earned respect on a parking lot full of pickup trucks.

Chapter Fourteen
P. S.

*"One learns that one must bend with the wind
if it's blowing your dollars away."*
—Steve Schneider's audio-visual tribute

On April Fool's Day of 1984, Clint's pet charity, the Boys Clubs of America, honored its pet philanthropist, him. The black-tie crowd filled a ballroom at the Anatole Hotel, the twin-towered affluent fortress on the edge of the city skyline. Much of the Dallas and Texas Establishment was present as Clint received the Herbert Hoover Humanitarian Award for his nearly 20 years as the clubs' benefactor.

The demographics of his tribute night were as diverse as those of his funeral would be—delegations from both of Clint's contrasting worlds: the unpreposessing Rev. Olen Griffing of the Shady Grove Church in Grand Prairie was there at Clint's request to deliver the invocation; on the dais he was sandwiched between power banker Robert Stewart III, the dinner chairman, and the leonine ex-Governor John B. Connally, who emceed the evening and introduced the speakers and entertainers. Even the choice of the music was arch: "Variations on a Theme by Corelli" was followed by Gershwin's "It Ain't Necessarily So," followed by Scarlatti's "Sonata in G Major."

The civic Murderers' Row of speakers included Tom Landry, Pete Rozelle, Tex Schramm, eventual Dallas mayor Annette Strauss, and Texas Governor Mark White.

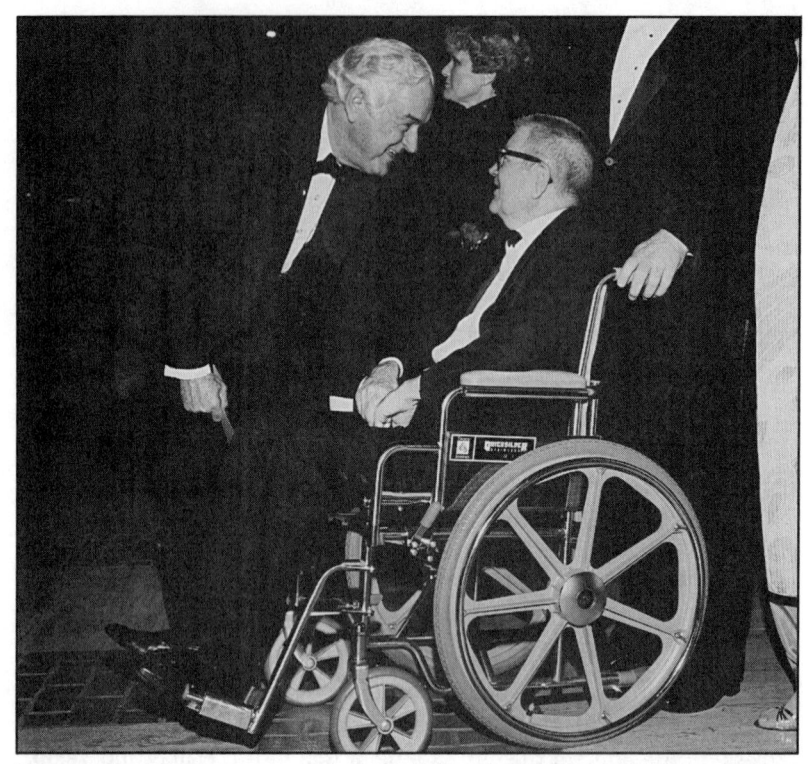

With former Texas Governor John B. Connally on the glittering and fateful night of the Boys Clubs' Herbert Hoover Award for Clint. It was the Dallas establishment's first view of the ailing Clint in his wheelchair. —photo courtesy of Bukki Erwin

But the biggest and most far-reaching stir that night was caused by the appearance of Clint himself. It confirmed the rumors of his seriously deteriorating health. That night was one of his first public outings in the wheelchair. The slur in his speech now was impenetrable. Bankers and lenders went home from the Anatole that night determined to start calling meetings.

The award Clint was receiving, the Herbert Hoover Humanitarian Award, had been given in the past to the likes of Lyndon B. Johnson, J. Edgar Hoover, Bob Hope, Dwight D. Eisenhower, Gerald Ford, Thomas J. Watson of IBM, and Robert Woodruff of the Coca-Cola Company. It was a distinguished honor, one not to be taken frivolously—an increasing concern of the night's planners once they heard that some friend of Clint's named Steve Schneider was going

P. S.

to be responsible for a major part of the program, the audio-visual presentation.

Cottontail, of course, had been Clint's own choice as tribute-maker. In the days before the event, the planners had made more and more calls to Schneider, asking exactly what he had in mind. "Oh, it'll just be a graphic and dignified overview of Clint's career and his successes in versatile areas of endeavor," Schneider said.

"Could we, er, perhaps see a copy of your script beforehand?" they kept asking anxiously.

"No, I don't think so," Schneider kept answering devilishly.

Had the writer been anyone but Schneider, Clint might have interceded and asked that a script or outline be sent over to stop the misery, but he was enjoying their anxiety too much.

Schneider's slide show for Clint was a howling success, its outrageous images and sardonic script running a roller-coaster of emotions in keeping with the tit-for-tat perversity of their own long friendship. In his narration, Schneider's laconic and gravelly voice wasn't quite able to mask the affection he felt.

The following are excerpts from the slide show:

Clinton Williams Murchison, Jr. A man, a myth, or, just another pretty face.

251

Classic Clint

Born at an early age, there was no question that he was destined for greatness. Naturally, as a young man, he was trained for his station in life, riding in limos, surrounded by "yes" men, protected by body guards.

Although all pictures have apparently been destroyed, it is said that young Clint was captain of the Texas Country Day football team for three years running, compiling a less-than-spectacular record of zero and thirty. However, Clint claims that they did once knock off the Hockaday Girls School field-hockey team in exhibition.

Going north to Lawrenceville School, his mental prowess he established. In the 1941 yearbook, Clint entered this somewhat less than modest description of himself: "Brains inversely proportional to size of body," which prompted some jealous classmates to observe, "There goes a guy with the big head."

As expected, Clint lettered in football, because his Daddy gave the money for the uniforms. And then is was on to MIT in Boston, where this 126-pound scatback touted himself as a "Texas Blue Chip." Checking his speed and watching his moves prompted the coaches to say, "I think someone sent us a Texas cowchip."

But the war cut short his budding football career. Clint joined the United States Marines. His contributions to the war effort were significant. This picture appeared as a recruiting poster for the Army Air Corp and was credited with luring many young men into the Corp. The caption challenging read, "Do you really feel that your wives and sweethearts are safe with this man guarding our shores?"

P. S.

Clint vaulted from the service into the business world sporting the then-popular Bryl Creem look. But this hairdo was shortlived and Clint switched to the crew cut, his trademark forever. Dapper, he reflected smugly upon himself, "The girls really go for my personality and charm, not my money." A little voice abruptly brought him back to reality, "It's your money, Clint."

Young Clint savored the power of the boardroom, where the important meetings were held, where the big decisions were made, and where the big boys would sometimes let him watch the stag movies.

From here it was on to New York, A cover story in *Time* Magazine, Wall Street, investment bankers, finance. Clint mischievously suggested, "We'll just tell 'em what they want to hear. Get the money. Then go out and buy a football team."

The Dallas Cowboys were born with a freshman headcoach and a mixed bag of players.

With Clint, a rare photo of our first quarterback, Eddie LeBaron, *standing*, for in those early days most of the time he was being beaten into the ground. "The Cotton Bowl," as Bob Cullum said "the stadium that Doak Walker built." Clint added, "And the Cowboys paid for too."

Classic Clint

For much needed rest and relaxation, he would get away to Spanish Cay, his island in the Bahamas, where he humbly thought of himself as, and was, a king. The unidentified bystander shown here was never seen again. Clint's last poignant words to him. "People don't lean on me. I lean on them."

Back to football. The fledgling years were past.

Grinning way up at Bob Lilly, and joyfully shouting, "Bob Hayes eats tamale pie!" the end of the rainbow was attained: a Super Bowl team at last. Now he could be somebody. No longer would Clint be just another fan lost somewhere in the crowd. This would be his finest hour, 1972, Miami, a Super Bowl victory was in hand.

Bolstered with a tad of the smart water, with Tom Brookshier, Clint, droopy-eyed, gave forth his infamous, but cryptic, victory speech, "We have had plenty of the thick. Now we can enjoy some of the thick." And 80 million viewers asked one another, "What in the hell does that mean?"

P. S.

His mysterious and still unknown speechwriter, standing close behind him, disappeared forever, quietly into the night.

His travels took him many places. In quest for foreign oil, a modern-day Lawrence of Arabia, he became. Clint's simple contribution to the Koran, "One learns that one must bend with the wind if it's blowing your dollars away."

Being summarily punished, when unexplainably caught wandering in a sultan's harem. Clint's words of wisdom to live by, "It is difficult to laugh at adversity, when your navel is full of sand."

The hatchet man. Ever watchful of pennies, he corrected the office problem of employees pilfering donuts from the coffee room. Clint hung this picture boldly above the donut dispenser with the succinct admonishment, "Go ahead. Make my day."

The politicians came to him often, and here Ted Kennedy sought his advice. Teddy wanted to form a touch football league for the more-refined less-violent New Englanders. His team would be named the "Hyannisport Goosers." The rules called for one hand below the belt.

255

Classic Clint

Here he is with Hubert Humphrey, and although he had every opportunity, and he should have, he did not say, "Hubert, your fly is open."

Celebrities were his bag, and after formal introduction, the big man, standing next to Gordon McLendon, said slowly, "You can call me Duke, Clint." With a little swagger and jut-of-jaw, Clint responded, "And you can call me king, Duke."

Clint had enjoyed it hugely. Ahead of him after that dinner would be the chaos of the lenders' panic, the bankruptcies, the distress sale of the Cowboys and Spanish Cay, the breakup of the companies, and his own plummeting health.

His letter to Steve Schneider would be one of his last thank-you notes to anyone. In its terseness and restraint, it was Classic Clint:

> April 4, 1984
>
> Dear Steve:
>
> The other night at the hotel somebody asked me who I was. I explained that I tagged along with Steve, and he seemed satisfied.
>
> Sincerely,
>
> CLINT

Afterword

By Stephen W. "Cottontail" Schneider

The publishers had hoped to get a friend of Clint's to do this part—I was the closest thing they could find.

That's a joke. Clint had lots of friends! Well, actually, if you knocked out all of the football kooks (and there were hordes) and all those who were trying to get into his wallet (this bunch scattered quickly when it became clear that "the cupboard was bare") and, of course, all the immediate family, Clint's friends would come down to a pretty tight group—say two or three.

That's not true either. Clint had lots of friends. Too many! That's because he never "culled 'em." If you were Clint's friend, you were Clint's friend. He took the rich with the poor—well, actually, not too many poor; the kings with the knaves—not too heavy on knaves either ("queens" were definately out); and the celebrities with the "nobodies"—no "nobodies." One can see that from such a broad selection, an occasional jerk could make the cut. The disgruntled have suggested that that's how I slipped in.

Through the years, Clint developed a nucleus of loyalists, old soldiers, good friends. They stuck. They were always around. Others would come and go, most having a hard time understanding Clint's personal pecularities. You see, he was a little weird.

Classic Clint

Small talk, for example, was not his bag. If the conversation wasn't of substance or of interest to him, his mind would wander off to ponder Chaos Theory, or fractals, or something further out in left field. While on these mental trips, he wouldn't talk. With his piercing cold blue eyes, Clint would just stare—right through you. It was unnerving, disturbing, a little like having lunch with a sphinx. Now if you wanted to talk about his beloved Dallas Cowboys, that was another matter. He could and would bore you to sleep with this subject in short order.

He prided himself on brevity. The one-liner, or the one-worder, was his thing. I don't believe I ever recall having heard Clint, on purpose, call me by name. Most of the time it was "Hey!" or, when in a more mellow mood maybe, "Hey, you!" He was a little weird.

The guy could laugh. He could laugh at something that he really thought was funny—like the time a friend, out drinking with "dollies" when he was supposed to be working, got trapped by his own son when, out riding with his mother, the young boy innocently exclaimed, "Look, Mama! There's Daddy's car!" This does not mean that Clint was insensitive. He understood tragedy and despair—like when his friend's wife didn't kill him, but she made sure that he'd never forget it, every day of his life.

When he did laugh, often it got away from him. In a giddy mood, Clint would sometimes actually talk—a very rare occurrence indeed—and word sounds mixed with convoluted giggling would gargle forth from his throat. No one could understand a damn word he was saying. But us "smart" guys, who were determined to stay on the "inside" (I wanted to hold on to my parking permit for Cowboy games), guffawed right along with him. As quickly as it would start, the laughter would stop. And Clint would revert to his reclusive state. The cold icy stare would return. A short sigh, then he would pick up his *Time* magazine and thumb through it, looking for his name again.

One day while visiting with him alone, my most cherished remembrance of Clint occurred. His malady was dragging him relentlessly down. His time, and he knew it, was getting short. Clint patiently was listening to my disjointed chatter—sitting there in his wheelchair—as I made light of his predicament, and we relived in our minds the good times that we had shared.

Afterword

On impulse, I remember, in a joking manner I asked him, "Clint, remember back when you could talk to me, but you wouldn't? Now that you can't talk, aren't you sorry that you didn't—and sorry that you can't talk to me now?" Mustering all his strength, inhaling deeply, he blurted out with resolution, "No!"

There was a glint in his eye and across his face glowed an impish grin. I think he wanted to. I wished he could have. He wasn't a bad guy. Maybe a little weird, but he was my friend.

Index

A

Acker, Ed, 48
Adams, Bud, 195
Al-Bader, Ali, 215
Al-Yagout, Mohammed, 51
Albert, Carl, 168
Ali, Muhammad, 152
Allen, George, 162
Altschuler, Dr. Ken, 216, 220
Anderson, Andy, 174
Anderson, Clinton P., 78, 153
Archbold, John D., 143
Archibald, John C., 143
Asher, Bob, 223
Armstrong, Neil, 13
Atmar, Mrs. Laura (Sugar), 146
Atmar, Dr. Robert, 146

B

Bailey, Joe, 63
Bailey, Paul G., 216
Baker, Bobby, 69, 182
Baker, Terry, 88
Barnes, Ben, 154
Barry, Dave, 178
Batista, Fulgencio, 41
Beatty, Warren, 107
Becket, Welton, 117
Berkowitz, Nathan, 223
Berry, Robert W., 139
Bettis, Holt, 225
Bettis, Roy H., 186
Bledsoe, Dr. Jim, 65
Boeke, Jim, 91
Bokmaier, Don, 213-214

Boyle, Deirdre, 162
Bradford, Hugh, 42
Bradshaw, Kathleen, 205
Brandt, Gil, 101, 236
Breedlove, William D., 2
Breem, John, 79
Breskin, Barnee, 6
Briggs, Ben, 186
Bright, Bum, 225
Brooks, Elston, 4
Brooks, Foster, 52
Brookshier, Tom, 254
Brown, Gov. Edmund G. (Pat), 167
Brown, Gov. Jerry, 167
Brown, John Y., 2
Brown, Paul, 104
Bryan, John Neely, 119
Buell, Tom, 186
Busby, Jim, 228
Byrne, Brendan T., 166
Busch, August A. Jr., 14-15
Byrd, Harold, 164
Byrd, Adm. Richard, 164

C

Cain, Mrs. Wofford (Effie), 222
Campbell, Sanders, 186
Cannon, Howard, 158
Carter, Guy, 186
Carter, Jimmy, 126, 163, 167
Cartwright, Gary, 247
Cashman, Pat, 52, 55
Caspary, Delo, 34
Castleberry, Delo, 34

Castro, Fidel, 159
Cavagnaro, Joe, 59, 109, 112, 247
Celler, Emmanuel, 158
Chambers, Jim, 122
Claborn, David H., 120
Connally, John D., 152, 249
Cooper, Kenneth, 170
Corrigan, Leo Jr., 186
Cosell, Howard, 81
Cox, Berry R., 210
Cross, Irv, 2
Cullum, Robert B., 115, 121-122, 124-125
Cverko, Andy, 107

D
Daniel, Price, 152, 167
Danner, Richard, 157
Dash, Sam, 156
Davidson, Irv, 71, 151, 188
Davis, Fletcher, 201, 203
Davis, Jefferson, 152
Davis, N. R. (Dick), 134
DeFermat, Pierre, 101
DeOrsey, Leo, 69, 71
Diab, Mohammed, 51
Dietrich, Marlene, 152
Dillinger, John, 179
Dinwiddie, William, 186
DiPerna, Vera, 144-145
Ditka, Mike, 106
Dodge, Dr. Henry W. Jr., 219
Dorandi, Pietro, 179
Dorsett, Tony, 58
Dowe, Ken, 168, 228
Downs, Ward, 7
Dunagan, Bill, 63

Duncan, Mark, 97
Durante, Sal, 178

E
Earhart, Amelia, 178
Eastwood, Clint, 160
Edwards, Roy, 123
Einstein, Albert, 152
Eiseman, Richard, 66
Eisenhower, Dwight, 151, 250
Eliot, George, 240
Elliott, George R., 176
Ellson, George, 52
Erwin, Bukki, 250
Ewing, Finley, 148, 186

F
Facenda, John, 180
Farris, Louis Jr., 230
Field, Kenneth E., 225
Fields, W. C., 101, 177
Fisher, Sir Ronald, 101
Fitts, Grant, 186
Fogelson, E. E. (Buddy), 17-18
Foley, Bob, 52, 206, 220
Foote, Guy (Murph), 186
Ford, Gerald, 250
Forner, Joe, 178
Foss, Joe, 108
Frase, Mrs. Bobby, 2

G
Gable, Clark, 240
Galbraith, John Kenneth, 159
Garrett, Jack Jr., 186
Garrett, Snuff, 45, 229
Garson, Greer, 17

Index

Gay, Jerald, 29
Gehrig, Lou, 217, 220
George, Phyllis, 2
Georges, Basil, 186
Georges, Bill, 14, 38, 39
Glieber, Frank, 92
Gluck, Maxwell, 183
Goldwyn, Sam, 164
Gooding, Gladys, 177
Grant, Ulysses S., 151
Griffing, Rev. Olen, 234, 249
Gulledge, Emory, 18

H

Haber, Jane Murchison, 234
Hagan, Walter, 48-49, 57
Halas, George, 68, 74, 78, 92
Halas, George Jr., 68
Hardin, Tom, 174
Harmon, Tom, 188
Hay, S. J., 204
Hayakawa, S. I., 180
Hayes, Bob, 105, 242
Heavner, Frank, 234
Heitzman, Raymond, 210
Hemingway, Ernest, 152
Henry, E. William, 94
Hershorn, Shel, 5
Hewett, Gene, 37, 40-42, 142
Higgs, Barton, 50
Hiland, George S., 186
Hill, Calvin, 178
Hirsch, Elroy, 11
Holland, 'Brud', 178
Hoover, Herbert, 250
Hoover, J. Edgar, 243, 250
Hope, Bob, 23, 250
Huff, Sam, 84
Hughes, Howard, 156-157

Hughes, Jerry, 212
Humphrey, Hubert, 164-165, 256
Hunt, Bunker, 81, 215
Hunt, Herbert, 214
Hunt, Jeanne, 56, 81
Hunt, Lamar, 75, 81-82, 93 197, 242
Hunt, Stuart, 56, 81
Hussein, Saddam, 152
Hutchinson, Willard, 15
Hutton, Betty, 23

J

Jackson, Michael, 225
Jacobi, Bruce, 48, 214
James, Harry, 22
Jarrell, Ramon, 139, 166
Jenkins, Dan, 3
Johnson, Lyndon B., 122, 151, 158, 160, 162, 164-166, 250
Johnson, Orrin W., 140
Jolson, Al, 152, 181
Jones, Jack, 65-66, 172-174,
Jones, John Paul, 24
Jonsson, J. Erik, 113-114, 123, 126, 128-129, 136, 159, 242

K

Katz, Sam, 6
Kennamer, Bobby Jack, 59
Kennedy, Sen. Edward, 151, 161-162, 255
Kennedy, John F., 114, 153, 236
Kilmer, Billy, 230
Kirby, Allan, 182
Kirk, Claude R. Jr., 154
Kissinger, Henry, 160

Kleifgen, Pete, vii, 50, 56
Kroc, Ray, 200, 202
Kuharich, Joe, 91
Kyser, Kay, 22

L

Lambert, Joe O., 181
Landers, Ann, 183
Landry, Alicia, 2
Landry, Gregg, 98
Landry, Tom, 2, 59, 74, 83, 86, 88, 90-91, 96, 100, 104, 162, 210, 235, 249
Laros, Tom, 186
Lawrence, Harding, 48
Lay, Herman, 105, 186
Lay, Mimi, 105
Leak, A. R., 186
Lear, Norman, 160
LeBaron, Eddie, 253
Lee, Robert E., 152
Lewis, Eugene, 85
Lewis, Hal, 77
Lewis, Mitch, 230
Lilley, Harold, 186
Lilly, Bob, 242, 254
Lindsley, Chandler, 216
Lindsley, Henry III, 149
Linen, James, 155
Linthicum, Virginia, 20-22, 29
Lipscomb, Gene, 107
Lively, Tom, 57
Lockhard, Joe, 179
Lockhart, Joe, 179
Loftin, Roy B., 43-45
Lom, Benny, 178
Lombardi, Vince, 80, 191-192
Long, Carolyn, 226
Long, Huey, 68

Long, Russell, 155, 157, 163, 226
Loy, Tommy, 90, 103
Luksa, Frank, 174
Lynch, James J., 109

M

Mabovitch, Moshe, 3
Madden, Bob, 42
Maheu, Robert, 157
Maloney, Larry, 71
Manders, Dave, 96
Marcus, Stanley, 7
Maris, Roger, 179
Marsh, Amos, 83-84
Marshall, George Preston, 67-69, 71, 78, 187
Martin, Jimmy, 52, 54
Martin, Spencer (Spinny), 39, 52-53, 177
Martinez, Cinca, 173
McCann, Dick, 188
McCarthy, Joseph, 164
McDermott, John R., 187
McDowell, John D., 3
McGonagill, Frank E. Jr., 142
McGovern, George, 166
McIlhenny, Walter S., 199
McKnight, Felix, 165
McLendon, Gordon, 43-45, 109, 223, 230
McPhail, William, 91
Meany, George, 159
Meir, Golda, 3
Menig, Mary, 16
Meredith, Don, 78, 84, 104, 243
Miller, Glenn, 22
Mills, Ogden, 46
Modell, Arthur, 92

Index

Moore, Kenneth, 186
Morton, Craig, 53
Mosher, Curt, 174
Murchison, Anne, 58, 215, 219, 227, 230, 234, 237, 244
Murchison, Burk, 34
Murchison, Burk Coleman, vi, 87, 194, 207-208, 221, 227, 230, 234
Murchison, 'Burkito,' 212, 228
Murchison, C. W. IV, 212, 234, 245
Murchison, Christine Elise, 234
Murchison, Clint III, vi, 13-14, 169, 234, 241, 245-246
Murchison, Clint Sr., v, 1, 21, 34, 41, 139, 148
Murchison, Coke Anne, vi, 6, 8, 9, 13
Murchison, David, 212
Murchison, Elise, 221
Murchison, Frank, 29
Murchison, Fred Cook, 146
Murchison, Fred S., 145
Murchison, George, 212-213, 234, 245-246
Murchison, Jane, 4, 8, 25-26, 28, 56, 77, 125, 181
Murchison, John Dabney, v, 7, 22, 25, 34, 36, 56, 181
Murchison, Lupe, 56
Murchison, Norinne, 29
Murchison, Ola Lee, 146
Murchison, Robert, vi, 61, 64, 86-87, 95, 99, 147-148, 160, 194, 200, 208, 234, 241
Murchison, S. L. (Sid), 146
Murchison, T. F., 214

Musberger, Brent, 2
Muss, Joshua, 37

N
Namath, Joe, 109, 155
Neely, Ralph, 59, 107
Neely, Stanley, 239
Nicoud, George Jr., 186
Nixon, Richard M., 156, 160
Noonan, Fred, 178

O
Oakie, Jack, 177
O'Brien, Davey, 188
O'Connell, Jack, 54, 237, 239
O'Donnell, Peter Jr., 186
Oliver, William B., 186
Olson, Jack, 12
Oostdyk, Harv, 240
Outlar, Jesse, 89
Owen, George, 220

P
Packer, H. Lynn, 197
Pahel, Ralph, 136
Pascal, Blaise, 101
Pearson, Karl, 101
Peeples, Jack, 2
Pei, I. M., 113
Pele (Edson Arantes do Nascimento), 178
Perkins, Don, 78
Perkins, Steve, 119, 174
Perry, George Sessions, 111
Perryman, Bill, 201
Pesci, Peter, 141-142
Petri, Louis, 46

Petrillo, James C., 22
Plank, C. Doug, 210
Platter, Niel W., 186
Poe, Edgar Allan, 152
Pope, Edwin, 98
Posner, Dr. Jerome, 220, 225
Potter, Mark, 5
Priddy, Ashley, 5

R
Ramey, Robert, 3
Ramsden, Dudley, 65-66, 183, 185
Rauscher, John Jr., 87
Reagan, Ronald, 167
Rebozo, Bebe, 156
Reed, Roy, 172
Reeves, Dan, 97, 138
Reinholm, Paul, 14
Reynolds, Burt, 160
Reynolds, Dick, 222
Rhome, Jerry, 88
Rice, Al, 6
Riegels, Roy, 179
Rimmer, Roy T., 132
Rizzo, Jilly, 53
Robertson, Walter, 174
Robinson, James F., vii-viii
Roma, Tony, vi, 54, 193, 221
Rooney, Dan, 198
Roosevelt, Franklin D., 151
Roosevelt, Theodore, 163
Rose, Bert, 133
Rote, Kyle, 141
Royal, Darrell, 159-160, 164
Rozelle, Pete, 81, 106-109, 118, 188, 249

S
Sabol, Ed, 180-181
Sanford, Ralph, 234
Sage, Anna, 178
Saunders, Coke Anne Murchison, 227
Saunders, Courtney Cain Murchison, 234
Saunders, Richard, 227
Sayers, Gale, 242
Schenkel, Chris, 86
Schmid, Smoot, 29
Schmitz, Bob, 246
Schneider, Martha Anne, 11
Schneider, Steve, 7, 10-11, 84, 121, 148-149, 163, 181, 230, 249, 251, 256
Schoellkopf, John L., 18, 226
Schramm, Tex, 64, 73-75, 92, 97, 100-101, 103, 123-124, 174
Scott, Norman, 143
Sears, John, 207, 245
Seiden, Billy, 56
Seiden, Janie, 56
Seiden, William, 56, 227
Semones, Jack, 86
Shanklin, Scott, 147
Sheehie, Lee, 156
Shephard, Robert, 62
Shepley, James R., 182
Sherman, Max, 224
Sherrod, Blackie, 3, 74, 85, 95, 134, 174, 176-177, 221
Shor, Toots, 84
Shore, Nat, 227
Shrake, Bud, 3-4
Shipp, Rev. Tom, 175

Index

Shula, Don, 2
Siegel, Morrie, 67
Simmons, Marshall, 58, 238
Sinatra, Frank, 53
Smith, E. Gordon, 16
Smith, Rankin, 89
Smith, Ray, 38
Snyder, Jimmy (the Greek), 2
Spadia, Lou, 93
Spencer, Sash, 223
Spivey, Marsha, 17
St. John, Bob, 174
Staubach, Roger, 138, 243
Stephens, Larry, 138
Stephenson, James, 147
Stevenson, Coke, 152
Stevenson, Donald W., 62-63
Stewart, James, 153
Stewart, Robert (Bobby), 65, 249
Strauss, Annette, 56, 128, 168-170
Strauss, Robert, 163
Strauss, Ted, 56, 128, 149, 169-170, 181
Stroman, Jim, 175
Sullivan, Billy, 81
Svare, Harlan, 88
Swanson, Kenneth, 33-35, 37

T
Tapley, Kenneth, 54
Tatum, C. A., 115, 118
Taylor, John, 110
Thieu, Nguyen Van, 108
Thomas, Danny, 45
Thomas, Max, 186
Thompson, Bob, 23, 41-42, 47, 57, 70, 243
Thompson, J. H., 121
Tittle, Y. A., 179
Trimble, George S., 12-13
Trousdale, Paul, 45-47, 140, 143, 184, 221
Tucker, Y. Arnold, 179
Turner, Joe M., 141

V
Vail, Charles, 3
Vallens, Ken, vii
Van Buren, Ernestine Van Orrick, 1
Van der Rohe, Mies, 6, 8-9
Vandergriff, Tom, 130
Vaughn, Jack, 149, 186

W
Wade, Henry, 44
Wade, Jim, 153-154
Walker, Doak, 253
Walker, Jerry Jeff, 104, 160
Walton, Jack, 207
Ward, Al, 174
Waters, Charlie, 96
Watson, Thomas J., 250
Webb, Carroll L. Jr., 186
Webb, Tom, 67, 69, 71, 151, 243
Webb, William G., 186
Welles, Orson, 128
White, H. W. B., 204
West, Bradley, 233
West, Bryan, 234
West, Loren, 234
West, Mae, 177
West, Wendy, 274
White, Mark, 249
Wigley, Robert, 186

Williams, Edward Bennett, 191
Wise, Wes, 159
Wolfe, Jane, 220
Wolman, Jerry, 117
Wood, C. V., 196
Woodard, Ruth, vii, 56, 58, 167, 171, 186, 219
Woodhull, Leonard, 100
Woodruff, Robert, 250
Woods, Harlan, 104
Works, Willard, 164
Wright, Frank, 206
Wright, Frank Lloyd, 6, 8
Wright, George, 196

Wyatt, Earle, 197
Wyatt, Oscar, 137
Wynne, Bedford, 71, 74, 138, 149, 153
Wynne, Toddie Lee Jr., 34, 186

Y

Yarborough, Don, 152
Yarborough, Ralph, 44
Yasgur, Max, 179-180

Z

Zeibert, Duke, 188

Regional Books From Wordware

Classic Clint: The Laughs and Times of Clint Murchison, Jr.
by Dick Hitt

Exploring the Alamo Legends
by Wallace O. Chariton

Forget the Alamo
by Wallace O. Chariton

The Great Texas Airship Mystery
by Wallace O. Chariton

100 Days in Texas: The Alamo Letters
by Wallace O. Chariton

Rainy Days in Texas Funbook
by Wallace O. Chariton

San Antonio Uncovered
by Mark Louis Rybczyk

Texas Highway Humor
by Wallace O. Chariton

Texas Tales Your Teacher Never Told You
by Charles F. Eckhardt

Texas Wit and Wisdom
by Wallace O. Chariton

That Cat Won't Flush
by Wallace O. Chariton

They Don't Have to Die
by Jim Dunlap

This Dog'll Hunt
by Wallace O. Chariton

To the Tyrants Never Yield
by Kevin R. Young

Unsolved Texas Mysteries
by Wallace O. Chariton